Managing Your Child's
Inhibitor

A Practical Guide for Parents

Laureen A. Kelley with Paul Clement

Dedicated to Joe Holibaugh

December 28, 1971 – June 13, 2006

A loving father, son, and fierce friend who lived every particle of his being with passion.

■■■

Contents

- Foreword 9
- Introduction 10

PART 1: MEDICAL ASPECTS OF INHIBITORS
1. A Surprising Diagnosis 15
2. What We Know about Hemophilia and Inhibitors 29
3. Treating Acute Bleeding 41
4. ITI: Eradicating the Inhibitor 55
5. Factor IX Deficiency and Inhibitors 71
6. Managing Pain 83
7. Ports, PICCs, and Pokes 103
8. Surgery and Inhibitors 119

PART 2: DAILY LIFE WITH INHIBITORS
9. Caring for Your Child Emotionally and Physically 139
10. Fostering Healthy Self-Esteem 153
11. Family, Friends, and Inhibitors 167
12. Keeping Joints Healthy 181
13. Insurance and Inhibitors 193
14. Attending School When You Have Inhibitors 209
15. Adolescence and Beyond 223

- Appendices A–D 239
- Glossary 246
- Acknowledgments 262
- Index 265

Points to Remember

You'll hear some parents and medical staff say "the inhibitor" and others say "inhibitors." The terms are often used interchangeably. Inhibitors are antibodies that your child's body produces, but you can also say that he has *an* inhibitor to factor VIII.

Although mainly boys get hemophilia, some girls do have hemophilia. For the sake of simplicity, in this book we'll refer to a child with hemophilia as "he."

We write NovoSeven®RT with its trademark symbol only once in the book, and then shorten it to NovoSeven or NovoSeven RT for easier reading. In this book, NovoSeven will always refer to NovoSeven RT.

■ ■ ■

Foreword

"Dr. Mathew, my son's bleeding knee is still swollen and painful." I will always remember receiving that panicky telephone call from a distraught mother. So began the journey of helping her family manage an inhibitor diagnosis for the first time.

Developing an inhibitor is a tough challenge for any person with hemophilia. *Managing Your Child s Inhibitor: A Practical Guide for Parents* goes to the heart of inhibitors, both from a medical standpoint and a parental perspective.

How can this book help you? Educated parents can make important treatment decisions along with their physicians and care team. Even if your child does not have an inhibitor, this book is worthwhile reading—an investment for your family—especially if you have young children who have recently started infusion of factor concentrates for their hemophilia treatment.

This book, the first of its kind, is divided into two parts: the first deals with medical aspects of inhibitors, and the second delves into day-to-day issues of care for patients and their families. You'll enjoy reading and learning from Laurie and Paul's clear, lucid, straightforward writing style. In these pages, you'll feel the pangs of a mother who has dealt with a child with hemophilia, and the anguish, frustration, and emotional rollercoaster of parents of children with inhibitors.

Though Laurie has written other books for parents of children with bleeding disorders, this book fills a critical void for parents who have no reference books on managing hemophilia and inhibitors. From coping with the initial inhibitor diagnosis to commonsense advice, *Managing Your Child s Inhibitor* will make you want to learn more, even in the most challenging circumstances.

As a person with an inhibitor, or a family dealing with a new inhibitor diagnosis, if you're worried, scared, and don't know where to turn, you'll find this book informative and resourceful. As a healthcare provider, I find it intellectually stimulating, and I appreciate that it considers inhibitors from the patient's and family's perspective. Fortunately my patient, whose mother called me in a panic, does not have an inhibitor at this time. But I will be giving this book to his mother, who reminded me that patients and families with inhibitors are different, unique, and wonderful!

Prasad Mathew, MD, Professor of Pediatrics
Director, Ted R. Montoya Hemophilia Program
Albuquerque, New Mexico
May 2010

Introduction

After twenty-two years in the hemophilia community, I thought I had seen it all. Since 1987, when my son with hemophilia was born, our community had been through HIV and hepatitis C contamination, factor shortages, and insurance crises. I had published books about hemophilia and von Willebrand disease (VWD), and many children's books, to educate people young and old about all aspects of bleeding disorders. I had visited more than twenty developing countries to help those with hemophilia who continue to suffer with no access to factor.

But up until four years before this book was written, I hadn't realized that we still had deep needs and tremendous suffering, right here in our own country. Like most of our community, I was ignorant of the plight of people with inhibitors. I was shocked—and ashamed—to learn that some of those who suffered quietly were families and individuals I knew personally.

My eyes were opened to this silent community when I was invited to join a Novo Nordisk consumer advisory panel composed of inhibitor patients and parents of children with inhibitors. The purpose of the panel was to reveal unmet needs. I had participated in various consumer councils in the past, and I knew that parents had standard consumer wish lists: they wanted different needle sizes, or peel-off labels on their factor, or coloring books for their kids—all legitimate requests. But the needs that were uncovered that day astounded me. Surrounded by twelve families with inhibitors for an entire day, I listened to some of the saddest stories I had ever heard.

I learned how hard it was to find product that worked to stop bleeds. I cringed at stories of unrelenting bleeds that kept child and parent awake for hours at night, for nights on end. Unresolved bleeds that confined children to wheelchairs. Days—weeks—lost from school or work. I listened to families who had burned though their insurance caps because of the high cost of treatment. Parents who hopped from job to job just to find new insurance policies. In tears, one mother even admitted that she and her husband had seriously considered asking her sister—who had no limits on her insurance—to adopt their son. Yes, the stories I heard left me stunned.

Why were we—the "regular" hemophilia community—so unaware of the suffering of inhibitor families?

The families themselves answered this question. Life is so good now, they explained, for those with "just" hemophilia that inhibitor families feel like a burden. "No one can relate to what we're going through," declared one father. Families without inhibitors simply couldn't understand their suffering, and often didn't want to hear it. "I went to one support group meeting and shared our stories, and everyone went silent," a mother recalled. Inhibitor families learned very quickly to hide their feelings, their stories, their suffering.

Isolation was perhaps the biggest obstacle. These families had no place to meet, no means to connect. Each family stayed in its own bubble of private hurt . . . until that consumer meeting, and the concurrent Inhibitor Education Summit, which also debuted in 2005. Two whole days in Philadelphia devoted to inhibitors: expert panels, presentations, social events. For the first time, a forum had been created to offer education, socializing, and networking just for inhibitor patients and families. I saw firsthand the inhibitor community transform and become empowered. And I hadn't seen so many tears since the HIV era of the late 1980s.

Since that first summit, the inhibitor community has been rapidly connecting and communicating. Scholarships for people with inhibitors are now available, as are brochures and other educational materials—and a regular spot in National Hemophilia Foundation (NHF) annual meetings. More information brings new choices, better decisions, more help, less isolation.

I decided that the community needed a book to bring these exciting new resources to all people with inhibitors. Not everyone can attend education summits. And all families need a reference book on inhibitors: a book that's comprehensive, yet written in plain language they can understand. A book to stick in a purse, briefcase, or backpack.

I also knew that Americans aren't the only ones suffering; inhibitor families in many countries remain disenfranchised and isolated. This book is a resource for them too, a resource that's unavailable anywhere else. It is the world's first book on inhibitors.

As a parent, you may feel frightened when you receive the inhibitor diagnosis, and perhaps even when reading this book. But I can't sugar-coat all that I've learned, because I believe that to be the best parent for your child, to make the best decisions about treatment and lifestyle, you need to hear the truth—straight from the families. Take it from Sonji Wilkes, mother of Thomas, who writes, "We visited other inhibitor families, and they kept saying, 'We don't want to scare you.' But we actually *wanted* to hear all their stories, good and bad, because we wanted to be prepared."

Debbie Porter, mother of Matthew, believes, "Information about inhibitors is not being given to the community at large, and some of what hematologists share with patients is glossed over for fear of alarming them." Both Sonji and Debbie craved information after the diagnosis, and only worried that they weren't getting *enough* information. Both have been through the trenches of inhibitor battles, and both have emerged stronger, more competent, and hopeful.

My own hope is that this book will become a tool for you to use in conjunction with your clinic visits, in discussions with your hematologist, and as a reference when you need an immediate answer. Bring it with you to clinic, to support group meetings, and to your local hemophilia chapter meeting. Bring it to your child's school, and share it with other inhibitor families.

The first half of the book dives directly into the medical aspects of inhibitors. There's a reason for this. While interviewing parents, I realized that they didn't have the luxury, like those of us dealing with just hemophilia, to sort out their emotions and take their time learning treatment. Instead, they were thrown to the inhibitor wolves: usually, as soon as they learned the diagnosis, they had to immediately begin making medical treatment decisions. Inhibitor parents must learn medical jargon and options pretty quickly, and learn about dosing in a different way. So this book stresses the medical aspects first, with family, social, and lifestyle aspects addressed in the second half.

Use the book as you need to use it: read the chapters in the order that works for you. Some chapters you might never need to read. Try reading it in short doses, a chapter or two at a time. There's a lot to digest!

Of course, I hope your child is one of the lucky ones who is eventually tolerized, and whose inhibitor is eradicated. But no matter what situation you face, take strength from knowing that in this book, you'll find many answers to your questions about inhibitors. And you'll realize, when you read the quotations of parents and patients, that you are not alone. There is a very special community of people who do know what you're going through, and what you will face. You'll benefit from their knowledge, so that your child can become an active part of a community that will no longer shun, ignore, or avoid him. Your child with an inhibitor—and all families with inhibitors—are now welcomed with open arms, at last.

Laureen Kelley
September 2010

Part 1

■■■

Medical Aspects of Inhibitors

1 A Surprising Diagnosis

"Your child has developed an inhibitor..." When your hematologist or nurse gives you this surprising diagnosis, you may feel curious, stunned, scared, or even relieved. So many questions run through your mind: *How can my child have two things wrong? What is an inhibitor? What does this mean for treating his hemophilia? How did he get an inhibitor? How can we get rid of it?*

An inhibitor is a major complication of hemophilia. When someone has hemophilia, his blood cannot clot properly because the blood is missing a protein needed for clotting. People with hemophilia need to infuse medicine called *clotting factor*, also called *factor* or *factor concentrate*, which contains the missing protein. An inhibitor develops when the body's immune system does not recognize the infused factor as a normal part of blood. Instead, the body thinks that factor is a foreign invader, like a virus or germ, and it develops antibodies[1] designed to attack the factor and make it harmless—and useless. So despite an infusion of factor, your child continues to bleed.

An inhibitor may have been the last thing on your mind while you were learning to manage your child's hemophilia. Some parents have never heard of inhibitors. Others have heard of inhibitors but never thought they would experience them. Some parents notice that their child's infused factor no longer works well, that bleeding doesn't respond to treatment, and that more frequent doses are needed. Even when parents suspect that something isn't right, they may hope that doctors will say the problem is only temporary.[2] The development of an inhibitor is almost always a surprise.

> *Coty was getting all this bruising. We just assumed he was not receiving enough factor. We were not well informed on inhibitors. The nurse suspected an inhibitor, and Coty was tested.* —Chasity, Mississippi

Fortunately, you're not alone in coping with the inhibitor diagnosis. You have expert medical care at your hemophilia treatment center (HTC). You have products to treat bleeding. You have treatments to try to eliminate the inhibitor. Although the diagnosis is a surprise, expert help is available.

> *We had felt hemophilia was manageable, but suddenly it didn't seem so manageable anymore. The risks had gone up. Could we effectively treat bleeds? We didn't know. There was much to learn and decisions to be made.*
> —Laura Shumway, Virginia

When Can an Inhibitor Be Diagnosed?

Inhibitors are relatively uncommon. If one develops, it's usually detected when a child with hemophilia is young, usually in the first one to three years of life. The median time to development of an inhibitor is about nine to eleven *exposure days*—days on which the child received one or more infusions of factor VIII or factor IX. Parents may suspect that something is wrong, usually because a bleed will not resolve, or takes significantly longer to resolve, after an infusion of factor. Several situations might indicate that a child has an inhibitor:

Unresolved bleeds

All HTCs routinely monitor their patients for inhibitors, and many do so more frequently in the first months of treatment. But not every child with hemophilia is seen at an HTC, and older children may go only once a year for their annual comprehensive visit. You may learn that your child has an inhibitor the hard way: when factor no longer works well to stop bleeds. How do you know when factor isn't working well? If you're new to hemophilia, this may not be easy—you may not be sure how long it should take a bleed to stop after an infusion. You're still getting used to identifying symptoms of different bleeds, learning about your child's individual bleeding pattern, and determining whether a "normal" muscle or joint bleed takes one day or four days to resolve. With so much to learn, it may not immediately dawn on you that the infused factor isn't working properly, and a bleed is taking much longer than it should to heal. It's common for parents to think that they simply need to give their child more frequent infusions, or give a higher dose per infusion.[3] Unresolved bleeding, even with repeated infusions of factor, is the primary way that parents discover their child has an inhibitor.

> *We suspected by age eight months that Jonathan might have an inhibitor. He had a leg bleed that we were treating every day with factor at 100% levels, for six days; it just wasn't getting better.* —Jackie, Massachusetts

> *Every time we infused, it would take more infusions to stop a bleed. Then we were giving him two to three doses for one bleed. Eventually, infusions didn't work at all.* —Debbie Branch, Kansas

Increased bruising

Bruising in young children with severe hemophilia is common. But if your child uses factor frequently and you notice increased bruising, this may be a sign of an inhibitor. One mother commented that her doctor noticed increased, repeated bruising at her child's infusion site, and suspected an inhibitor.

> There was a huge increase in the number of bruises and their severity. My son started having a lot of soft tissue bleeds. Wasn't he getting enough factor? I thought, maybe it's the product we're using, or maybe he needs a different product. We did not suspect an inhibitor, but the HTC ordered blood tests. —Chasity, Mississippi

Routine clinic visit

Ideally, you'd like to learn that your child has an inhibitor *before* an emergency happens and before he gets a major bleed. A blood test at your child's HTC comprehensive clinic visit can identify an inhibitor. It's wise to have a child with hemophilia tested for inhibitors routinely: learning that he has an inhibitor in advance of surgery or a major bleed allows parents to have a plan in place and the correct treatment on hand.[4]

> We did not suspect or even think about an inhibitor. Noah had his first comprehensive visit at age ten months, where they drew blood. I later received a phone call from our HTC nurse. She said that Noah's inhibitor test was positive. The HTC team was just as shocked as I was! —Cicely Evans, Massachusetts

Breakthrough bleeds while on prophylaxis

Prophylaxis is the scheduled infusion of factor to help prevent bleeding. Many children with hemophilia on prophylaxis receive factor two to three times a week, enough to keep the lowest level—called the *trough level*—of factor in the blood above 1%. Children on "prophy" usually will have enough circulating factor to prevent most spontaneous bleeds and abnormal bruising. When a child on prophy starts bruising or even bleeding more often than usual, an inhibitor may be inactivating some of the factor, thus lowering his factor level and increasing his risk of bleeding.

> Logan was on prophy but had lots of bruising. I told our HTC nurse that Logan looked as though someone had thrown him down a flight of stairs. He ran a blood test for an inhibitor, and there it was. —Anonymous

Bleeding after surgery

Because surgery often involves blood loss, it requires special precautions for children with hemophilia. A common first surgery is circumcision. In families with no history of hemophilia, elective circumcision is usually performed soon after birth, and prolonged bleeding that results from the surgery may indicate hemophilia. A blood test will confirm the diagnosis. Depending on the circumcision method, some babies with hemophilia have no bleeding problem with circumcision—even without an infusion of factor.[5] Others bleed profusely and need factor to control bleeding. Any kind of surgery on a child with hemophilia requires careful planning and monitoring of factor levels, and any child who continues to bleed following surgery, even with adequate factor, should be immediately tested for an inhibitor. Ideally, all children with hemophilia should be tested for an inhibitor *before* any surgery of any kind.

> *Caeleb was circumcised at age eleven months. The clots that formed on his penis fell off, and it wouldn't stop oozing. We returned to the hospital, and although the doctor infused him with an enormous amount of factor VIII, the oozing continued. So they tested his levels and realized he had developed an inhibitor. —Cazandra Campos-MacDonald, New Mexico*

> *When Reuben was one year old, he had urological surgery for an undescended testicle. Postoperatively his factor levels corrected only to 20% instead of 100%. The wound continued to ooze. Our HTC staff suspected an inhibitor, but we didn't know for sure until a blood test during his second hospitalization. —Wendy Sass, New York*

> *Matthew's first exposure to factor was at age six months during surgery to correct his clubfeet. His feet swelled a lot after surgery, and he was in pain despite a continuous infusion of factor. The first labs showed that his factor level was low, although he was receiving the continuous infusion. I suspected he might have an inhibitor, but this was not confirmed until a week later. —Debbie Porter, California*

Following a major bleed

Parents may suspect inhibitors during a major bleed that does not resolve.

> *Lee was five when diagnosed with an inhibitor. He had collapsed on the floor in the bathroom, and we didn't know what was wrong. We gave him factor but had no idea that he had an inhibitor. He got much worse. The next day he was in excruciating pain. We had to call an ambulance and rush him to hospital. It was an internal bleed inside his spinal column; our hematologist had only seen three such bleeds. Lee was hospitalized for three weeks. Within two days of admittance, they had done an inhibitor test, and he had one, very high. —Eleth Ridenhour, Kansas*

Reaction following infusion

Inhibitor development in children with hemophilia B is rare—only 1% to 3% of people with hemophilia B get them. Unlike people with hemophilia A and inhibitors, about 45% of people with hemophilia B and inhibitors also develop allergic reactions at about the same time that they develop inhibitors.[6] Allergic reactions may start out mild, and then increase in severity after repeated exposure to products containing factor IX, often to the point of a serious, life-threatening allergic reaction called *anaphylaxis*. Allergic reactions in hemophilia B patients are not in themselves an inhibitor, but are a sign that an inhibitor has developed (see chapter 5).

> *At age eleven months, Jay had a spontaneous head bleed. He had intracranial surgery and was started on daily doses of plasma-derived factor IX. After about a month, we were treating at home and he started getting hives with each infusion. His reaction progressed each time until it was anaphylactic. I knew what inhibitors were, but I had never heard of anyone having an inhibitor and anaphylactic reaction.* —Shari Luckey, Michigan

Later in life

If a person with hemophilia is going to develop an inhibitor, he'll usually do so while he's a child, often within twenty exposure days, and almost always before the hundredth exposure day. And he'll probably have severe hemophilia. Only about 1% to 2% of people with mild hemophilia develop inhibitors. Although most inhibitors occur early in life, in rare cases an inhibitor develops when a child is older, sometimes a teen or an adult. Unlike people with severe hemophilia, people with mild hemophilia who develop inhibitors tend to develop them later in life, usually after intensive exposure to factor during and after surgery or traumatic injury.

> *I developed an inhibitor while a sophomore in high school. I had a bleed in my psoas, and I was put on prophylaxis. I haven't had too many bleeds in my life. I was diagnosed with mild hemophilia when I was thirteen, when I had hurt my elbow and it swelled. I'd never heard of hemophilia. I was on prophylaxis for my psoas bleed when they diagnosed me with the inhibitor.* —John Salierno, New Jersey

> *I was diagnosed with an inhibitor when I was seventeen. I knew I had mild hemophilia, but I never understood the depth of it. I wasn't affiliated with an HTC and never had any factor. But after I had four wisdom teeth out, the gums started oozing, and then one night, the bleeding was steady. I was rushed to the hospital. A hematologist gave me a large bolus of factor. I spent a week in hospital, and I got large amounts of factor. The inhibitor was diagnosed soon after.* —Richard Pezzillo, Rhode Island

Regardless of how you discover your child's inhibitor, the diagnosis can be both a relief—now you know what's wrong—and a worry. What will happen next? It helps to know what to expect during this time, and to know that feelings of anxiety, fear, and anger are normal and can be managed.

Reactions to the Inhibitor Diagnosis

Following an inhibitor diagnosis, a lot will happen in a short time. The diagnosis requires parents to learn about bleed management, immune system responses, treatment, and product choices—much more than when they had to deal with "just" hemophilia. There's a whole new level of medical information to be learned, and learned quickly.

But there's also a lot of emotional change. Because inhibitors usually happen early in a child's life, parents may be dealing simultaneously with the hemophilia diagnosis. This can trigger a wide range of emotions.

> We were just getting over the fact that our son has hemophilia, and then this happened—our world was crashing down. These were the three worst days of my life: the day he was diagnosed with hemophilia, the day he was diagnosed with severe hemophilia, and the day he was diagnosed with an inhibitor. —Jackie, Massachusetts

> The inhibitor diagnosis came four months after his hemophilia diagnosis, when we were still in survival mode from the first diagnosis. —Richard and Lynley Scott, New Zealand

You may go through the same emotional tumult that you experienced when you learned your child had hemophilia.

> What did I feel? Fear, panic, overwhelmed, lost, grief, guilt, anger. Incredibly protective of my son. An overwhelming feeling of responsibility to ensure his life. That the life I had envisioned and had hoped for us as a family, but especially for Eshton, had been stolen. —Joyce Hewitt, Michigan

These feelings are often referred to as *stages of acceptance*—a series of common emotions resulting from a sudden loss or major life change. Not everyone progresses through these stages in order or feels them in equal intensity. Everyone reacts a bit differently. As with any major life change, you need to work through your chaotic feelings to arrive at a place of mental and emotional acceptance.

Shock

Shock is emotional numbness. It's also called dissociation. Dissociation is a psychological defense that protects you from sudden and overwhelming emotional trauma. You may seem to have no feelings, no reaction. This defense allows you to continue to care for your baby or yourself, while putting your emotions on hold, to be dealt with later.

My oldest son, who was ten at the time Caeleb was diagnosed with his inhibitor, also had an inhibitor at age one. Regardless, I was stunned. —Cazandra Campos-MacDonald, New Mexico

Denial

Eventually shock wears off. You may experience denial, believing that the diagnosis is a mistake. Denial is a normal defense mechanism that gives you a temporary feeling of control. Denial creates an almost invisible, protective emotional barrier around you, pushing the problem away. This doesn't last too long with an inhibitor, though, as you'll be able to clearly see bruising or know that an infusion isn't working—and you'll have to make treatment decisions.

Anger

As you accept and process the diagnosis, you may think, *Why did this have to happen? It's not fair!* Your anger may be directed at God, Mother Nature, fate, your spouse or partner, even yourself. Anger is recognition that something undesirable happened, and that nothing you can do—for now—can change it.

I was angry because I couldn't play basketball. I was stuck home all day and didn't go to school. I felt like I was missing out on a lot. My parents were worried because they saw the change in my personality. Staying home with them didn't make it better. For all of us, it was a huge transition. —John Salierno, New Jersey

Sadness

After your anger subsides, you may feel sadness. You may cry and feel hopeless or despondent. This is grief. You may be grieving about the pain your child might suffer; the disruption the inhibitor brings to your life; the lack of control you may feel; and the overwhelming responsibilities that inhibitor treatment requires. Your sadness is a sign that you are beginning to accept the diagnosis.[7]

It was horrible, frightening, and devastating. We had known about Reuben's hemophilia for less than a month, and this new information was overwhelming. I sobbed in the hall of the hospital. —Wendy Sass, New York

Guilt

When you hear the inhibitor diagnosis, it's normal to want to blame something or someone. After all, you didn't ask for this! Blaming others means that you want them to feel responsible for the situation. But if you blame yourself, you may feel tremendous guilt—guilt for giving him hemophilia, and possibly guilt for giving him an inhibitor. Or you may feel you are being punished for something. In reality, it's no one's fault when a child develops an inhibitor.

> *I found myself bargaining: please just give him mild hemophilia! That didn't work, and I'd cry again. I said to my husband, "What did I ever do to deserve this? Were we bad parents to our first child?" —Jackie, Massachusetts*

> *I often blamed God, and felt He was punishing me for something that I did in the past. But Kyler is a special little boy, and I accept the diagnosis now. —Anonymous*

Isolation

You may feel more isolated emotionally: having an inhibitor makes you different from other hemophilia families. Regular hemophilia support groups may not seem relevant.[8] Until you locate other families with inhibitors, you may continue feeling isolated, even shunned, as your problems seem so much larger than other families can handle or want to hear.

> *We really struggled to find understanding and support. At times we felt very isolated, with little support from anyone other than our family and friends. Within the hemophilia community, people seemed to pity us rather than offer support. —Richard and Lynley Scott, New Zealand*

Relief

It might seem strange, but some parents feel relieved to know their child has an inhibitor. They finally know exactly what's wrong and why he continues to bleed. And they now know they can attempt treatments to stop the bleeding.

> *Days after we found out about the inhibitor, a nurse at the HTC told us that she had suspected an inhibitor. That was of great comfort after the fact. We didn't even know that the inhibitor was a possibility. —Sasha Cheatham, Oklahoma*

All these feelings are normal. You may feel them all, or only one. You may go through these stages of acceptance in the order just listed, but most people don't experience them in sequence. You may experience some stages simultaneously. Some may be brief, and others may persist stubbornly. It helps to identify the stage you're in. Tell yourself it's okay to feel angry, sad, or overwhelmed. Give each stage time: time for you to process new information, adjust to the huge shift in your expectations, and let the diagnosis sink in. The key to regaining your emotional balance is to recognize that you are in a stage but still moving toward acceptance. But if you're stuck for too long in one stage, you may need to reach out for help from a counselor or trusted friend, from someone in your faith, or from your HTC. You need not—and should not—travel this road alone. Support and help are available.

How Fathers and Mothers Learn to Accept

An inhibitor diagnosis is a source of intense stress, and each person copes with stress in different ways. A mother and father may discover that they process and react to the diagnosis differently. For example, one parent may seem too emotional, the other too distant. We all handle life's challenges differently, based on our biological makeup as males and females, our cultural conditioning, and our own upbringing.

> *My husband is not an open book. He felt he had to be strong for me. Hemophilia, an inhibitor—this is all new. I think it was too much for him to grasp. He works, so I was home with the kids all the time, and the burden fell on me. He acted like, "If I don't think about it, it's not true." But it's all I thought about. —Jackie, Massachusetts*

Mothers traditionally tend to take on emotional processing for the family. A mother may openly express her emotions: crying, talking, or worrying. Her intense feelings may lead her to *enmesh*, or fuse, herself with the family problem (see chapter 10). This overly intense involvement often has negative consequences. She may ask, *Why me?* as if she did something to deserve this situation. Or she may feel guilty for personally "causing" the disorder.

> *I am much more emotional than my husband. He says, "Let's figure it out and deal with what comes." He didn't like the diagnosis, but he said, "We'll deal with it." I was worried, imagining a worst-case scenario. He likes to do his own research and then figure things out, while I have to talk to others with similar issues, and become as proactive as possible. —Kari Atkinson, Iowa*

Fathers traditionally want to be rational problem solvers. To such a father, an inhibitor is a problem affecting his family—something to solve. To accomplish this, he may withdraw emotionally for a while, not showing his feelings. He may focus more on medical facts than on emotions, appearing strong and stoic. Or he may distance himself from his feelings by attending intensely to work, hobbies, sports, or the financial concerns surrounding inhibitors.

> *My first reaction was mild, because I didn't know too much about it and didn't understand the implications. You think, it's just another medication we need to be on.* —Shari Luckey, Michigan

In a two-parent family, there is usually a balance: one parent is more outwardly calm, and the other more openly emotional. Yet as gender roles have changed significantly in America over the past decades, the father may be the obviously distressed parent, and the mother the calmer parent. The key point: both parents experience a full range of emotions but express them in different ways. If fathers and mothers don't understand how they each cope with stress, they may experience tension, resentment, conflict, or distancing. For example, a mother may not understand at first that the inhibitor diagnosis can rob the father of his feeling of competence: he can't make this go away. And she may feel hurt or resentful if he withdraws from her. A father may not understand that the diagnosis causes the mother to seek comfort through relationships: she needs to talk. He may feel neglected when she spends less time with him and more time with other family members or friends. It's important for parents to maintain their relationship—their partnership—during this stressful time.

When parents understand the way each partner copes with stress, they can learn to respect the other's needs, and they can respond appropriately and lovingly to meet those needs. Remember that the reactions of fathers and mothers may differ. Try not to take each other's reactions personally. Finally, remember that people go through stages of acceptance at different speeds and in different sequences. The father might be in denial while the mother has moved on to anger. Remind yourself that these stages usually pass, and that your partner will soon move on at his or her own pace, with support and compassion.

> *My husband Shawn was great about the diagnosis. He said, "Our life didn't end when our sons were born with hemophilia. So what? There's a lot the boys can do. This is not a pity party." He was a great support for me.* —Carri Nease, Maryland

Stages of acceptance can take anywhere from a few weeks to months, or even years, especially if an inhibitor is stubborn and requires long-term treatment. Try to determine if you're stuck in a stage. If negative emotions seem to persist for months, consider some form of counseling. Children with inhibitors need emotionally stable, reliable parents who can work through periods of stress.

> *Krisdee tends to worry more, while I'm a little more optimistic: let's try this, get rid of this. She is more protective, and I am more gung-ho. This didn't cause any conflict, but it definitely reflected different coping styles. She was*

more prone to prevent bleeds, and I felt we should treat when they happen. We talked about it, and we balanced each other out. —Derek Nelson, Utah

After Acceptance: Getting Informed

When you are emotionally ready, you'll want more information about inhibitors. You'll make better decisions when you understand your treatment options. And with more decision-making experience, you'll feel more confident.

Your primary source of information should be your HTC. There are about 140 of them in the United States. If you are not currently being seen at an HTC, now is the time to request a referral, because treating inhibitors is beyond the scope of most hospitals or medical centers without an HTC. HTCs are centers of excellence that specialize in diagnosing and treating bleeding disorders. The physician who diagnosed your child can refer you to the nearest center, or you can locate HTCs on the Centers for Disease Control and Prevention (CDC) website or National Hemophilia Foundation (NHF) website. The HTC has a multidisciplinary team of specialists to

treat the family and patient as a whole. The focus isn't solely on treating individual bleeding episodes, but on offering acute and long-term care, family and genetic counseling, surgery, education, physical therapy (PT), clotting factor, and supplies specific to hemophilia patients.

At the time of this writing, no other books on inhibitors exist for patients and families, so for other print material you'll need to read booklets, brochures, and newsletters. Search for information on the Internet: most hemophilia organizations and pharmaceutical companies post informational articles. Mailing lists, forums, and social networking sites exist where families dealing with inhibitors can interact and learn from each other. Remember that information from the Internet can sometimes be unreliable: anybody can post articles, so misleading or incorrect information is not uncommon. If you have questions about what you read, call the nurse at your HTC to help find the answers.

Shock, disbelief, relief, anxiety. It wasn't until we spoke to more people in the hemophilia community that we realized the full implication of inhibitors. After the shock, we just wanted to learn as much as possible. —Richard and Lynley Scott, New Zealand

You'll get some of the best everyday information from other parents. It may be hard to find other parents in your area who have children with inhibitors, but the Internet and mailing lists can broaden your horizon and make it easier to find contacts. Ask your HTC to put you in touch with other parents in your area who have experience with inhibitors. You'll need to make an effort to find them and to stay in touch. But when you do, you'll learn that you are not alone.

To connect with inhibitor families, contact these resources:

- Your HTC, first and foremost

- National Hemophilia Foundation (NHF)
  800-42-HANDI or www.hemophilia.org

- Register as a member to receive the magazine *HemAware*
  www.hemaware.org

- Your local hemophilia foundation or association

- Hemophilia Federation of America (HFA)
  800-230-9797 or www.hemophiliafed.org

- Sign up to receive the *Parent Empowerment Newsletter* (PEN)
  LA Kelley Communications, Inc.
  800-297-9877 or www.kelleycom.com

The dual diagnosis of hemophilia and an inhibitor is challenging. Don't be overwhelmed by trying to absorb too much too soon. Your desire for knowledge may not keep pace with what's available: inhibitor education resources are being produced slowly, and other parents or support groups may be hard to locate. No single source can prepare you completely. When you're ready, read the available literature, meet with your HTC, check with hemophilia organizations, and meet other parents. Little by little, you'll become fluent in the language of inhibitors, and you'll feel more competent as the parent of your special child. ■

■NOTES

1. Antibodies are explained in chapter 2.
2. An inhibitor may be temporary when it is a transient inhibitor. See chapter 2.
3. Never alter your child's dosage regimen without first consulting your hematologist, who needs to know whether the prescribed dose is working.
4. Inhibitor tests should always be performed at an HTC-recommended laboratory. Inhibitor tests done outside an HTC may not be accurate and may need to be repeated at an HTC.
5. A bleeding disorder should be suspected in a baby who bleeds excessively after a circumcision. But a lack of bleeding does not rule out a bleeding disorder—the amount of bleeding after a circumcision may also depend on the circumcision method.
6. Lusher J. Inhibitors in young boys with haemophilia. *Best Practice & Research Clinical Haematology*. 2000;13(3):457–68.
7. Sadness is a normal reaction to life's unexpected blows. When sadness persists for weeks, even months, and interferes with normal activities that used to give you joy, you could be suffering from depression. Up to 80% of women who have recently given birth experience some sadness. Postpartum depression is more serious and can affect up to 25% of women after childbirth. The diagnosis of hemophilia and an inhibitor can further impact women who are already suffering mild to severe depression. Please speak to a social worker, clergy, or licensed therapist to determine if you are depressed. Depression can and should be treated.
8. From 2005 to 2010 a series of successful Inhibitor Education Summits was held, bringing members of the inhibitor community together. Please ask your HTC or NHF for updates about future inhibitor consumer meetings.

SUMMARY 1
A Surprising Diagnosis

- The inhibitor diagnosis is almost always a startling surprise for families.

- An inhibitor is usually detected when a child with hemophilia is young, usually in the first twenty exposure days and rarely after the hundredth exposure day.

- In rare cases, an inhibitor can develop in older children, teens, or adults.

- An inhibitor is usually diagnosed when a bleed does not resolve after regular treatment or during routine screening at an HTC clinic visit.

- It's normal for parents to experience a range of intense feelings after an inhibitor diagnosis: shock, denial, anger, and sadness.

- Fathers and mothers may react differently to the diagnosis.

- Make sure you are seen at an HTC, which specializes in treating people with hemophilia and their families, and has the expertise to deal with inhibitors.

- Contact other families with inhibitors through your HTC, local hemophilia organization, and Internet mailing lists and social networks.

- Read as much as you can about inhibitors without overwhelming yourself. Start with www.hemophilia.org and use the Internet to search for inhibitor information.

2 What We Know about Hemophilia and Inhibitors

Although an inhibitor diagnosis may seem to come out of the blue, inhibitors are really a normal reaction of the body's immune system. The immune system is our body's defense force, designed to protect us from foreign invaders. These foreign invaders include bacteria, viruses, and foreign proteins—in other words, anything that our body identifies as not belonging inside us, and as potentially harmful. Our immune system protects us in many ways, but one way is by creating specialized proteins that travel in the blood: *antibodies*.

Antibodies are custom-made proteins, specifically designed to recognize and attach only to a specific chemical or molecule on the surface of a foreign invader such as a virus or bacteria. But first, the immune system must recognize the foreign molecule, and to do that, the molecule must be introduced into the body. This is how vaccines work.

As a child, you probably received a polio vaccination. The polio vaccine is made of inactivated polio virus particles, given in a subcutaneous or intramuscular injection. A weakened virus may be given orally, but this is rarely done in the United States. Your immune system recognizes the virus particles as a foreign invader and, to combat the invader, begins to make antibodies that are specific to the polio virus. These antibodies, produced in response to the inactivated or weakened polio virus, are then capable of inactivating the infectious polio virus if you are exposed to the virus in the future. Although the number of polio antibodies produced by your immune system decreases over time, other cells in your immune system "remember" the polio virus, and are ready to rapidly produce more antibodies if you are ever again exposed to the polio virus. It's an efficient way to guard the body against *pathogens*, or disease-causing organisms.

Sometimes the immune system makes mistakes or becomes confused. For example, when you have allergies, your immune system is overreacting to essentially harmless stuff like dust or pollen. Sometimes the immune system mistakenly attacks the body itself, resulting in an autoimmune disorder such as lupus or acquired hemophilia.[1] And sometimes the immune system mistakenly identifies helpful agents, such as factor concentrate, as something harmful.

What Is an Inhibitor?

In hemophilia, an inhibitor is an antibody directed against factor. It develops when the immune system doesn't recognize either factor VIII or factor IX, and identifies infused clotting factor as a foreign and possibly dangerous protein. The immune system mounts an attack against the factor by creating antibodies. The antibodies are custom-made to attach to one or more of several areas on the infused factor molecule and neutralize, or *inhibit*, its action. The factor molecule is now unable to take its part in the clotting process. Consequently, the infused factor doesn't work, a clot can't form, and bleeding continues.

> I tell people my boys have a great immune system: it recognizes that they don't make factor, and when factor is infused, the immune system says, "Let's go get it!" —Carri Nease, Maryland

It's easy to understand why inhibitors may develop, especially if your child has severe hemophilia. A baby born with severe hemophilia lacks functional factor VIII or factor IX. As a result, his body never learns to recognize a complete factor molecule as a normal component of blood. Without normal factor circulating in the blood, his immune system never "learns" that factor is a useful protein—and infused factor appears truly foreign. That's why inhibitors happen mostly to people with severe hemophilia. People with moderate or mild hemophilia have some factor circulating in their bloodstream; the body recognizes its own factor as a normal part of the body, and usually recognizes infused factor as familiar, so no antibodies develop. But rarely, and for reasons we don't completely understand, some mild hemophilia patients do develop inhibitors, and bleed like patients with severe hemophilia and inhibitors.

Diagnosing Inhibitors

There are usually no external signs that your child with factor VIII deficiency has developed an inhibitor. Most commonly, inhibitors are discovered after you or your HTC team notice that infusions of factor fail to adequately stop bleeding. It's also common for children with factor IX deficiency to develop an allergic reaction to factor IX at the same time they develop an inhibitor. Inhibitors are sometimes diagnosed by routine blood tests at regular HTC clinic visits. Your HTC staff will want to screen for inhibitors often during the first year or so of treatment with factor, when the development of an inhibitor is most likely, and then about once a year after that. Your child will also be screened anytime he is scheduled to have surgery.

Your child's hematologist might want to test for an inhibitor more often if there is a family history: perhaps your father, uncle, or brother with hemophilia had inhibitors. If inhibitors are suspected, the hematologist will order a diagnostic screening test to determine the presence of an inhibitor. This initial diagnostic test for inhibitors is a *mixing study*, a test that mixes your child's blood plasma with normal plasma to see if the addition of the normal plasma will correct the clotting time. If your child doesn't have an inhibitor, the test will yield a normal clotting time, because the factor from the normal plasma will form a clot. But if he has an inhibitor, then the inhibitor from his blood will attack the factor in the normal plasma, and the clotting time will be prolonged. If this happens, your hematologist will order a more complex test called the *Bethesda Inhibitor Assay* (or Bethesda assay) to determine how much of the antibody is present.

Strength of the Inhibitor

The Bethesda assay does not directly test for the presence of an inhibitor, but instead measures an inhibitor's ability to inactivate factor.[2] The assay's results are expressed in numbers to allow a comparison or measurement of the inhibitor level—the higher the inhibitor level, the more factor the inhibitor is capable of inactivating. The strength or concentration of the inhibitor is reported as a *titer*, which is expressed in *Bethesda Units* (BU).[3] Your child could have a titer, or inhibitor level, of 1 BU, 10 BU, or even as high as 10,000 BU, though titers this high are rare.

Unfortunately, the Bethesda assay isn't foolproof. Results can vary widely from one lab to another, depending on how the blood sample was collected or the experience of technicians performing the assay. Also, the assay can't accurately detect very low levels of inhibitors, especially below 0.4 BU. And for some patients, the test does not work as expected, and the technician cannot accurately measure the level of an inhibitor. But overall, the Bethesda assay is a very useful, reliable indicator of the strength of an inhibitor.[4]

Inhibitor levels are usually grouped according to their BU numbers:

Low-titer inhibitor: less than or equal to 5 BU

High-titer inhibitor: greater than 5 BU

Of course, it's better not to have an inhibitor at all, but a low-titer inhibitor is preferable because you may be able to infuse larger-than-normal doses of standard factor concentrate to effectively treat bleeds. With high-titer levels, even large doses of factor won't be enough to control bleeds.

> *We found out a few days after the blood test. Our son's titer was 177 BU. I understood a little about inhibitors because the book Raising a Child With Hemophilia had a chapter on it.* —Jackie, Massachusetts

> I'm surprised by what I've learned about inhibitors since the diagnosis. I've learned exactly how close to the immune system the inhibitor works. Sometimes when my son gets sick, his inhibitor jumps by 10 BU to 15 BU.
> —Chasity, Mississippi

Inhibitors are classified in two ways:

1. By the inhibitor titer (BU)
2. By the response type (how the immune system responds to infused factor)

We've already discussed inhibitor level, or titer, as measured in BU. But there's another concern: How does the immune system respond to infused factor? Does the titer stay more or less constant over time after an infusion? Or does the titer increase within a week or so after the infusion?

- If your child's inhibitor titer is less than or equal to 5 BU, and it remains at that level even after an infusion, your child is a *low responder*.

For other people, when factor is infused, the immune system ramps up inhibitor production in an effort to eliminate or inactivate the infused factor. This results in an increased inhibitor titer within a week after exposure to factor.

- If your child's inhibitor titer rises above 5 BU over a few days after an infusion, your child is a *high responder*.

High-responding inhibitors are more challenging to treat, because the infused factor that is intended to resolve a bleed actually stimulates the immune system to fight the infusion at the same time (see chapter 3 for more on treatment).

> Caeleb's BU was over 2,300. I didn't realize that levels could get so incredibly high. We found out that levels in the thousands don't normally stay that high for long, but getting to 10 BU and below can take time. —Cazandra Campos-MacDonald, New Mexico

So it's important to understand both *inhibitor titer* and *response type*. Your child could have one of two combinations of titer and response:

- low titer / low responding
- high titer / high responding

In general, most people with low-titer inhibitors are also low responders, and those with high-titer inhibitors are high responders. High responders generally show an *anamnestic response*, or "memory response," after an infusion of factor. This means that following an infusion, the inhibitor titer will rise substantially after four to six days. Low responders do not show an anamnestic response after an infusion of factor: the inhibitor titer stays more or less stable.

Low-responding inhibitors sometimes disappear spontaneously after weeks or months: these are *transient inhibitors*. But high-responding inhibitors will not go away on their own. They are permanent unless eradicated by specialized treatment programs called *immune tolerance induction* or ITI (see chapter 4).

> Hayden demonstrated an inhibitor at one point, but it was transient. His titer was 1.0 BU at its highest, only for one month. —Derek Nelson, Utah

In some cases, a high responder can temporarily have a low inhibitor titer. How can this be? If a high responder is not exposed to factor for a long time (often a year or more), the immune system slowly decreases the number of antibodies produced against the factor. Eventually, with no exposure to factor, the inhibitor level may drop below 5 BU. Avoiding infusions of standard factor and using *bypassing agents* like *recombinant* factor VIIa (which does not cause anamnesis) to treat bleeds is a useful strategy to lower the inhibitor titer when preparing for elective surgery.

Make sure you know your child's inhibitor titer and response type. These help determine which therapy will be useful in treating a bleed.

How Many People Get Inhibitors?

What's the chance that someone with hemophilia will develop an inhibitor? It's hard to say. You may see widely differing numbers in various reports or brochures that list the percentage of people at risk for inhibitors. There are a number of reasons for this. First, hemophilia is a rare disorder, and hemophilia with inhibitors is even more rare—meaning the number of patients studied is small, so it's hard to get conclusive data. Second, different studies often use different methods—including how often they test for inhibitors—so the data produced by these studies can't be compared.[5] So far, there haven't been enough controlled studies of enough patients, using comparable methods, to state with certainty the risk of developing inhibitors.

Still, it's important to understand current research, and to stay informed on the latest study results. To do that, you'll need to understand two terms used in reporting rates of inhibitors: *incidence* and *prevalence*.

Incidence

Incidence means the number of *new* cases of a disease or disorder in a population during a specific time period. For example, the incidence of hemophilia is one in

5,000 male births per year, or about 400 American babies born with hemophilia every year. So for inhibitors, incidence means the number of new cases of inhibitors during a specific time period. This may be one year, but when studying inhibitors, it's usually cumulative: that is, results are collected from the entire time the study was conducted, possibly ten or fifteen years. Incidence shows how a disease changes over time, or when it's most likely to develop.[6]

Most researchers agree that the incidence of inhibitors in severe hemophilia A patients is about 20% to 30%. This means that about 2 in 10 people with severe hemophilia A develop inhibitors. The incidence of inhibitors in mild to moderate hemophilia A patients is much lower, about 1 in 15, or about 3% to 13%.[7] People with mild or moderate hemophilia generally don't develop inhibitors until adulthood. This may have to do with the fact that they infuse factor infrequently. Many people with mild or moderate hemophilia develop inhibitors after being exposed to large doses of factor after a major injury or during surgery, and large doses of factor delivered when the immune system is on high alert are thought to be a risk factor for developing an inhibitor. Unfortunately, when mild or moderate hemophilia patients do develop inhibitors, the antibodies can destroy not only the infused factor but also the body's *own* factor. This converts mild or moderate hemophilia to severe hemophilia. The good news is that about 60% of inhibitors in mild and moderate patients disappear on their own within an average of nine months.[8, 9]

Prevalence

Prevalence describes the proportion of individuals in a population who have a disease or disorder at a specific point in time—like a snapshot. For example, the prevalence of hemophilia in the United States is about 17,500 people, or about .01% of the general population. Roughly 1,200 of these people have inhibitors, which is a prevalence of about 7% of the American *hemophilia* population.[10] Prevalence numbers for inhibitors in people with hemophilia A are lower than incidence because these numbers do not include people with transient inhibitors that disappeared on their own, or those who have eliminated inhibitors through ITI.

The overall prevalence of inhibitors in hemophilia A is about 7% to 15% of all patients at any given time. This translates to about 1,200 to 2,600 people in the United States who currently have inhibitors. The prevalence of inhibitors in hemophilia B is about 2% to 3% of the total hemophilia B population.

> **How Common Are Inhibitors?**
>
> *Incidence: What are the chances of getting an inhibitor?*
> 20% to 30% of severe hemophilia A patients
> 1% of hemophilia B patients
>
> *Prevalence: How many people have inhibitors now?*
> 7% to 15% of hemophilia A patients
> 2% to 3% of hemophilia B patients
>
> The prevalence of inhibitors in hemophilia A is a lot lower than the incidence because it does not include transient inhibitors that disappear on their own, and the success rate of ITI in hemophilia A is high. The prevalence of inhibitors in hemophilia B is several times higher than the incidence. Why? Because few hemophilia B inhibitors are transient, and ITI is less successful than in hemophilia A; this means more inhibitor cases over time.

Why know the odds of getting an inhibitor when your child already has one? It might help you cope better if you know you're not alone. It may help you when making family plans for the future. And it helps to know that many inhibitors are low responding, and that patients can still use factor for treating bleeds. Some inhibitors can be overcome by ITI, and some even go away by themselves.

Risk Factors for Developing Inhibitors

We don't know exactly why some people get inhibitors and others don't. Even within a family, one child with hemophilia might get an inhibitor, while a sibling does not. We do know that certain circumstances, events, or traits might increase the risk of developing an inhibitor:

Type of factor deficiency. People with hemophilia A are ten times more likely to get inhibitors than are people with hemophilia B.

Severity of factor deficiency. People with severe hemophilia A or B are much more likely to get inhibitors than are people with moderate or mild hemophilia.

Type of mutation. People with certain genetic defects in the gene coding for factor VIII or IX are more likely to develop inhibitors. In hemophilia A, people with nonsense mutations, intron 22 inversions, and large deletions in the gene for factor VIII are at greatest risk of developing inhibitors.[11] The type of mutation is one of the most significant risk factors for developing inhibitors.[12]

Family history of inhibitors. The type of mutation that causes hemophilia in a particular family is the same for all family members who inherit the defective gene. So if your father, uncle, or brother had inhibitors, your child has an increased risk of developing an inhibitor. But keep in mind that although the family history and type of mutation are major risk factors for developing inhibitors, mutation and family history alone are not enough to predict for certain whether anyone will develop inhibitors.

I learned that both my uncles had inhibitors. It was comforting to know that Tristan was not an anomaly in our family. —Jessica Herren, Pennsylvania

Race. African Americans develop inhibitors at twice the rate of Caucasians. This is believed to be due to slight differences in the makeup of the factor VIII molecule. Most *plasma-derived* factor VIII concentrates, and all current recombinant factor VIII concentrates, contain a variant of the factor VIII molecule found mainly in Caucasians. These products may be more likely to trigger an immune system response in African Americans.[13]

Environmental effects. The possibility of developing an inhibitor may be slightly higher if your child receives an infusion of factor when his immune system is already on high alert. This might happen when your child is infused while he's fighting an infection, or perhaps just after an immunization.

Exposure to factor. Most inhibitors occur soon after exposure to factor, usually within the first twenty infusion days, with a median of nine to eleven exposure days. After 100 infusions, inhibitor development is very rare, but the risk is never completely gone: any hemophilia patient can develop an inhibitor at any time.

■ ■ ■

Some studies report that patients who receive their factor through a pump (called *continuous infusion*) have higher rates of inhibitors when compared to patients who receive factor through a single infusion, or *bolus*. We don't know the reason, but it may be related to *when* factor is delivered and not necessarily *how* it's delivered. Patients on continuous infusion are normally in hospitals recovering from major surgery or injury, and their immune systems may be on high alert, so they're more likely to develop inhibitors.[14, 15]

What Parents Need after the Diagnosis

As you can see, there's a lot to learn with an inhibitor diagnosis. You want information, even though you may feel overwhelmed and stunned. One mother couldn't recall anything her HTC staff had told her initially about inhibitors—everything happened as in a fog or slow motion. She simply wasn't absorbing the information. Still, the best way to receive the diagnosis is in person at the HTC, where you can ask questions, get educational materials, and be reassured that you'll be able to manage the inhibitor. Remember that understanding this material and accepting the diagnosis takes time and patience.

> We were given heaps of information, but we needed time to process the diagnosis before much learning took place. The doctors and hemophilia nurses were willing to answer our questions. But the information was overwhelming, and though it was supposed to comfort us, it seemed totally confusing. The doctors empowered us to learn about the inhibitor diagnosis, and over time, we got on with life and realized that this was another mountain to climb and conquer! —Richard and Lynley Scott, New Zealand

> The doctors had never spoken to us about the possibilities of inhibitors. We rarely met with our son's doctor until his comprehensive clinic, four months after his inhibitor diagnosis. What I really wanted was to speak to others who were going through or had already experienced what we were facing now. —Sasha Cheatham, Oklahoma

The measurements and statistics presented in this chapter can give you a sense of the bigger picture of inhibitors. The Bethesda assay will give you a measurement that helps to determine the best treatment for your child's inhibitor. Now it's time to decide which treatment he'll receive. ■

■NOTES

1. Acquired hemophilia is not genetically inherited but is an autoimmune disorder that may suddenly occur, typically in women after giving birth or in the elderly fighting cancer or an infection.
2. Always have the Bethesda Inhibitor Assay performed at an HTC because lab technicians there are familiar with the test. Have repeat tests done at the same HTC because the assay results may differ slightly from lab to lab.
3. An inhibitor plasma that contains 1 BU of antibodies per mL will neutralize 50% of factor VIII or factor IX activity in an equal volume of pooled normal plasma after the mixture is incubated at 37 degrees C for 2 hours. Hillarp A. Basic *in vivo* coagulation and laboratory aspects of hemophilia [Internet]. Malmö, Sweden: Dept of Clinical Chemistry, University Hospital [cited 2010 Feb. 10]. 59 p. Available from:

    http://www.wfh.org/2/docs/Programs/IHTC-Lab-Training-module.pdf; Kitchen S, McCraw A. Diagnosis of haemophilia and other bleeding disorders: a laboratory manual [Internet]. Montréal: World Federation of Hemophilia; 2000 [2010 Feb. 10]. 108 p. Available from: http://www.wfh.org/2/docs/Publications/Diagnosis_and_Treatment/Lab_manual_web.pdf
4. Some laboratories perform a modified Bethesda assay, referred to as the Nijmegen Modification of the Bethesda assay, or the Nijmegen method, that produces fewer false positives at low inhibitor levels as compared to the standard Bethesda assay.
5. Another issue to consider is that often the people citing risk levels have a preexisting bias, and they may be selecting the numbers that bolster their perspective. For example, proponents of recombinant products have often downplayed results that could be interpreted as suggesting higher rates of inhibitor formation in patients using recombinant factor, while proponents of blood-derived products have chosen to highlight the higher number of inhibitors detected in those studies, without acknowledging that the results may simply be a case of looking more closely at patients with more sensitive assay methods.
6. Be careful when trying to compare the incidence rates among different studies. The population's age, the sample size, and the length of time the study was conducted may produce wide variations that are not comparable. And different studies may calculate the incidence in different ways.
7. Hay CR. Factor VIII inhibitors in mild and moderate-severity haemophilia A. *Haemophilia.* 1998;4:558–63.
8. Hay CR, Ludlam CA, Colvin BT, Hill FG, Preston FE, Wasseem N, Bagnall R, Peake IR, Berntorp E, Mauser Bunschoten EP, Fijnvandraat K, Kasper CK, White G, Santagostino E. Factor VIII inhibitors in mild and moderate-severity haemophilia A. UK Haemophilia Centre Directors Organisation. *J Thromb Haemost.* 1998 Dec;80(6):1036–37.
9. Hay CR. Factor VIII inhibitors in mild and moderate-severity haemophilia A. *Haemophilia.* 1998 Jul;4(4):558–63.

10. Because inhibitors are about ten times more common in hemophilia A than in hemophilia B, this combined prevalence overestimates the prevalence of inhibitors in hemophilia B patients and underestimates the prevalence of inhibitors in hemophilia A patients.
11. A mutation is a change in the genetic material (DNA) of an organism. In hemophilia, there are several types of mutations that can result in factor deficiency. A nonsense mutation in a gene tells the cell to stop assembling the protein before the factor molecule is finished, resulting in a shortened, nonfunctional factor molecule. An inversion happens when a section of a gene is reversed, and the gene cannot code for functional factor. An intron is a non-coding section of gene important in assembling the final protein. A deletion is a loss of part or all of the section of the gene that codes for factor, resulting in the inability to produce factor.
12. Ragni MV, Trucco M, Jaworski K, Yan J, Feng J, Hashimi H, Hill KA, Sommer SS, the Hemophilia Inhibitor Study. Large deletion mutations are linked with hemophilia inhibitors of high titer and short tolerance induction. *Blood.* 2003;102:162a.
13. Viel KR, Ameri A, Abshire,TC, Iyer RV, Watts RG, Lutcher C, Channell C, Cole SA, Fernstrom KM, Nakaya S, Kaspe CK, Thompson AR, Almasy L, Howard TE. Inhibitors of factor VIII in black patients with hemophilia. *N Engl J Med.* 2009;361(5):544.
14. White B, Cotter M, Byrne M, O'Shea E, Smith OP. High responding factor VIII inhibitors in mild haemophilia: is there a link with recent changes in clinical practice? *Haemophilia.* 2000;6:113–15.
15. Von Auer CH, Oldenburg J, Von Depka M, Escuriola-Ettinghausen C, Kurnik K, Lenk H, Scharrer I. Inhibitor development in patients with hemophilia A after continuous infusion of FVIII concentrates. *Ann NY Acad Sci.* 2006 Jan 9;1051; Issue Autoimmune Diseases and Treatment Organ-Specific and Systemic Disorders:498–505.

SUMMARY 2
What We Know about Hemophilia and Inhibitors

- Inhibitors are a normal reaction of the body's immune system.

- Inhibitors are antibodies, custom-made proteins designed to inactivate factor. They develop when the immune system doesn't recognize factor concentrate, and produces antibodies to neutralize it. The infused factor does not work, a clot can't form, and bleeding continues.

- The Bethesda Inhibitor Assay is a test to measure the strength, or titer, of the inhibitor, described as Bethesda Units (BU). An inhibitor titer can be 1 BU, 10 BU, or even as high as 10,000 BU.

- Inhibitors are classified in two ways: by titer and by the immune system's response to infused factor.

- An inhibitor less than or equal to 5 BU is a low-titer inhibitor; an inhibitor greater than 5 BU is a high-titer inhibitor.

- Low-titer inhibitors are preferable because you may be able to effectively treat bleeds by infusing larger-than-normal doses of standard factor concentrate.

- If your child's inhibitor titer is less than or equal to 5 BU, and it remains at that level even after an infusion, your child is a low responder.

- If your child's inhibitor titer rises above 5 BU several days after an infusion of factor, he's a high responder. High-responding inhibitors are more challenging to treat because standard factor concentrates are not effective at stopping a bleed.

- Low-responding inhibitors that disappear spontaneously after weeks or months are called transient inhibitors.

- The incidence of inhibitors in severe hemophilia A patients is about 20% to 30%.

- Certain people with hemophilia have a higher risk of developing inhibitors: people with severe hemophilia A or B; people with certain genetic defects in the gene coding for factor VIII or IX; people with a family history of inhibitors; African Americans; and people receiving infusions while fighting an illnesses or infection.

- The greatest risk of developing an inhibitor is within the first twenty infusions of factor.

3 Treating Acute Bleeding

As a parent, you are probably most concerned with knowing how to stop a bleed when your child has an inhibitor. Controlling bleeds with an inhibitor present is a challenge, but it's not impossible. There are two main treatments for acute bleeds in the presence of inhibitors:

- High doses of standard factor concentrate
- Infusion of special factor concentrates called bypassing agents

Your hematologist will determine which treatment to use based on two observations:

- Your child's inhibitor titer: the Bethesda Units
- How his inhibitor level responds to infused factor: high responding or low responding

Our HTC called and said Bode has an inhibitor: "Don't give him more factor. We'll call you and let you know what to treat him with." I didn't understand what they meant. Why not give him factor? —Ashley Druckenmiller, Iowa

Treatment with High Doses of Factor

As we discussed in chapter 2, there are two types of inhibitors: low responding and high responding. Hemophilia patients with low-titer, low-responding inhibitors are easier to treat. Because even after exposure to factor, the inhibitor level in low responders remains fairly low—less than 5 BU—meaning that bleeds can usually be controlled with frequent, large doses of standard factor concentrate.

How does that work? Large doses of infused factor overwhelm the inhibitor. As the inhibitor tries to neutralize or inactivate the circulating factor, there simply aren't enough antibodies to do the job. Some of the factor is neutralized, but not all. Enough factor is left in the bloodstream to participate in the clotting process. A dose of factor two to three times higher than normal is often enough to control bleeding. Of course, the higher the inhibitor level, the higher the dose of factor needed to control a bleed. If your child's inhibitor titer is more than 5 BU, this type of treatment will not be not effective.

Factor must also be infused more frequently if your child has an inhibitor. Why? Because the inhibitor is constantly inactivating some of the factor, so the factor will disappear more quickly.

Sometimes, high doses of factor can successfully control bleeds in high responders. How? If your child hasn't been exposed to factor for a long time (possibly a year or more), the immune system will slowly decrease antibody production, and his titer may drop to a level low enough to allow a standard factor concentrate to be effective for a few days. In this case, a few high doses of factor may successfully control a bleed before the anamnestic response, or memory response, kicks in and the body begins to ramp up production of inhibitors. Knowing this, you can plan strategically with your HTC: if your child is having elective surgery, you can avoid exposure to factor by using one of the bypassing agents described in the next section; this will allow the inhibitor titer to decrease. Then, when surgery day arrives, you can successfully control bleeding by using a standard factor concentrate for a few days, followed by a bypassing agent after the inhibitor titer rises. Of course, once the inhibitor has rebounded, or peaked, about five to seven days later, the high inhibitor makes infusions of standard factor useless.

Treatment with Bypassing Agents

If your child has a high-titer, high-responding inhibitor, standard factor concentrates will be useless in treating his bleeds. Why? Because the inhibitor will inactivate virtually all of the factor, regardless of how much factor is infused. In this case, your hematologist will prescribe a bypassing agent. A bypassing agent is a clotting factor, or combination of clotting factors, designed to skip the need for—bypass—a particular clotting factor.

To visualize how bypassing agents work, think of the clotting process, or *clotting cascade*, as a line of standing dominoes.[1] Clotting factors circulate in the blood in an "inactivated" form, ready to participate in the formation of a clot. When an injury occurs, a chemical reaction causes the first clotting factor to be "activated"—imagine it knocking over the first domino in line. The first factor then activates the second factor—as the first domino falls, it knocks over the second domino. If all the factors were functional, with none destroyed by inhibitors, this chain reaction process would continue—the line of dominoes would fall, one after another.

Using this analogy, when the last domino is knocked over, fibrin fibers are produced, making a strong fibrin clot. If one of the factors (dominoes) is removed, then the process will stop at the gap in the line, and no fibrin will be produced. A bypassing agent allows the clotting process to continue by "jumping" the gap. Imagine knocking down the next domino after the gap using your finger as the bypassing agent.

There are two types of bypassing agents, and each jumps the gap in a different way:

1. *Activated prothrombin complex concentrates* (aPCCs) are plasma-derived products containing several clotting factors, some of which are already activated. These factors are ready to activate the next clotting factor in the cascade without the need for the missing clotting factor. These products are usually used for patients with factor VIII deficiency who have developed an inhibitor to factor VIII, although some patients with inhibitors to factor IX also use them.

2. *Recombinant factor VIIa* (rFVIIa) uses a different pathway in the clotting cascade to bypass the need for the missing clotting factor. Using the domino analogy, it skirts around the gap and continues to knock over the dominoes, until the end—formation of a fibrin clot.

Activated prothrombin complex concentrates

The only aPCC currently available in the United States is FEIBA VH, produced by Baxter BioScience.[2] FEIBA stands for *factor eight inhibitor bypassing activity*. FEIBA contains activated clotting factors II (prothrombin), VII, IX, and X, which have been naturally activated during processing. FEIBA has been available in America for more than thirty years, and it has a good track record of *efficacy*—how well it works to clot blood.

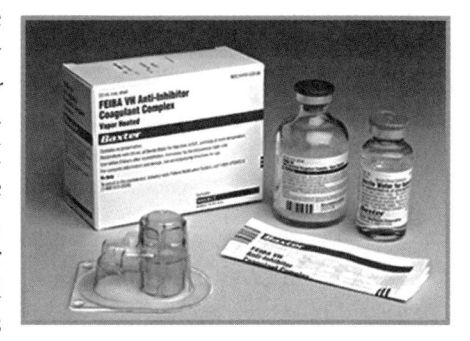

FEIBA does carry the risk of some side effects. One possible side effect is anamnesis. FEIBA contains very small amounts of factor IX and factor VIII *antigen*. An antigen is anything that produces an immune response by the body. FEIBA can produce anamnesis in about 20% of patients with hemophilia A and can also cause anamnesis in hemophilia B patients, causing the inhibitor level to rise or stay elevated.[3] Despite this, FEIBA is effective in controlling bleeds for most people with inhibitors.

Managing Your Child's Inhibitor

Dosing of FEIBA must be closely monitored and should not exceed 100 units per kilogram of body weight (written U/kg) at twelve-hour intervals, or 200 U/kg per day. More frequent or higher dosing may increase the risk of an uncommon but dangerous and sometimes fatal side effect called *disseminated intravascular coagulation* (DIC), in which unwanted clotting occurs throughout the body. The risk of DIC is normally very low—less than one half of one percent. But the risk of DIC may be increased by certain injuries, such as crush injuries or blunt trauma. The presence of a *port* (see chapter 7) or other risk factors for blood clots, such as recent surgery, blood infection, or severe liver disease, may also increase the likelihood of unwanted clots developing when FEIBA is used. Your HTC team should monitor your child for blood clots and DIC in the event of serious injuries, when using high FEIBA doses, or during prolonged use of FEIBA.

> We treated bleeds every twelve hours with FEIBA and used ice as much as possible. FEIBA would eventually get rid of the bleed. —Sasha Cheatham, Oklahoma

Recombinant factor VIIa

Recombinant factor VIIa is known in America by its brand name, NovoSeven® RT, manufactured by Novo Nordisk Inc. It is not derived from human plasma, but is a recombinant product, made through DNA technology. NovoSeven uses a different pathway in the clotting cascade than FEIBA does, which eventually results in the formation of fibrin and the production of a strong fibrin clot at the site of the injury.

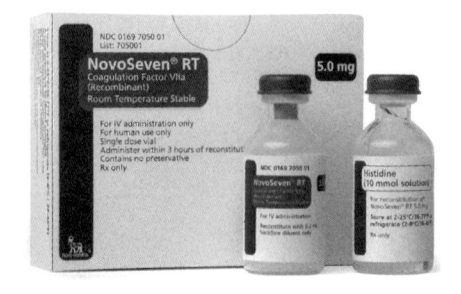

Because NovoSeven contains no clotting factors other than recombinant factor VIIa, there is no risk of an anamnestic response to factor VIII or IX, which would provoke the inhibitor to rise. For this reason, NovoSeven is the product of choice for people with factor IX inhibitors who have allergic reactions to factor IX. As with FEIBA, the risk of DIC with NovoSeven is very low. In fact, because NovoSeven operates mainly at the site of the injury, it's thought to be even less likely than FEIBA to cause DIC.[4] But with prolonged treatment, or when treating certain types of injuries (such as crush injuries or blunt trauma), your child should be monitored for this possible complication. Finally, because NovoSeven is not produced from blood plasma, it is free from human blood-borne viral infection.

We had misinformation from our HTC. They scared us about using NovoSeven because of thrombotic events, which we learned was unfounded.
—Anonymous

We made sure we gave Jonathan NovoSeven right after an injury, quickly: 1.2 mg[5] every two to three hours, at least for a few days, even if we thought the bleed was resolved. —Jackie, Massachusetts

On the negative side, NovoSeven has a very short *half-life* of a little over two hours. The body uses up infused factor over time: half-life refers to the time it takes for half of the infused clotting factor activity to disappear. The half-life for most standard factor VIII concentrates is about twelve hours. With NovoSeven's short half-life, half the activity is gone in about two hours, so frequent infusions are needed to keep factor levels high. If your child needs repeated infusions, this can be expensive and can disrupt daily routines.[6]

FEIBA versus NovoSeven

Both NovoSeven and FEIBA are effective at stopping bleeds. Which product will work best to stop your child's acute bleeds? There are several reasons for choosing one product over another.

One reason is *potential reactions*. If your child has hemophilia A and experiences anamnesis when exposed to the factor VIII antigen in FEIBA, or if he has hemophilia B and suffers from severe allergic reactions when exposed to the factor IX in FEIBA, he will need to use NovoSeven.

Another reason is *unequal response* to these products. NovoSeven works best for some people, but for others, FEIBA works best. Your child may have varying responses to one or both products. Some patients have found they must use both products, alternating doses between one product and the other: for example, first an infusion of NovoSeven; then perhaps several hours later, an infusion of FEIBA, or vice versa. This strategy is normally used when one product doesn't effectively stop a bleed.[7] *Caution: Alternating products in this manner should only be done under the supervision of your HTC.*

A third consideration is *convenience*. FEIBA is infused only once every twelve hours, and NovoSeven is infused every two to three hours. On the other hand, with FEIBA the infusion time is thirty to forty-five minutes, due to the higher volume, while NovoSeven can be infused in just a few minutes, due to its lower volume. Each family, with their HTC, should choose the product that best treats a bleed, while also considering frequency of infusions and insurance coverage.

> We started treating Bode's bleeds with FEIBA, but his titer went from 2,000 BU to 2,500 BU. The factor VIII in FEIBA was spiking it. Sometimes FEBIA works for us, sometimes it doesn't. —Ashley Druckenmiller, Iowa

> We've tried both FEIBA and NovoSeven. There was no significant improvement in bleeds with either one. For me, the convenience of NovoSeven was greater, even though it was every two to three hours. FEIBA had to be pushed over an hour because of the higher volume. —Sonji Wilkes, Colorado

Also note how the two products are dosed. FEIBA is dosed in units (U) and comes in different assay sizes:[8]

500 U

1,000 U

2,500 U

Dosing is determined by your child's weight (in kilograms, not pounds) and by the severity of the bleed. Your doctor can explain dosing and tell you how much factor to use for each type of bleed.

NovoSeven is dosed differently than FEIBA. It's measured in micrograms, not units. One microgram is one millionth of a gram—or about thirty-five billionth of an ounce! Microgram is abbreviated as mcg or μg, with mcg more commonly used in medicine to avoid errors in reading scripts. Many parents just refer to micrograms as "mikes." And you might need to brush up on your math: vials of NovoSeven are not labeled in micrograms, but in milligrams (mg). Currently, NovoSeven is available in four assay sizes:

Measurements to Memorize

1 pound (lb) = 0.45 kilograms (kg)
1 kg = 2.2 lb
1 milligram (mg) = 1,000 microgram (mcg)
0.09 mg = 90 mcg

1.0 mg (1,000 mcg)

2.0 mg (2,000 mcg)

5.0 mg (5,000 mcg)

8.0 mg (8,000 mcg)

The standard NovoSeven dose is 90 micrograms per kilogram of body weight, written as 90 mcg/kg. You can say, "ninety mikes per kilo." Depending on the type of bleed and the efficacy of NovoSeven, your child's dose may range from 35 mcg/kg to 120 mcg/kg, and sometimes substantially higher than this for those who employ *megadosing* (see next section).

For example, a child weighing 60 lb (27 kg) who is prescribed 90 mcg/kg should get 2.4 mg of NovoSeven every two to three hours. How to do the math? Convert 90 mcg to mg by moving the decimal point three places to the left, and then multiplying by the weight in kg. In other words,

0.09 mg x 27 kg = 2.43 mg/kg

Because NovoSeven does not come in a 2.4 mg dose, your HTC will tell you whether to use a 2 mg vial, or 1 mg and 2 mg vials, for each dose.

Megadosing with NovoSeven

We've found that with severe bleeds, an initial triple dose of NovoSeven, followed by regular doses for a couple of days, is the only thing that works to get a hold on the bleed. —Cicely Evans, Massachusetts

At times, even the recommended dose of NovoSeven may not do the trick. Parents and physicians have found that doubling or tripling the initial dose, and infusing less often, can sometimes help stop a bleed more effectively than using a lower dose spread out over several hours. Although studies show that NovoSeven resolves 90% of bleeds after one or two infusions, it's sometimes more effective to use a higher single dose, or megadose.[9] But some studies have also found that this method can be more expensive than using the standard 90 mcg/kg dose. Still, you might do this simply for convenience: it's hard to infuse every two hours when you need to work, your child needs to go to school, and you all need to sleep.

We've been doing megadosing. A year ago, we would dose our son at 90 mcg/kg with NovoSeven and repeat every two hours, as prescribed. This was a lot of factor and a huge disruption in life. Depending on the severity of bleed, we dosed every two hours through the night. Our HTC recommended every two hours for forty-eight hours! Each infusion took ten to fifteen minutes, start to finish. Now, with higher dosing, we've seen a big difference: if we got right on top of it and gave a higher dose of 240 mcg/kg initially, followed by another dose of 160 mcg/kg after four to six hours, it would stop all the bleeding. —Anonymous

Recent studies have shown that giving a single megadose (200 to 300 mcg/kg) every six to eight hours may be more effective than giving a series

---

Recommended Dosing

NovoSeven: 90 mcg/kg every 2–4 hours

FEIBA: 75–100 U/kg every 12 hours

of three 90 mcg/kg doses (one dose every two hours), and may eliminate the need for frequent infusions.[10, 11] If you are giving more than three doses of 300 mcg/kg, contact your HTC for further instructions.

> *A pharmaceutical medical liaison spoke to our HTC about megadosing. Now the HTC will write a prescription for it. We did prophylaxis dosing with NovoSeven: one 160 mcg/kg dose per day, or one 2 mg vial. If there is breakthrough bleeding, our doctor leaves it up to us. We'll use a 1 mg vial, or a 1 mg vial plus a 2 mg vial to make 3 mg. —Anonymous*

Megadosing is considered an *off-label* use of NovoSeven, not approved by the United States Food and Drug Administration (FDA). Although megadosing has been clinically studied, it has not been approved by the FDA and may increase the risk of thrombotic complications (excessive clotting at other sites). Because of this, *you should not try any dosing changes without first consulting your hematologist.* It's important to talk to your HTC about individualizing the dosing regimen to fit your child's needs and your family's lifestyle; but at the same time, it's essential to protect your child by using proper and safe dosing under HTC supervision. You can't sacrifice an effective treatment just because it's inconvenient.

> *We give NovoSeven in a double dose on first infusion, and follow up every two to three hours with a single dose, but only up to six doses per day.[12] —Jane, Massachusetts*

Using Both Products to Treat a Bleed

Manufacturer guidelines recommend that when your child has a bleed, he should receive either NovoSeven *or* FEIBA. Yet as we discussed earlier, some families with inhibitors are instructed by their physicians to alternate dosing using FEIBA *and* NovoSeven. This is also considered off-label use, not FDA approved. Novo Nordisk and Baxter BioScience both warn that this practice may increase the risks of DIC and thrombotic complications. Still, some parents have found it to be the only treatment regimen that works.

Jackie Russell Photo

> *One product alone won't stop bleeds for us. Now we give doses of FEIBA, which takes forty minutes; then in six hours, we give NovoSeven; then in six hours, we give FEIBA; and so on, until the bleed stops. —Debbie Porter, California*

If we pretreat for activities, we use FEIBA—like the time Leland flew to Texas, or when he went snowmobiling. When he has a bleed, we start with NovoSeven for three to four days. If the bleed hasn't resolved, which it often does not, then we switch to FEIBA. —Jane, Massachusetts

When a bleed is serious or life-threatening, contact your HTC hematologist immediately, especially when one product doesn't seem to be controlling it, no later than twelve to twenty-four hours after the onset of the bleed and administration of product.

Adjunct Therapies

Along with factor concentrates, of course, you can always use ice when your child has a bleed. Parents know that following RICE (see chapter 11) helps slow bleeds and aids in healing.

Factor, rest, ice, compression, elevation, and the occasional lollipop for comfort. —Jessica Herren, Pennsylvania

But additional medicines and treatments, called *adjunct therapies*, can also help reduce bleeding, increase factor's effectiveness, improve clotting, and retain clots.

Antifibrinolytic agents

Antifibrinolytic agents inhibit the breakdown of clots by preventing the body's natural enzymes from dissolving the fibrin fibers in the clot. These products often are used to help retain clots on mucous membranes, as with bleeds in the mouth or nose, where clots may be easily dislodged. But their effect isn't limited to mucous membranes: they also help retain clots throughout the body. Of course, for antifibrinolytics to be effective, a strong fibrin clot must already be in place. This means that antifibrinolytics are effective only *after* a dose of factor, or after a clot has formed.

Antifibrinolytics are for short-term use only—usually less than seven days and sometimes up to ten days. They should not be taken when a kidney bleed is in progress, or when blood appears in the urine, because they may prevent the normal breakdown of blood clots in the kidney and cause kidney damage or severe pain from the clot, much like a kidney stone.

Currently, two antifibrinolytics are available in the United States: (1) epsilon aminocaproic acid, sold under the brand name Amicar®, available as an elixir (syrup) and in tablet form; and (2) a more potent antifibrinolytic called tranexamic acid (TXA), sold under the brand name Lysteda™ and available in tablet form. Another brand of TXA is Cyklokapron®, available in the United States as an intravenous injection, but not as tablets.

We treat our son Tristan with NovoSeven, 2.4 mg every two to four hours depending on the type of bleed. We also elevate and ice the area when necessary. We give 7 mL of Amicar every four to six hours for mouth bleeds. We have used FEIBA to help with breakthrough bleeds. —Jessica Herren, Pennsylvania

Always check with your HTC hematologist *before* using any antifibrinolytics when you are using FEIBA or NovoSeven. Use with FEIBA may increase the risk of DIC. For this reason, Baxter recommends that you do not use antifibrinolytics until twelve hours after administering FEIBA. Amicar has been used along with NovoSeven, but the use of Amicar with NovoSeven has not been studied in a clinical trial. It's currently not known if an increased risk of DIC exists when an antifibrinolytic is taken with NovoSeven.

Porcine (pig) factor VIII

Until 2004, some patients with factor VIII inhibitors used porcine factor, derived from pigs. Porcine factor VIII is similar enough to human factor VIII that it functions well in the human clotting system, yet it's different enough that it largely escapes detection by inhibitors to human factor VIII.

Unfortunately, repeated exposure to porcine factor VIII often causes the immune system to produce more inhibitors to human factor VIII. It also stimulates the development of new inhibitors targeting the porcine factor VIII and making it ineffective. The previously available porcine factor VIII product sometimes caused severe allergic reactions and a drop in platelet counts. Even worse, it often was contaminated with porcine parvovirus, common in pigs, which is resistant to viral inactivation methods. Because of concerns about this virus and the frequent side effects, the product was discontinued in 2004. As of this writing, Ipsen Limited is working with Octagen Corporation to test a recombinant porcine factor VIII. Early results from the clinical trials are promising, and the incidence of allergic reaction is low.

Immunosuppressive drugs

In some cases when time permits—as before elective surgery or ITI—inhibitor levels can be reduced by giving immunosuppressive drugs, such as steroids or immunomodulatory drugs like rituximab or cyclophosphamide, or high doses of human gamma globulin (often called IVIG for *intravenous immunoglobulin*). These drugs depress the immune system, reducing the level of inhibitors produced (read more about immunosuppression in chapter 4). Temporarily reducing the inhibitor level may allow more effective bleeding control during surgery, or may increase the success rate of ITI.

We went to the hospital, put our son in the intensive care unit, and were there for a month and a half. Our HTC team started him on steroids while giving him low doses of factor IX, and then slowly started to wean him off the steroids while increasing the factor dose. Eventually he tolerated the factor IX and had no reaction. It worked! —Anonymous

Plasmapheresis

It's also possible to reduce the inhibitor level by removing the inhibitor through a process called plasmapheresis, also known as therapeutic plasma exchange. The basic procedure involves passing the blood through a machine that separates blood cells from plasma. The blood cells are returned to the patient, and the plasma is replaced with fresh plasma (from another donor) or with a saline solution containing albumin. Saline solution is preferred over fresh plasma because of concerns of anamnesis, viral infection, and allergic reactions from fresh plasma. Because the inhibitors (antibodies) are found in the plasma, removing some plasma lowers the inhibitor level. Two or three liters of plasma may be removed during a single plasmapheresis session, which can reduce the inhibiter titer by as much as 40%.[13] The treatment may consist of a single session, or several sessions per week over several weeks. Reducing the inhibitor through plasmapheresis allows a patient to use standard factor VIII or factor IX concentrate to control bleeding.

Plasmapheresis reduces inhibitor levels only temporarily, but the two or three days of lowered inhibitor levels permit effective factor replacement therapy, possibly making it easier to control bleeding or allow surgery with less risk to the patient.

Immunoadsorption

Immunoadsorption is similar to plasmapheresis: the blood is slowly passed through a machine that separates blood cells and plasma. But in immunoadsorption, the plasma is also passed through a column of beads coated with *monoclonal antibodies*, which selectively remove the inhibitor from the plasma before it's returned to the patient.

Compared to plasmapheresis, immunoadsorption can reduce the inhibitor titer to a lower level. It's also faster because the treatment *selectively* removes the inhibitors and can process more than two or three liters of blood. Although immunoadsorption is available in Canada and several European countries, it's not readily available in the United States outside of clinical trials. The FDA considers immunoadsorption experimental.

■■■

Treating bleeding episodes in the presence of an inhibitor is always a challenge. Currently, none of the products used to treat bleeds in people with inhibitors is as effective as pure factor VIII or IX in people without inhibitors. As a result, your child with an inhibitor tends to bleed for a longer time. This increases his risk of complications including *hemophilic arthropathy* (joint destruction caused by repeated bleeds) and life- or limb-threatening hemorrhages, plus the possible side effects of their treatment.

A relatively new treatment option for patients with inhibitors is prophylaxis, or regular infusions, with bypassing agents to help prevent bleeds. Although very expensive, prophylaxis with bypassing agents has been shown to reduce the frequency of joint bleeds and help maintain joint health and range of motion (ROM).

> *From the middle of fourth grade until the end of tenth grade, Reuben was on daily NovoSeven prophylaxis. For the past two years, he has been on daily FEIBA prophylaxis. For acute bleeds, especially joint bleeds, he takes the steroid prednisone to reduce inflammation at the injury site. He has also applied ice packs to injuries to ease pain and swelling.* —Wendy Sass, New York

Using FEIBA and NovoSeven, along with some of the adjunct therapies (see chapter 6), you and your hematologist can experiment to find the treatment that works best for your child. And while you look for that, your hematologist may also ask you to consider trying another approach: *eradicating* the inhibitor with ITI. This therapy attempts to "retrain" the immune system so it produces fewer or no inhibitors, allowing regular infusions of factor VIII or IX to treat bleeds. For many families, ITI is the key to eliminating inhibitors. ■

Which Bypassing Agent for Your Child?

Product Characteristics	NovoSeven RT	FEIBA VH
Immune response	no anamnestic response	may elicit anamnestic response
Source	recombinant	plasma
Volume	small	larger
Infusion time	5 minutes	30–45 minutes*
Frequency of infusion	every 2–3 hours	every 8–12 hours
Side effects	blood clots, DIC	in factor IX patients: allergic reactions, blood clots, DIC
Safety	no risk of viral contaminants	risk of viral contaminants considered extremely low

*without a port

■ NOTES

1. The domino analogy of the clotting cascade is for illustration and does not accurately represent the actual clotting process.
2. Both aPCCs and a related product, prothrombin complex concentrates or PCCs (also called factor IX complex), have been used to treat bleeding in patients with inhibitors for more than thirty years. But PCCs are rarely used because several studies have shown them ineffective in controlling bleeds.
3. Ewing NP, Pullens L, De Guzman C. Anamnesis in patients with hemophilia and inhibitors who receive activated prothrombin complex concentrates for prophylaxis. *J Thromb Haemost.* 2007;5(Sup 2): P-T-158.
4. Some off-label uses of NovoSeven—not approved by the U.S. FDA—such as use in heart surgery, have shown an increased risk of DIC.
5. This dosing was appropriate for the original NovoSeven, no longer on the market, but not for NovoSeven RT, the current product of Novo Nordisk.
6. Clinical trials of an extended half-life form of recombinant factor VIIa are underway as of this writing.
7. Using NovoSeven and FEIBA sequentially or in combination is considered off-label use. Please do not attempt this without your HTC hematologist's supervision.
8. Remember that an assay is a laboratory test that determines what is present and how much is present in the blood. Here it refers to the amount of factor present in the vial.
9. Lusher JM, Roberts HR, Davignon G, Joist JH, Smith H, Shapiro A, Laurian Y, Kasper CK, Mannucci PM. A randomized, double-blind comparison of two dosage levels of recombinant factor VIIa in the treatment of joint, muscle and mucocutaneous haemorrhages in persons with haemophilia A and B, with and without inhibitors. rFVIIa Study Group. *Haemophilia.* 1998;4:790–98.
10. Parameswaran R, Shapiro AD, Gill JC, Kessler CM, HTRS Registry Investigators. Dose effect and efficacy of rFVIIa in the treatment of haemophilia patients with inhibitors: analysis from the Hemophilia and Thrombosis Research Society Registry. *Haemophilia.* 2005 Mar;11(2):100–106.
11. Ng H, Lee L. Recombinant activated clotting factor VII (rFVIIa) in the treatment of surgical and spontaneous bleeding episodes in hemophilic patients. *Vasc Health Risk Manag.* 2006 Dec;2(4):433–40.
12. Using NovoSeven in this way is not approved by the FDA and should be considered only if recommended by your doctor or HTC.
13. Kasper, C. Diagnosis and management of inhibitors to factors VIII and IX: an introductory discussion for physicians [Internet]. Treatment of hemophilia monograph #34. Montréal: World Federation of Hemophilia, 2004 Sep. [cited 2010 Feb 16]. 26 p. Available from: http://www.wfh.org/2/docs/Publications/Inhibitors/TOH-34_English_Inhibitors.pdf

SUMMARY 3
Treating Acute Bleeding

- There are two main treatments for acute bleeds in the presence of inhibitors:

    High doses of standard clotting factor concentrate

    Infusion of bypassing agents

- A bypassing agent is a clotting factor, or mixture of clotting factors, designed to skip the need for, or bypass, a particular clotting factor.

- FEIBA is a plasma-derived bypassing agent. Dosing should not exceed 100 U/kg of body weight at twelve-hour intervals, or 200 U/kg per day.

- NovoSeven RT is a recombinant bypassing agent that contains only factor VIIa and operates mainly at the site of the injury. It requires infusions approximately every two to three hours. The standard NovoSeven dose is 90 mcg/kg.

- NovoSeven and FEIBA are not equally effective for all inhibitor patients. Reasons for choosing one or the other include efficacy, dosing convenience, anamnesis, and risk of allergic reactions (factor IX).

- Megadosing means using a single high dose of NovoSeven (200 to 300 mcg/kg) instead of a series of three standard doses (one 90 mcg/kg dose every two hours). *Always check with your HTC hematologist before using a megadose.*

- Antifibrinolytic agents help retain clots, often on mucous membranes, as with bleeds in the mouth or nose, where clots are easily washed away. *Always* check with your HTC hematologist *before* using any antifibrinolytics when you are using FEIBA or NovoSeven.

- Immunosuppressive drugs, plasmapheresis, and immunoadsorption are other ways to lower the inhibitor temporarily, and may be useful for elective surgeries.

4 ITI: Eradicating the Inhibitor

The ultimate goal in treating inhibitors is to eradicate your child's inhibitor. With the inhibitor titer low, you may be able to use large doses of your child's standard factor concentrate to treat bleeds without worrying that all the factor will be destroyed by the immune system. With the inhibitor gone, you will once again be able to use normal doses of your standard factor concentrate. Standard factor resolves bleeds more effectively, reduces the incidence of complications like joint disease, and greatly improves quality of life.

Immune tolerance induction (ITI)[1] is a treatment protocol that attempts to eradicate the inhibitor. ITI requires frequent infusions of factor VIII (if your child has hemophilia A) or factor IX (if he has hemophilia B) in an attempt to overwhelm or desensitize the immune system so that it no longer produces the inhibitor. Your HTC hematologist may want to start your child on ITI soon after he's diagnosed with an inhibitor. There is no standard regimen or protocol for ITI. Protocols are individualized to fit the type and level of inhibitor, and to meet the unique needs of the patient and family. Also, each HTC usually has a preferred protocol. Even so, if your child's initial round of ITI is not successful, your HTC may try additional rounds of ITI using different protocols, hoping that one can eradicate the inhibitor. You'll need to be patient and flexible, as this may be a long and difficult process.

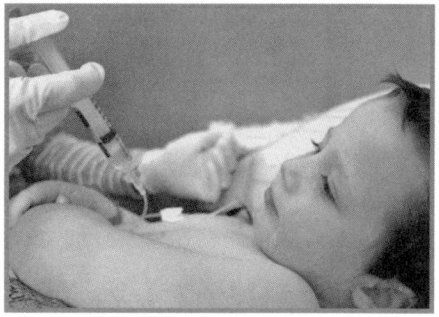

Jon Orlando Photo

Immune Tolerance Induction

Regardless of which ITI protocol your HTC tries, all protocols are designed to teach the immune system to recognize factor VIII or IX without eliciting an immune response—that is, without producing an inhibitor. ITI is similar to *allergy immunotherapy*, used for people with allergies to desensitize them to certain allergens, such as pollen. In allergy immunotherapy, regular injections of the allergen are given over a long period. Eventually, after repeated exposures to the allergen, the body learns to recognize the foreign substance without mounting an allergic response. In other words, the body gets used to the allergen.

With ITI, frequent infusions of factor are given for months, even years. This helps the immune system to either (1) tire of producing antibodies, or (2) learn to recognize factor as a normal body protein, eventually lowering or stopping the production of inhibitors. How this really works is still unclear. The ultimate goal of ITI is to eliminate the inhibitor altogether, or to reduce it to titers low enough that standard factor concentrates may be used for treating bleeds.

> **What Does Inhibitor Tolerance Mean?**
>
> A patient who successfully completes a course of ITI is said to be *tolerized*. The goal of ITI is complete tolerance: a sustained undetectable inhibitor titer, with the infused factor having a normal half-life and recovery.
>
> The term *partial success* is sometimes used to describe someone whose inhibitor titer has dropped below 5 BU but will decrease no farther. In this case, infused factor has a recovery of less than 66%, a half-life of less than six hours, and no anamnestic response over six months of on-demand treatment or twelve months[2,3] on prophylaxis. Partial success can also describe people who have an undetectable inhibitor, but with an inadequate half-life and recovery.

We think the inhibitor went down within days of starting ITI, because he never got bruises or bleeds. Nine months later, his titer was less than 0.5 BU! —Kari Atkinson, Iowa

Paul was five when we started ITI. He had daily infusions at 100 IU/kg. Within a year, his titer was down to zero; Paul was tolerized. —Kerry Fatula, Pennsylvania

Although ITI was first used successfully in 1977 in Bonn, Germany, there still is no general consensus about the best or most effective protocol to eradicate an inhibitor. Because of the limited number of patients with inhibitors available for studies, no randomized trials have yet been published comparing one protocol to another. Each protocol varies by the amount of factor VIII prescribed per dose and by how frequently doses are administered.[4] And some protocols call for adjunct therapies, such as immunosuppressive drugs, to be used simultaneously. Protocols may vary from twice-daily infusions of factor to as few as three infusions per week. The ideal factor dosage for ITI is also a matter of debate. Worldwide, here are the best-known protocols:

Bonn protocol. 200 IU/kg of factor VIII every day. This is the highest dosage of the ITI protocols.[5]

Dutch protocol. 25 IU/kg of factor VIII every other day. This is the lowest dosage of the ITI protocols.

Malmö protocol. This intensive, two- to four-week inpatient protocol uses high doses of factor VIII in conjunction with immunosuppressive drugs in an attempt to shorten ITI treatment time and achieve immune tolerance in about a month.[6, 7]

Most American HTCs prescribe daily doses of 50 to 100 IU/kg of factor. But they will adapt the protocol to fit the needs of the patient, and will consider the family's ability to participate in very aggressive treatment regimens. Some HTCs start with high doses once or twice daily, and then reduce the dose when the patient begins to respond. Others begin with a lower or less-frequent dose, and then increase the dose or frequency if they see no progress. Most American HTCs reserve the Malmö protocol for patients who fail all other regimens.

> *We tried the Malmö protocol in October 1995, when Leland was age two years, six months. His titer was 66 BU. Before starting Malmö, we started plasmapheresis to get his titer down. It was an outpatient treatment of four visits over ten days; each visit took several hours. That got his titer below 5 BU. —Jane, Massachusetts*

Which protocol will your HTC recommend? Because there is no conclusive evidence to guide your physician or HTC, this decision is often based on your hematologist's personal preference or "gut feeling." Here, the art of medicine transcends the current science. Your hematologist may refer to a study of ITI protocols, called the International ITI (I-ITI) study, conducted from July 2002 to October 2009. As of this writing, the final results of the I-ITI study are not yet available. Until these results are published, you and your hematologist will be taking some shots in the dark, trying to find the protocol that works best for your child.[8] Even after the results of the I-ITI study are known, the best ITI regimen will still be a matter of debate for many patients who are not considered good risks.

Most ITI regimens last one to two years. But if slow, steady improvement occurs, ITI may be continued for more than four years. Many HTCs will switch ITI protocols if no progress is seen on a particular protocol after twelve to twenty-four months. Technically, ITI failure is defined as no success in eliminating the inhibitor after thirty-three months, or when there is no consistent (at least 20%) fall in the inhibitor titer every six months.[9]

Regardless of which treatment you try, ITI is intense, challenging for the family, and expensive. But it's almost always the first step in treatment when trying to control an inhibitor.

When to Start ITI

It's generally agreed that it's best to start ITI as soon as possible after your child is diagnosed with an inhibitor, especially if the inhibitor titer is less than 10 BU. And ITI seems to work best in young children.[10] Still, some HTCs may wait several weeks or months before implementing ITI, to see if the inhibitor is transitory and will resolve on its own, or to allow the inhibitor to drop below 10 BU.

It's also generally agreed that the best time to start is when the inhibitor titer is low. If your child's titer is below 10 BU, your HTC may recommend starting ITI right away. If it's higher, your HTC may want to wait until the titer drops below 10 BU. Normally, without further exposure to factor, the inhibitor titer will fall over time. This can be a very slow process because the inhibitor decreases by 50% every three to four weeks. For example, if the inhibitor titer is 1,000 BU, it would take about seven months for it to fall below 10 BU. This means that you'd need to use a bypassing product, such as NovoSeven or FEIBA, to treat bleeds while waiting for the inhibitor titer to drop. ITI is more successful when the patient's historic maximum inhibitor titer is below 200 BU and his peak titer while on ITI is below 500 BU.[11] The level of the inhibitor at the start of ITI has been shown to be more important than the timing of starting ITI.

What Type of Factor Concentrate for ITI?

ITI regimens are varied and individualized, and debate continues about which product is best to use. Often, American HTCs begin ITI using the product on which the inhibitor developed. In most cases, this is recombinant factor VIII. If this strategy doesn't lower the titer, some HTCs will next consider a plasma-derived product containing *von Willebrand factor* (VWF).

Why might factor VIII products with VWF be more successful at inducing tolerance? Perhaps because the body is less likely to recognize the factor VIII protein as being foreign when VWF is attached. That's because factor VIII occurs naturally with VWF. VWF is like a chauffeur: its job is to protect, drive, and deliver factor VIII to its destination—the injured blood vessel. When VWF attaches itself to factor VIII, it hides some of the areas on the factor VIII molecule that attract inhibitors. In this way, VWF may reduce the risk of inhibitor formation.

How Long to Try ITI?

There is no consensus on how long to try ITI. Of course, the goal is to stay on ITI until the inhibitor is eradicated—that is, until the titer falls below detectible levels, and the recovery and half-life are normal or nearly normal. But this may never happen.

If your child is not responding well to ITI, how long should you continue before calling it quits or trying another protocol?

Be patient: you may need to stay with one protocol, or one type of factor concentrate, for twelve to twenty-four months before you abandon it for another. And if all ITI attempts are unsuccessful after thirty-three months, ITI should be stopped.

Typically, when your child begins ITI, the inhibitor titer will start to rise within two or three days after exposure, and spike sometime within the first month because of anamnesis. Recall that in anamnesis, the immune system "remembers" the offending antigen (factor) and rapidly ramps up the immune system to produce antibodies (inhibitors) to attack the invader (the infused factor).

What happens over the next few months after the initial anamnestic spike may be the most important part of any ITI program, indicating how successful your program will be. Shortly after the inhibitor spikes during the first month, an equally sharp *drop* in the titer often happens during the second month. Then, following the second month, the titer may continue to drop for another two months or longer. After this, the titer tends to stabilize.

For most patients on ITI, the inhibitor titer will drop below detectable limits within four to six months after starting ITI (or sooner on some protocols) and remain undetectable. When the inhibitor titer is undetectable, and the recovery and half-life of infused factor is at least near normal, patients are said to be completely tolerized. In the United States, after patients are tolerized, they are rapidly weaned off their regimen and placed on prophylaxis, often for life. For example, a hemophilia A patient may be prescribed factor VIII at 100 IU/kg daily; then 50 IU/kg daily; then 50 IU/kg every other day; then 25 IU/kg daily until he is infusing factor two or three days a week. Exactly what to do after tolerization is achieved remains debatable, but most physicians agree that without an ongoing prophylaxis regimen, there's a higher chance that the inhibitor will reoccur.

For another, smaller group of patients on ITI, the inhibitor titer may drop to low levels during ITI but never become undetectable: this is called partial success.[12] As we discussed earlier, partial success means that the inhibitor acts like a low-responding inhibitor so these patients can use high doses of standard factor concentrate to control bleeds. Patients who have partial success on ITI usually don't repeat ITI if they can easily and effectively be treated for bleeding with high doses of factor VIII and are not bleeding on prophylaxis.

For others on ITI, there is no significant drop in inhibitors after the first month. This happens most often in patients who have high-titer inhibitors at the start of ITI, and whose peak titer after initiating ITI climbs over 500 BU. These patients are at high risk of failing ITI. In the United States, some HTCs add a short course of low-dose prednisone or another corticosteroid if the drop in the inhibitor titer is slow.

Managing Your Child's Inhibitor

> *We tried ITI on Tristan immediately; his titer was well over 100 BU. We began treating him with factor VIII every day for the first six months. Tristan stayed on ITI for about eighteen months with no success.* —Jessica Herren, Pennsylvania

ITI requires frequent blood tests to monitor the inhibitor titer and half-life of the infused factor. Recall that the half-life is the time it takes for the body to use up half of the circulating factor. The normal half-life of factor VIII is about ten to twelve hours, and the half-life of factor IX is about twenty-four hours. For factor VIII, half-life means that about twelve hours after an infusion, you should have about half of the infused factor still circulating in your bloodstream. If an inhibitor is present, then at twelve hours you will have significantly *less than* half of the initial dose of factor still circulating in your bloodstream. For example, if your child receives a dose of 50 IU/kg of factor VIII, the expected factor level is 100% a few minutes after the dose is infused. Twelve hours later, it's expected to be half that, or 50%. If the circulating factor level is far below 50%, then the inhibitor is still present.

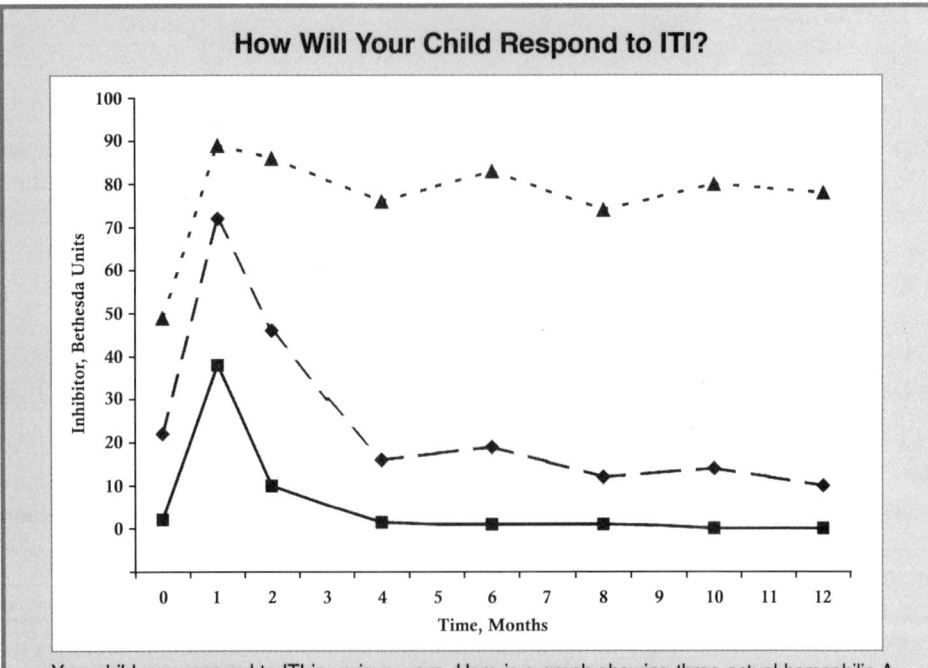

How Will Your Child Respond to ITI?

Your child may respond to ITI in various ways. Here is a graph showing three actual hemophilia A patients on immune tolerance, using 50 IU/kg/day. The solid line (bottom) shows a patient whose inhibitor titer rose sharply during the first month, fell sharply in the second, and then gradually fell to zero. The dashed line (middle) shows a patient whose titer rose in the first month and fell slowly. This patient still had some inhibitor detectable after two years. The dotted (top) line shows a patient whose inhibitor never fell notably, and who later was found to have a large factor VIII gene deletion.[13]

Part of me wants to stop my son's ITI, but part of me says we cannot. It's our best chance. If we stop, his body would respond with a vengeance. The inhibitor would come back stronger. —Sonji Wilkes, Colorado

When ITI Is Most Successful

ITI succeeds most often when the patient's inhibitor titer is below 10 BU at the start of ITI. Patients with an inhibitor titer above 10 BU at the start of ITI are not considered good candidates for ITI.[14] To increase the chance of success, doctors sometimes wait before starting ITI until the inhibitor titer drops below 10 BU naturally, which can take up to several months.[15] Or they may encourage a short-term drop in inhibitor titer through plasmapheresis, or by suppressing the immune system with drugs so ITI can be started. Depleting the inhibitor with plasmapheresis is short term, lasting only a few days. Plasmapheresis is usually reserved for emergency situations, such as surgery, to help manage life-threatening bleeding.

The good news? Today, ITI is effective 60% to 80% of the time in factor VIII inhibitor patients.

The downside is that other factors influence ITI's success. Infections during ITI reduce the success rate. This is a particular concern for patients with ports, because port infections are common. And most children on ITI have ports. Port infections during ITI may reduce the success rate; but it's hard to do ITI *without* a port, because venous access is more difficult for the many infusions needed (see chapter 7). Temporarily stopping or interrupting ITI also greatly decreases the success rate. Once started, ITI therapy should not be interrupted.

> ITI is considered to have failed when . . .
>
> it doesn't eliminate the inhibitor after 33 months
>
> *or*
>
> a consistent (at least 20%) fall in the inhibitor titer doesn't occur every 6 months while receiving ITI.

Nate was four when we started ITI. But his body has never accepted the port well. When you get a port infection, the immune system is aroused, and then the inhibitor goes high. We had him on ITI at 100 IU/kg every day. He had several port infections, and [during the infection] the inhibitor would shoot to 300 BU or even 600 BU. —Kerry Fatula, Pennsylvania

Still, once achieved, tolerization is lasting, and few people relapse and find their inhibitor returning.

From Failed ITI to Immunosuppression

ITI doesn't work in 20% to 40% of patients. If your child's titer is not decreasing on ITI after twelve to twenty-four months, then your HTC might recommend using a different factor concentrate or different protocol, or including adjunct therapies to help lower the inhibitor. The most important adjunct treatment to increase the success rate of these stubborn cases may be immunosuppression.

Because an inhibitor is the result of an immune response, it makes sense that drugs designed to depress the immune system might also help decrease inhibitor production. Immunosuppressive drugs used to treat hemophilia inhibitors fall into four main categories:

1. Chemotherapy drugs
2. Steroids
3. Immunoglobulins (IVIG)
4. Rituximab

Occasionally, two other immunosuppressive drugs may be used: cyclosporin A and mycophenilate mofetil, both used in transplant medicine.

Chemotherapy drugs

The most commonly used chemotherapy drug for inhibitor treatment is cyclophosphamide (generic for the brand names Endoxan, Cytoxan®, Neosar, and Revimmune). It works by stopping or slowing cell growth and depressing the immune system. Cyclophosphamide has several side effects and is a carcinogen—it may cause cancer. Because it lowers the body's ability to fight infection, people with hepatitis C (HCV) or human immunodeficiency virus (HIV) should not take this drug.

> Under Malmö we administered Cytoxan and IVIG. There sometimes is a peak [in inhibitor titer after starting ITI], but I don't think anyone expected it to reach 1,700 BU, as Leland's did. It was frightening. The doctors were surprised at how high it went. Every week it started coming down, and we went in weekly for tests, then every month. I don't think his titer went below 100 BU, and we kept getting more aggressive [in our treatments]. It would plateau, and then we'd up the dose . . . it finally wouldn't budge. And we had to accept that we wouldn't beat it. —Jane, Massachusetts

Steroids

Drugs like prednisone reduce inflammation but also suppress the immune system.

Immunoglobulins

Immunoglobulins are mixtures of antibodies isolated from plasma obtained from blood donors. Administration of IVIG leads to a temporary reduction in the inhibitor. Exactly why this works is unknown. Not all patients respond to IVIG, and inhibitor titers rarely decrease to undetectable levels when using IVIG.

Rituximab

This monoclonal antibody anti-cancer drug is approved for treating lymphoma. Its use for inhibitors is considered off-label, but early trials suggest that it may be helpful in treating factor VIII inhibitors. Currently no standardized protocol exists for using rituximab, but several trials have administered one dose weekly for two to five weeks. Although the effects of rituximab may last for several months, the reduction in inhibitors doesn't seem to be permanent. Several HTCs have had some success using rituximab in patients who have failed conventional ITI. Although rituximab seems to have few side effects, as with any immune suppression regimen, systemic infection—which affects the entire body—is a major concern and may cause death.

> *Andrew was on ITI for twenty-two months. One year after stopping ITT, he continued to have a level of 6 to 10 BU. He was having frequent bleeds in his knee. We had difficulty maintaining a port free of infection, and venous access was not happening. We made a collective decision to trial a course of rituximab. The strain of recurrent hospitalization was affecting us as a family and Andrew as an individual. We started rituximab in June 2005. The protocol was weekly infusions of rituximab for four weeks, then monthly infusions for five months; total treatment course was six months. On September 25, 2005, Andrew was inhibitor-free. He continued his treatment and had his last dose of rituximab in January 2006. He continues inhibitor-free two years later, with all his cell counts returning to normal. —Richard and Lynley Scott, New Zealand*

> *The administration of rituximab involves four-hour infusions, if you are lucky. The first dose was inpatient, with subsequent doses outpatient. Thomas watched Spider-Man and sat quietly through it all. We also gave him Benadryl®, which knocked him out. Rituximab nauseated him, and he'd throw up for a day or two afterward. —Sonji Wilkes, Colorado*

■■■

All immunosuppressive drugs increase the risk of systemic infection. This is especially worrisome for patients with ports, which includes the vast majority of people on ITI. Doctors probably won't administer these drugs to patients with HCV or HIV. People infected with hepatitis B (HBV) absolutely must not use rituximab because it often causes "reactivation" of the hepatitis B infection, possibly resulting in fatal hepatitis.

Most immunosuppressive drugs have significant short-term and long-term side effects. Except for low-dose, short-term courses of steroids, immunosuppressive drugs are not commonly used in the United States. Although rituximab seems promising, more data are needed before the drug becomes accepted in America. In Europe, immunosuppressive drugs are used more often to treat inhibitors: the Malmö protocol uses high-dose factor replacement in combination with cyclophosphamide and high-dose IVIG to shorten the time needed for tolerization.

> *Chemotherapy is a four-week course, once a week. We did ours on a Friday, so if our son was sick, it was over the weekend, but then he was well enough to attend preschool on Tuesday through Friday. He had an anti-nausea pill, which worked sometimes. The protocol halved his titer from 60 to 30 BU. So we were pleased. And we took a month off, just ITI and no chemotherapy.*
>
> *We did a second course and added Cytoxan, which is infused via an IV. The whole thing takes about eight hours. Administering the drug takes thirty minutes, but they hydrate you two hours before, two hours after—and there are the typical hospital delays. It made our son a little sicker than did the rituximab. We used lower doses so he didn't lose his hair. He received Cytoxan only once a month, for six months. At month five, he had a zero titer. But we did month six anyway. He had a zero titer for three months, and then it came back at 1.4 BU. —Sonji Wilkes, Colorado*

After ITI: Prophylaxis

If ITI is successful, and the inhibitor is eradicated or reduced to low levels, your child probably will be placed on prophylaxis. Prophylaxis is the scheduled infusion of factor concentrate, usually two or three times per week, to maintain a constant presence of factor in the bloodstream. It makes sense: once the immune system is trained to recognize factor as part of the body, you'll want to ensure continued exposure to factor. If you stop prophylaxis, and factor levels go down, the body may "forget" what factor is, and the inhibitor can come back when you next infuse. Prophylaxis helps keep the inhibitor at bay, and has the added benefit of preventing bleeding episodes!

We weren't clearly told that once we had eradicated the inhibitor, our son would be on some sort of standard factor replacement for a very long time or even life. —Sasha Cheatham, Oklahoma

After Paul was tolerized, we went to 50 IU/kg every other day. Even now, when his dose gets too low, his inhibitor will go up. —Kerry Fatula, Pennsylvania

Treating to eradicate the inhibitor will be a challenging time in your life. No single treatment protocol is guaranteed to work. You'll have frequent trips to the hospital, consistent monitoring of inhibitor titers and factor half-life, long waits, and unpleasant side effects. It's inconvenient and expensive. It's also mentally and physically draining on the patient and family. Yet most families gladly endure the hardships of ITI because if it's successful, quality of life improves immeasurably. ∎

ITI went fine, but it was tough. The HTC would give Ethan massive doses of factor. Every day we went to the HTC. We'd come home every day, and Ethan didn't want to be touched because he was so sore; we'd put him in his baby bed. He has a bird feeder outside his window, and he would watch the birds. ITI went on for two years—every day for two years. Ethan has a high tolerance to pain, and he learned to deal with ITI. God gives these kids a special gift of strength to deal with this. —Kim Stubbs, Mississippi

Matthew's Story

Matthew tried ITI three separate times: at age six months, four years, and eight years.

The first time, we started at age six months and continued until Matthew was age two years, six months. It began with daily infusions of recombinant factor VIII at 100 IU/kg. We then switched to a monoclonal product at the same dosage. Then we switched to continuous infusion: Matthew wore a portable pump that delivered 100 IU/kg over a twenty-four-hour period. The protocol was then switched from the continuous infusion to twice-daily infusions at 100 IU/kg. That was the first attempt—all failed.

The second attempt, when Matthew was four, was the Malmö protocol. First we did plasmapheresis to remove antibodies; this took six hours, three days in row. Then Matthew received IVIG, Cytoxan, and daily infusions of a monoclonal factor VIII at 200 IU/kg. This caused the inhibitor to rise "off the charts," and we stopped when the inhibitor was around 48,000 BU. Matthew was also having severe reactions to the IVIgG, and it was difficult to get enough blood donations to do the plasmapheresis. It was horrible.

The third attempt, at age eight, used a [plasma-derived factor VIII] product containing VWF. We started at daily doses of 50 IU/kg, and then later increased to 100 IU/kg. The inhibitor initially dropped to around 60 BU but began rising steadily afterwards. This was ended after one year of treatment because of trouble with venous access.

On all attempts except the Malmö, we first saw a rise in inhibitor level, followed by a drop in the level, then followed by a steady rise in the level. The inhibitor has never gone away. It has never dropped below 30 BU, which was where it was at the time of Matthew's initial diagnosis.

— *Debbie Porter, California*

■NOTES

1. Sometimes called immune tolerance therapy or ITT.
2. DiMichele D, Hoots W, Pipe S, Rivard G, Santagostino E. International workshop on ITI: consensus recommendations. *Haemophilia*. 2007;13:1–22.
3. The pharmacokinetic parameters currently used to define ITI success in patients with severe and mild haemophilia A were established by consensus at the Second International Conference on Immune Tolerance held in Bonn, Germany, in 1997. These parameters include an undetectable inhibitor level (<0.6 BU), FVIII plasma recovery >66% of predicted, FVIII half-life >6 h after a 72-h FVIII washout period, and the absence of anamnesis upon further FVIII exposure [57]. This definition has been adopted by the I-ITI study [23], which defined partial success as a reduction of the inhibitor titer to <5 BU; FVIII recovery of less than 66% of predicted; and FVIII half-life of <6 h after a 72-h FVIII washout period associated with clinical response to FVIII therapy and no increase in the inhibitor titer exceeding 5 BU over a six-month period of on-demand treatment or twelve months of prophylaxis. Dimichele D. Immune tolerance therapy for factor VIII inhibitors: moving from empiricism to an evidence-based approach. *J Thromb Haemos*. 2007 Jul 9;5(Sup 1):143–50.
4. These protocols only mention factor VIII patients because only factor VIII patients were used in the original studies. Fewer hemophilia B patients develop inhibitors and thus there is less data on how to perform ITI for factor IX inhibitors.
5. In the original Bonn regimen, patients were also treated with another medication (FEIBA) to suppress or prevent bleeding. It was thought that this was an important way to diminish stimulation of the immune system due to bleeding. IU stands for International Unit, a measurement of standard factor VIII or factor IX. FEIBA is measured in units (U) only.
6. The Malmö protocol was developed at the University of Lund, Malmö University Hospital, Sweden. The protocol uses intravenous immunoglobulin (IVIG) and cyclophosphamide to depress the immune system.
7. Kasper, C. Diagnosis and management of inhibitors to factors VIII and IX: an introductory discussion for physicians [Internet]. Treatment of hemophilia monograph #34. Montréal: World Federation of Hemophilia, 2004 Sep [cited 2010 Feb 16]. 26 p. Available from: http://www.wfh.org/2/docs/Publications/Inhibitors/TOH-34_English_Inhibitors.pdf
8. Prior to its closure in December 2009, the international Immune Tolerance Induction Study compared two dosing regimens of factor infusion: a low-dose, three-times-per-week versus a high-dose daily infusion. Researchers and HTCs worldwide hope that the data from this study, when released, will reveal the best dosing regimen for ITI. Hay RM, DiMichele, DM, Mauser-Bunschoten EP. Immune tolerance induction study [Internet]. [place, publisher unknown] [cited 2009 Jan 4]. Available from: http://www.itistudy.com
9. Hay CRM, Yoshioka A, Rivard G, Goldstone J, Keegan J, Goldberg I, DiMichele DM. International Randomized Immune Tolerance (ITI) Study: Progress Report [Internet]. [place unknown]: Central Manchester Children's University Hospitals [cited 2010 Feb 16]. 1 page. Available from: http://www.itistudy.com/HayPoster1.pdf

10. Some studies have found no correlation between the success of ITI and the time interval between inhibitor detection and start of ITI. Lenk H; ITT Study Group. The German Registry of Immune Tolerance Treatment in Hemophilia–1999 update. *Haematologica.* 2000 Oct;85 (Sup 10):45–47.
11. Mariani G, Ghirardini A, Bellocco R. Immune tolerance in hemophilia-principal results from the International Registry. Report of the factor VIII and IX Subcommittee. *J Thromb Haemost.* 1994 Jul;72(1):155–58.
12. Santagostino E, Coppola A, Tagliaferri A, Mancuso ME, Scaraggi FA, Biasoli C, Schinco PC, Iorio A, Latella C, Di Minno G. Immune tolerance induction (ITI) in patients with hemophilia A and inhibitors: the Italian Retrospective-prospective Registry: the Profit Study. *J Thromb Haemost.* 2007;5(Sup 2): P-W-128.
13. Kasper, Carol K., Diagnosis and Management Of Inhibitors To Factors VIII and IX: An Introductory Discussion for Physicians. World Federation of Hemophilia. 2004; #34. http://www.wfh.org/2/docs/Publications/Inhibitors/TOH-34_English_Inhibitors.pdf
14. Mariani G, Ghirardini A, Bellocco R. Immune tolerance in hemophilia-principal results from the International Registry: report of the factor VIII and IX Subcommittee. *J Thromb Haemost.* 1994 Jul;72(1):155–58.
15. ITI Study Newsletter [Internet]. 2007 March; (4). 8 pages. Available from: http://www.itistudy.com/Newsletter%20March%202007.pdf

SUMMARY 4
ITI: Eradicating the Inhibitor

- The ultimate goal in treating inhibitors is to eradicate or eliminate the inhibitor.
- With the inhibitor titer low or gone, you may be able to use high doses of your child's standard factor concentrate to treat bleeds.
- ITI requires frequent infusions of factor in an attempt to overwhelm or desensitize the immune system and eliminate the inhibitor.
- There is no standard ITI regimen or protocol. Protocols are individualized to fit the type and level of inhibitor, and to meet the individual needs of each patient and family.
- A patient who loses his inhibitor through ITI is said to be tolerized.
- There are several ITI protocols. The most common: Bonn protocol (200 IU/kg of factor VIII every day); Dutch protocol (25 IU/kg of factor VIII every other day); Malmö protocol (high doses of factor VIII in conjunction with immunosuppressive drugs).
- ITI is most successful if started when the inhibitor titer is below 10 BU.
- Although ITI is often started as soon as possible after an inhibitor diagnosis, there is no scientific basis for this approach. Waiting for the inhibitor titer to drop below 10 BU will increase the chance of successful tolerization.
- Waiting to start ITI may allow some low-titer inhibitors to resolve on their own (transient inhibitors).
- You may need to do one ITI protocol for twelve to twenty-four months before trying another protocol or another type of factor concentrate.
- ITI requires frequent blood tests to monitor the inhibitor titer and half-life of the factor.
- ITI doesn't work in 20% to 40% of patients. Your HTC might recommend another round of ITI using a different factor concentrate, a different protocol, or adjunct therapies to help lower the inhibitor.
- Immunosuppressive drugs, designed to depress the immune system and reduce inhibitor titers, may be the most important adjunct therapy to increase the chance of success for a second round of ITI.

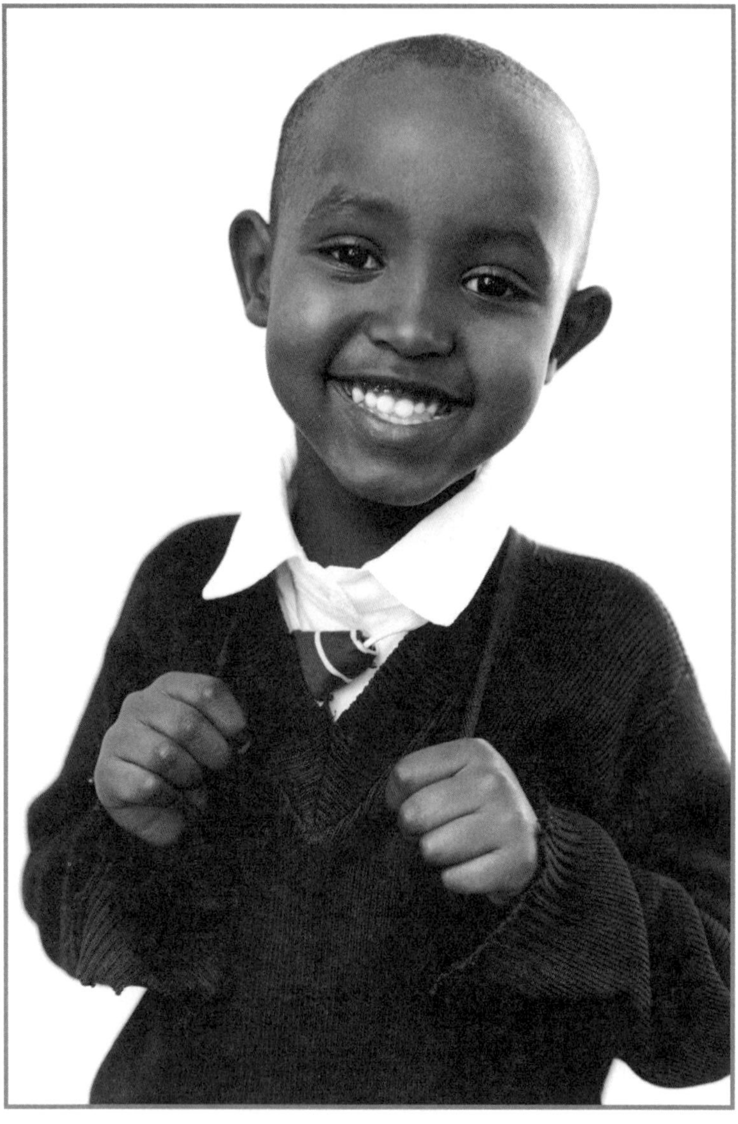

5 Factor IX Deficiency and Inhibitors

Your child with hemophilia B is very special. First, it's a rare thing to have hemophilia at all. Hemophilia A, known as classical hemophilia or factor VIII deficiency, affects only about one in 5,000 males. And hemophilia B, known as factor IX deficiency or Christmas disease, is even more rare, affecting only one in 30,000 males.[1] About 15% of people with hemophilia have hemophilia B.

If your child has hemophilia B *and* an inhibitor, that's even more rare. Although inhibitors can develop in patients with hemophilia A or B, their prevalence is about ten times lower in hemophilia B. About 20% to 30% of people with hemophilia A have inhibitors, while only 2% to 3% of people with hemophilia B have inhibitors.[2]

> *Everything I'd read said that usually people with factor VIII deficiency, not factor IX, had inhibitors. So I was confused and wasn't sure what to think.*
> *—Anonymous*

Hemophilia B and Inhibitors

Why are inhibitors less common in hemophilia B? No one is really sure. One theory is that certain genetic mutations (partial and complete gene deletions) that often cause hemophilia A, and that carry a higher risk of inhibitor development, are less common in factor IX deficiency. So this may contribute to the lower risk of inhibitors in people with hemophilia B. Or perhaps when compared to the factor VIII protein, the factor IX protein is less *immunogenic*—less likely to trigger an immune response. It could be that because the structure of factor IX is similar to that of other vitamin K–dependent factors (like factors II, VII, and X) the body is less likely to identify it as foreign. In general, researchers believe that the body probably doesn't consider factor IX as foreign as factor VIII, so it's less likely to attack it. But no one knows why.

We do know some things about factor IX and inhibitors. Almost all factor IX inhibitors occur in patients with severe hemophilia B.[3] They are commonly associated with the *complete absence* of factor IX as a result of large gene deletions or nonsense mutations.[4] These inhibitors are rarely transient, as they can be in some people with factor VIII deficiency. Indeed, 60% to 80% of inhibitors in factor IX deficient patients are high responding.[5, 6, 7]

Perhaps the most important fact to remember is that an inhibitor in a hemophilia B patient carries a potentially serious risk: the threat of severe allergic reactions to infused factor IX.[8]

Allergic Reactions in Hemophilia B Inhibitors

Allergic reactions to infused factor IX are a serious complication in hemophilia B inhibitor patients. Up to 50% of patients who develop an inhibitor will also develop allergic reactions, sometimes severe, to infused factor IX at the same time they develop the inhibitor. In fact, an allergic reaction after a factor IX infusion is sometimes the first indication that an inhibitor to factor IX has developed. In contrast, factor VIII inhibitor patients rarely develop severe allergic reactions to infused factor VIII.

> At eleven months, Jay had a spontaneous head bleed. He had intracranial surgery and was started on daily doses of factor IX concentrate. After a month, he started to get hives with each infusion. Our HTC drew labs to check for an inhibitor. Meanwhile, his reaction worsened each time until it was anaphylactic.[9]
> —Shari Luckey, Michigan

Because of the risk of allergic reactions, if your child has severe hemophilia B, his first twenty (at minimum) infusions of factor IX concentrate should be done in a hospital or clinic with expertise in treating severe allergic reactions.[10] If you're not infusing at a medical facility for the first twenty infusions, then it's especially important to learn the symptoms of an allergic reaction. Most can be handled easily, but some can be serious or life-threatening. *Be prepared.* Signs and symptoms of allergic reactions may include any or all of the following:

- hives (wheals or welts)
- itching
- rapid swelling (edema) of skin, mucosa (such as the lining of nose and mouth)
- edema of the tissues underlying the mucosa
- edema around neck and face (angioedema)
- chest tightness
- shortness of breath (dyspnea)
- wheezing

- faintness

- low blood pressure (hypotension)

- fast heart rate (tachycardia)

Anaphylaxis (see chapter 1) is the most serious kind of allergic reaction. It's an acute, severe, systemic allergic reaction with a rapid onset. Anaphylactic shock, the most severe type of anaphylaxis, causes a decrease in blood pressure, which leaves the brain starved for oxygen, resulting in confusion, weakness, pale color, and sometimes unconsciousness. Often there is swelling in the throat and inflammation in the lungs, causing severe shortness of breath. In children, you might hear a croaky voice when the airway is beginning to constrict. *Anaphylactic shock is a medical emergency.* If not treated immediately, it can lead to death from respiratory and cardiac arrest within minutes.

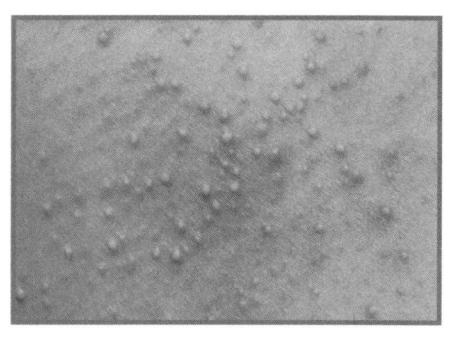

And watch for signs of a mild allergic reaction—itching, for example—that could later turn into a more serious complication. Repeated exposure to factor may cause mild allergic reactions to become more severe. Always report any reaction, even mild ones, to your hematologist immediately!

> *Jay was getting his factor in a pump for ten minutes, while he was watching cartoons. When it was done, he got red spots—blotchy, not raised. I called our HTC and they said to bring him in right away. I got in a traffic jam, and by the time I arrived, all the symptoms were gone! The next day I infused again, and he got blotchy again. Eventually the reaction progressed to raised hives, swelling of the nose, and all the way to vomiting. —Shari Luckey, Michigan*

Always have antihistamines, such as Benadryl, on hand for hard-to-treat mild to moderate allergic reactions. Give Benadryl or its equivalent at the first sign of an allergic reaction. For most mild to moderate reactions, Benadryl is often enough to alleviate the symptoms. If your child has trouble breathing, this could be anaphylaxis—a true medical emergency. Your child's airway could rapidly constrict, making it even harder to breath and resulting in respiratory arrest. This is life-threatening. *Do not take a wait-and-see approach to anaphylaxis.* Get help immediately!

Some of the most dangerous symptoms of anaphylaxis can be relieved at home, before your child is transported to a hospital, by the prescription drug epinephrine (adrenaline). Epinephrine will help keep the airway open and increase blood pressure until you can get to a medical facility. Ask your hematologist for a prescription for epinephrine to fill and keep on hand.

Managing Your Child's Inhibitor

If your child has trouble breathing following an infusion of factor IX, follow these rules:

1. Don't attempt to drive your child to the ER.
2. Call 911 immediately for emergency transport.
3. Give your child epinephrine.
4. Call the ER and HTC so they can prepare for your arrival.

At age nine months, Tyler had port surgery. He got factor IX through the whole surgery with no problems. In clinic, a few days after the port was inserted, the nurse gave him his factor IX and he went into anaphylactic shock. He turned grey, got hives, and his breathing was labored . . . no one even mentioned that these kids could go into shock! Next thing I knew, six paramedics appeared and took Tyler to the ER. They gave him Benadryl and epinephrine, and put him on oxygen. —Anonymous

Remember: ask your hematologist for a prescription for epinephrine, such as EpiPen® or Twinject®. These are prefilled epinephrine syringes that should be stored with your factor. You can inject your child with epinephrine yourself, with a simple intramuscular injection in the thigh, right through clothing. The syringes are *auto-injectors*, meaning that you don't have to push a plunger. Because no one can predict who might get a mild allergic response and who might go into anaphylactic shock, you should be prepared for any reaction. Always keep Benadryl and at least two doses of epinephrine on hand.

How to Measure Inhibitors to Factor IX

Inhibitors to factor IX are measured just like inhibitors to factor VIII, using the classic Bethesda Inhibitor Assay (see chapter 2), and are reported in BU. The inhibitor titer is also classified in the same way as factor VIII titers: a low titer is less than 5 BU, while a high titer is 5 BU and greater.

Eshton developed an inhibitor after his very first dose: he had an inhibitor titer of 7 BU. On his second dose, he developed an anaphylactic reaction to factor IX. I learned quickly that the inhibitor was the least of our worries—it was the severe allergy that was of the utmost importance to treat. —Joyce Hewitt, Michigan

Tyler's highest BU was only 1.3. Normally it's not even measurable! —Anonymous

Treatment of Bleeding Episodes

Patients with low-responding, low-titer inhibitors to factor IX can use high doses of factor IX concentrate to treat bleeding if they do not have a history of allergic reactions to factor IX.

This is not an option for patients with high-responding, high-titer inhibitors to factor IX, or for patients who develop severe allergic reactions to factor IX. For these patients, treating a bleed can get complicated. Treatment normally involves using a bypassing agent and possibly immunosuppressive drugs. You might need to try several treatment regimens before finding the one that's right for your child.

High doses of factor IX products

This treatment works best with a low-responding, low-titer inhibitor (less than 5 BU) because the titer stays low even after exposure to factor IX. And when the titer stays low, you can infuse high doses of factor IX to overwhelm the inhibitor, leaving enough factor remaining to form a clot.

But it's always hard to predict exactly what will happen to factor when it's infused in a person with an inhibitor. For this reason, your hematologist will often do recovery and half-life studies of the factor (see chapter 2) after an infusion of factor IX to accurately determine how the inhibitor affects the infused factor. Although there is no standard treatment protocol for controlling a bleed in someone with a low-titer inhibitor, your hematologist may give an initial "neutralizing dose" of 200 IU/kg, and then measure the factor IX levels; this helps to determine if the dosage must be increased. For example, if your child weighs 44 lb (20 kg), then he might be prescribed 4,000 IU every day for a certain number of days. The inhibitor titer should also be monitored after several days to see whether it increases due to anamnesis. Doses may need to be doubled or tripled, and factor may need to be administered more frequently. Talk to your HTC staff and discuss the exact protocol that may be best for your child.

Bypassing agents

With high-responding, high-titer inhibitors, an infusion with high doses of factor IX concentrate is not an option—it will be ineffective and will only cause your child's titer to spike. So treatment means using one of two bypassing agents: FEIBA or NovoSeven. Which one is best for factor IX deficient patients with inhibitors?

Initially we tried plasma-derived factor IX, but because of the allergic reaction, we can't use it. The only product that works for Jay is NovoSeven.
—Shari Luckey, Michigan

Currently, there are no controlled studies comparing the effectiveness of these two products in factor IX patients. Your choice of product should be a joint decision between you and your hematologist. The two products can work with differing degrees of effectiveness in different patients. Your choice of product to treat bleeds in the presence of factor IX inhibitors will also be affected by three primary safety concerns:

1. Risk of allergic reaction
2. Risk of anamnesis
3. Risk of thrombosis

Anamnesis, the immune system's memory response, may occur when FEIBA is infused. Why? Because FEIBA contains factor IX, which causes the inhibitor to spike after an infusion in high responders with hemophilia B and inhibitors. Also, if your child develops allergic reactions to factor IX—recall that almost half of all factor IX inhibitor patients do—even the low level of factor IX in FEIBA can cause an allergic reaction. For these patients, treatment is usually restricted to NovoSeven, which sidesteps the possibility of anamnesis and allergic reactions to factor IX.

Our insurance company required us to try FEIBA first, but it raised our son's inhibitor from 1.2 to 5.9 BU! We had to switch to NovoSeven. —Anonymous

Thrombosis, or the formation of an unwanted blood clot, is a rare complication that can occur with either FEIBA or NovoSeven. Thrombotic complications have been reported when either FEIBA or NovoSeven is infused repeatedly in large amounts. This risk increases if there is extensive tissue damage, as in a crush injury. Heart attacks caused by overdosing have been reported, even in young people with inhibitors. Careful dosing can help reduce your child's risk of thrombosis. Be sure to review with your HTC staff the exact dose and frequency of infusion recommended for your child for various bleeds. Thrombotic complications may include the following:

- Disseminated intravascular coagulation (DIC; see chapter 3), a condition associated with bleeding and clotting
- Deep vein thrombosis (DVT), where clots occur in the major veins of the body
- Pulmonary embolism (PE), where clotting occurs in the lungs
- Fatal or life-threatening acute myocardial infarction (MI), or heart attack

Repeated doses of bypassing agents should be done at your HTC, with your hematologist present, where your child can be monitored for thrombotic complications.

Temporary reduction of titer

As we discussed in chapter 3, if your child has a high-responding inhibitor and faces a life-threatening bleed or a scheduled surgery, the inhibitor titer can be reduced temporarily by plasmapheresis or immunoadsorption, allowing for the use of standard factor IX concentrates.

To review: plasmapheresis is a process that routes the patient's blood through a machine that removes some of the plasma—and along with it, some of the inhibitor—and replaces it with an albumin solution, or sometimes with plasma from another donor.[11] This is short-term therapy only, useful for emergencies. Within a few days of plasmapheresis, the inhibitor titer starts rising again.

Immunoadsorption is another short-term therapy in which the blood is cycled through a machine. But instead of removing the plasma from the blood, the machine passes the plasma through a column or cylinder filled with many tiny beads. Attached to the beads in the column are monoclonal antibodies against human immunoglobulins (the inhibitors). While the plasma passes through the column, the monoclonal antibodies selectively *adsorb* the inhibitors, removing them from the plasma, which is then returned to the patient. Immunoadsorption is a long process—a single treatment may take three to six hours. Immunoadsorption is typically not available at American HTCs.

Immune Tolerance Induction

As we discussed in chapter 4, ITI attempts to overwhelm the inhibitor with frequent, large doses of infused factor over an extended period, from several months to several years.[12] For patients without an allergic response, this usually means a daily regimen of factor IX infusions.

The risk of anaphylaxis in factor IX patients with an inhibitor complicates ITI, usually making this strategy possible only for hemophilia B inhibitor patients who do *not* experience allergic reactions to factor IX. In some cases, patients with factor IX inhibitors and allergic reactions can be desensitized to the factor over a period of months by administering escalating doses of factor along with the immunosuppressive drug rituximab, allowing them to start ITI.

> *Tyler's hematologist started him on recombinant factor IX, then we tried NovoSeven. But his quality of life continued to deteriorate. Then we gave him steroids, and started him on low doses of recombinant factor IX. As we*

slowly weaned him off steroids, we increased his factor dose, and now we give him 1,500 IU of recombinant factor IX daily. It worked! —Anonymous

The chance for successful tolerization is higher if ITI is started when the inhibitor is below 10 BU. For those with high-titer inhibitors, the inhibitor level will often drop below 10 BU if the patient is not exposed to factor IX for one or two years. For this reason, people with high-titer inhibitors may be treated with recombinant factor VIIa, avoiding anamnesis and allowing the inhibitor titer to drop below 10 BU so that ITI can be started.

Remember that ITI is successful in only 25% to 40% of factor IX patients, compared to the success rate of 60% to 80% for factor VIII patients.[13] ITI is even less successful in people whose titers were greater than 200 BU at some time in the past. It's also less successful in people whose inhibitors spike above 500 BU during ITI, and in people who have had an inhibitor for more than two years.

But there's another risk for patients undergoing ITI for factor IX inhibitors: a kidney disorder called *nephrotic syndrome.*

Nephrotic Syndrome: A Dangerous Complication

For factor IX inhibitor patients, ITI can lead to nephrotic syndrome.[14] This kidney disorder occurs in about 34% of patients with factor IX deficiency who are on ITI. Nephrotic syndrome is more likely if your child has a history of allergic reactions to factor IX.

In nephrotic syndrome, the kidneys become plugged with microscopic solids, or *precipitates,* that form when inhibitors combine with factor IX. As a result, the kidneys begin to lose their ability to filter waste products out of the blood, and they start dumping proteins into the urine. This causes fluid retention and high blood pressure. Patients may look swollen. Nephrotic syndrome usually develops eight to nine months into a course of ITI. Although steroids often help treat nephrotic syndrome, factor IX inhibitor patients with allergic responses generally respond poorly to steroids. If your child develops nephrotic syndrome, you'll probably have to stop ITI. Fortunately, kidney function often improves after ITI ends.

Eshton was admitted to the ICU to begin ITI with infusions of factor IX. We then spent six months trying to convince his body to accept it. We learned that children who previously had allergic reactions and had tried ITI with factor IX had developed nephrotic syndrome. We had to discontinue. —Joyce Hewitt, Michigan

We were on ITI for nine to ten months, when one morning Jay woke up and said, "My face feels funny." His face was huge, swollen, and puffy. I took him to our HTC, but by then the problem had resolved. Our hematologist later called and said that while attending a hemophilia event in Ireland, she overheard a doctor talk about nephrotic syndrome, then thought, oh my God! We returned to the HTC, and she ordered a urine sample. I got nervous. We were sent to a nephrologist. We learned that Jay, age two, was retaining fluid, his kidneys weren't emptying out, and he was losing proteins through his kidneys.
—*Shari Luckey, Michigan*

If your child is on ITI, your HTC will probably be checking for nephrotic syndrome by giving him frequent urine tests. But you should still be familiar with the symptoms of nephrotic syndrome, so you can monitor your child at home and alert your physician at the first sign of trouble. These are the most common signs of nephrotic syndrome:

- swelling
- puffiness around the eyes, especially in the morning, and facial swelling
- fluid retention (edema) in the legs, especially the feet and ankles
- fluid in the lungs
- foam in the toilet after urinating (indicates that the kidneys are passing protein)
- poor appetite
- swollen abdomen
- high blood pressure

Nephrotic syndrome can cause permanent kidney damage. Some people may respond to steroids like prednisone, but if this isn't successful, ITI must be discontinued. Fortunately, the prognosis is good for a full recovery for children after ITI ends.

At first our hematologist said he couldn't do ITI with boys with factor IX deficiency and allergies, due to neuphrotic syndrome. But then the HTC put four-year-old Tyler on a pump twenty-four hours a day, which infused factor IX; he wore it around his waist for eighteen months. They were going to tolerize him. He was having a bad ankle bleed and was on morphine. We couldn't get it to stop bleeding. The ankle bleed finally stopped when it compressed itself shut. He was on pain meds, and had a port. We had tickets to go to the circus, but Tyler developed a fever. I knew he had to go to the hospital, but I didn't let that stop us from going to the circus! Halfway through, Tyler started pooing blood. I called our hematologist and said, "There's only twenty minutes left. Can we stay?" The doctor said, "Sure, stay! See you in half an hour." Tyler sat with the biggest smile! When the circus was over, we went to the HTC. He was in ICU for six weeks. They started him on steroids, then started giving him low doses of factor IX, and slowly started to wean him off steroids while increasing the factor dose. He eventually tolerated the factor IX, and had no reaction. It worked! —Anonymous

■ ■ ■

Treating inhibitors is complicated. If your child has hemophilia B and an inhibitor, it's further complicated by the worry about allergic reactions and nephrotic syndrome. Based on the risk of complications, patients with allergic reactions to factor IX are *not* good candidates for ITI.

Despite this, all hope is not lost. Inhibitors in children with hemophilia B and allergic reactions have been eliminated using the immunosuppressive drug rituximab. This drug targets white blood cells in the immune system called B-cells, which produce inhibitors. Rituximab also may be used in combination with prednisone or cyclophosphamide. These and other treatment regimens have helped some patients with factor IX deficiency and inhibitors who have allergic reactions. Eventually, these patients have seen their inhibitors eliminated or reduced enough to resume successful treatment with their usual factor IX concentrate.

Together with your HTC staff, you'll be able to try a variety of treatment protocols until you find one that works for your child. Remember, it's fine to ask questions and seek answers. Don't stop until you're satisfied with the answers you receive. ■

Inhibitors by Factor Deficiency

Factor IX	Factor VIII
1 in 30,000 males	1 in 5,000 males
3% to 5% develop inhibitors	20% to 30% develop inhibitors
possible allergic reactions to infused factor IX	allergic reactions rare
associated with large deletions in factor IX gene	associated with genetic deletions and other genetic defects
ITI: poor response	ITI: good response

◼ NOTES

1. Soucie M, Evatt B, Jackson D, Hemophilia Surveillance System Project Investigators. Occurrence of hemophilia in the United States. *Am J Hematology.* 1998;59:288–94.
2. Katz J. Prevalence of factor IX inhibitors among patients with haemophilia B: results of a large-scale North American study. *Haemophilia.* 2007 Jun 28;2(1):28–31.
3. At the time of the survey, inhibitors were present in 28 of 735 patients with severe hemophilia B, 1 of 644 with moderate hemophilia B, and none of 588 with mild hemophilia B. The overall prevalence was 1.5%, or 3.8% in severe hemophilia B. Katz J. Prevalence of factor IX inhibitors among patients with haemophilia B: results of a large-scale North American study. *Haemophilia.* 1996;2:28–31.
4. A gene deletion, as the name implies, means that the entire gene is missing and therefore unable to code for the production of a protein. A nonsense mutation is a change in the DNA that prematurely stops the "reading" of the DNA, resulting in a shortened and nonfunctional protein.
5. One survey found that 62% of factor IX patients with inhibitors had high-titer inhibitors. Katz J. Factor IX inhibitors in patients with haemophilia B: survey results from 82 treatment centres in the United States and Canada. *Blood.* 1994;84:63.
6. Another U.S. survey identified 11 of 29 (38%) factor IX inhibitor patients as having inhibitor titers of 5 BU or lower, with the remainder having higher-titer inhibitors. DiMichelle D. Hemophilia: a new approach to an old disease. *Hematology/Oncology Clinics N Am.* 1998 Dec 1;12(6):1315–44.
7. Chitlur M, Warrier I, Rajpurkar M, Lusher J. Inhibitors in factor IX deficiency: a report of the ISTH-SSC international FIX inhibitor registry (1997–2006). *Haemophilia.* 2009 Sep;15(n5):1027–31.
8. Franchini M, Lippi G, Montagnana M, Targher G, Zaffanello M, Luca Salvagno G, Franca Rivolta G, Di Perna C, Tagliaferri A. Anaphylaxis in patients with congenital bleeding disorders and inhibitors. *Blood Coagulation & Fibrinolysis.* 2009;20(n4):225–29.
9. Jay recovered and is now thriving.
10. Lusher J. Inhibitor antibodies to factor VIII and factor IX: management. *Semin Thromb Hemost.* 2000;26(2):179–88.
11. Plasmapheresis requires specialized equipment that may not be available at all HTCs.
12. See chapter 4 for more about protocols and dosing for ITI.
13. Rodriguez N, Hoots W, Brown D, Womack M, Cantini M, Escobar M. Failure of immune tolerance induction in haemophilia B patients with C, T 6460 nonsense mutation. *J Thromb Haemost.* 2007;5(Sup 2):P-T-130.
14. Nephrotic syndrome does not occur in hemophilia A patients undergoing ITI.

SUMMARY 5
Factor IX Deficiency and Inhibitors

- Inhibitors in hemophilia B are about ten times more rare than inhibitors in hemophilia A.

- Most inhibitors in hemophilia B patients occur in those with severe hemophilia and are associated with the complete absence of factor IX.

- Almost 50% of hemophilia B patients develop allergic reactions to factor IX at the same time they develop inhibitors.

- Although some allergic reactions may start out mild, after repeated exposure to factor they may become more severe.

- Anaphylactic shock is a severe, systemic allergic reaction with rapid onset. It is a medical emergency and may cause death from respiratory arrest within minutes.

- Always be prepared for any level of allergic reaction: keep antihistamines (Benadryl) on hand for mild to moderate reactions, and fill a prescription for epinephrine (EpiPen or Twinject) for severe reactions.

- Because of the risk of severe allergic reactions, children with hemophilia B should receive, at minimum, their first twenty infusions at an HTC or medical facility capable of dealing with anaphylactic shock.

- Hemophilia B patients with low-responding inhibitors can often use high doses of factor IX to treat bleeds.

- Hemophilia B patients with high-responding inhibitors must use bypassing agents such as FEIBA or NovoSeven to treat bleeds. Because NovoSeven contains no factor IX, its use will prevent anamnesis and allergic reactions.

- ITI is less successful in hemophilia B patients (25% to 40%) than in hemophilia A patients (70% to 80%).

- About a third of hemophilia B patients on ITI develop nephrotic syndrome, a dangerous complication that plugs the kidneys, about eight to nine months into a course of ITI. This usually means that ITI must be stopped.

- In some cases, patients with hemophilia B, inhibitors, and allergic reactions may still be able to try a course of ITI by taking immunosuppressive drugs during ITI.

6 Managing Pain

Pain may be one of the biggest challenges you'll face when dealing with an inhibitor. Why? Bleeding into joints and muscles is often more prolonged for people with inhibitors, causing acute pain at the bleeding sites. Repeated joint bleeds cause the joint cartilage to deteriorate, resulting in arthritis—and chronic pain.

How much pain will your child experience? It's hard to say. There is a direct relationship between joint damage and pain. He may experience significant pain if he tries to "tough it out" and avoid using pain medications. He may develop a tolerance to high levels of pain. But if he does experience a lot of pain, here's the problem: most physicians are not well trained to treat ongoing, chronic pain. HTCs rarely include pain specialists in their comprehensive care staff, and many hospitals housing HTCs do not have pain clinics. And many physicians avoid prescribing *opioids* (narcotics), the most effective painkillers, fearing scrutiny under the policies and regulations of federal and state drug enforcement agencies.

> Andrew seemed to have inadequate pain relief with a knee bleed. Doctors were reluctant to give him narcotics. We found this traumatic: Andrew was in intense pain, and we were unable to help him. I still shudder when I think of that time. Now we always want to have an adequate pain relief strategy.
> —Richard and Lynley Scott, New Zealand

Good pain management can help your child get through severe bleeds as well as chronic pain. Many options exist for treating pain, from ice to opioids, to make life easier for you and your child.

Your Child's Pain Level

It's hard to know exactly what your child is feeling when he's in pain. Pain is purely subjective: there is no scientific, objective way to measure his type, level, or intensity of pain. Compounding this dilemma is the trouble your child may have reporting his pain: how do you interpret a nonverbal toddler's pain? Different patients use the same terms to describe widely differing types of pain. And because we all register pain uniquely, what may be excruciating to one person may be only moderately painful to another.

> *Logan deals with pain well. Tylenol® for ankle bleeds, and he's fine. The first few ankle bleeds, he wouldn't tell me that it hurt. He doesn't complain, and he doesn't whine or cry. —Anonymous*

In an attempt to quantify the level of pain, doctors often ask patients older than age eight to rate their pain on a scale of 0 to 10, with 10 being the worst pain. Again, it's subjective: one person's 2 may be another person's 8. A young person who hasn't experienced pain at level 10 may rate his pain higher than would someone who has suffered severe pain. But the main goal is to find consistency for the individual patient. To help children describe their pain, many physicians use the Wong-Baker FACES Pain Rating Scale©: a row of simple faces wearing expressions ranging from a frown to a big smile. Children point to the face that best represents how they feel. Or they may be asked to compare their pain to something: "It feels like when I have a really bad headache."

Instructions for using the Wong-Baker FACES Pain Rating Scale©

0	2	4	6	8	10
No Hurt	**Hurts Little Bit**	**Hurts Little More**	**Hurts Even More**	**Hurts Whole Lot**	**Hurts Worst**

Explain to the person that each face is for a person who has no pain (hurt) or some, or a lot of pain. Face 0 doesn't hurt at all. Face 2 hurts just a little bit. Face 4 hurts a little more. Face 6 hurts even more. Face 8 hurts a whole lot. Face 10 hurts as much as you can imagine, although you don't have to be crying to have this worst pain. Ask the person to choose the face that best describes how much pain he has.

Reprinted with permission. The Wong-Baker FACES Foundation, 2010. www.wongbakerfaces.org

---

> *Matthew is in pain all the time. He describes his pain at a constant level of around 6. His acute pain ranges from 8 to 10 depending on the bleed. —Debbie Porter, California*

> *I think Thomas has chronic pain, but he won't tell me. Generally he says he does not have pain, but I think he has high pain tolerance. The happy-face pain scale works well when he tries to describe his pain.* —Sonji Wilkes, Colorado

How can you teach your child to report and respond to pain promptly? First, try to find out if he's in pain. Very young children can't verbalize their pain, and older children may try to hide it, so you must learn to read body language and moods. Is your child grumpy or irritated? Is he crying, limping, or favoring a limb? Has he lost his appetite? Is he having trouble sleeping? Has he lost interest in normal activities? Verbal children may not report the onset of a bleed as painful, but they may say something feels "tingly," "hot," or just "funny." Ask questions, gently helping your child find the right words to describe his pain: Where does it hurt? How does it feel? Does it feel like . . . ?

Remember, your child's pain is *his* pain. No one else really knows how he feels. If your child reports pain, don't disregard or downplay it. Don't tell him to tough it out. Trust him, and teach him to interpret his pain so he can describe it to others. Post the Wong-Baker FACES scale on your refrigerator at his eye level, and encourage him to point to a face that best describes how he feels. Over time, he'll develop a greater awareness of his own levels of pain. Work with your HTC to appropriately treat your child's pain based on what *he* is feeling, not on what you or anyone else *thinks* he is feeling.

> *The school nurse sees Leland attending class and thinks his pain can't be that bad. But we must trust him when he tells us about pain. We trust Leland's pain assessment 100%.* —Jane, Massachusetts

Types of Pain

Pain is categorized as either *acute* or *chronic*. Acute pain lasts hours, days, or even months, while the body is healing. Chronic pain is ongoing, and lasts six months or longer. Acute pain is considered necessary and even beneficial—it alerts our bodies to danger or injury, and prompts us to protect ourselves or get treatment. Acute pain goes away after the body has healed. But chronic pain does not go away and is often destructive and debilitating, harming quality of life.

As a result of hemophilia and inhibitors, your child may experience

> ***acute pain:*** usually caused by bleeding that leads to swelling in joints and muscles.
>
> ***chronic pain:*** usually caused by arthritis, a consequence of repeated bleeds that have damaged the joint's cartilage.

By treating your child at the first sign of pain, you may avoid the use of prescription-strength painkillers.

> When Thomas has acute pain, we give him Children's Tylenol chewables. It was trial and error figuring out which painkiller worked best. Stay on top of it! Once pain manifests, it's 2:00 am, and you're at the ER getting morphine. When a bleed starts, it's factor and Tylenol, regularly, every four to six hours.
> —Sonji Wilkes, Colorado

Acute pain and chronic pain require different treatment approaches. Acute pain is usually treated promptly and effectively by both physicians and parents. For acute pain, treatment involves not only reducing the level of pain, but also seeking to eliminate the *cause* of the pain. For chronic pain, treatment usually seeks to reduce the *level* of pain, and may include surgery.

Chronic pain is often underappreciated and undertreated. When young people with hemophilia first experience chronic pain, they often haven't learned to distinguish between acute and chronic pain. Believing their pain is due to a bleed, they treat with factor—which doesn't reduce chronic pain. Parents should suspect chronic pain if their child has had repeated bleeds into a joint or has developed a *target joint*. A target joint is one that suffers repeated bleeding and usually develops arthritis. Chronic pain often creeps up slowly over time, usually first apparent as joint pain that tends to be more severe in the morning and then decreases as the day wears on.

Managing Acute Pain

Bleeding into joints and muscles causes acute pain. To limit acute pain, it's imperative that you *stop the bleeding as soon as possible* with your prescribed factor concentrate or bypassing agent.[1]

Also investigate using adjunct or additional therapies to help reduce swelling and pain. Adjunct therapies are designed to increase the effectiveness of the primary therapy, often allowing you to use a lower dose of drugs or use them for a shorter time. In some cases, adjunct therapy can reduce or eliminate pain without using drugs. One adjunct treatment that helps reduce pain from bleeds and speeds healing is RICE: Rest, Ice, Compression, Elevation.

- *Rest* the injured body part for twenty-four to forty-eight hours to prevent reinjury of the site.
- *Ice* the site for ten to fifteen minutes at a time using a gel-filled cold compress, Cryo/Cuff®, bag of frozen peas or crushed ice wrapped in a towel, four to eight times a day. Wait at least forty minutes before reapplying.[2] Icing

reduces blood flow to the injured area, which helps control bleeding and swelling. Ice also helps numb pain. To avoid freezing and damaging the skin, be careful not to place the ice or cold object directly on the skin.

- *Compress* the affected area with an elastic bandage to help reduce bleeding and swelling.[3]

- *Elevate* the injured body part above the heart to help reduce swelling and the throbbing sensation common in lower extremity bleeds.

I lived through a lot of severe pain as a teen because I wasn't managing my bleeding properly. Not icing fast enough, no factor available. It made me smarter: I learned not to do certain things again, whatever caused the pain.
—R. H., Connecticut

If RICE alone doesn't reduce your child's pain sufficiently, he may need a pain medication, or *analgesic*. Most people with hemophilia use over-the-counter (OTC) analgesics to treat mild to moderate acute pain. For more intense pain, your child may need more potent, prescription-only analgesics.

Pain medications to treat acute and chronic pain are often divided into three groups:

1. *Non-opioids*, including acetaminophen and non-steroidal anti-inflammatory drugs (NSAIDs).

2. *Opioids* (narcotics), including hydrocodone and morphine.

3. *Adjuvant analgesics*, a loose term for many medications, including some antidepressants and anticonvulsants, originally used to treat conditions other than pain.

Non-Opioids for Acute Pain

Non-opioids are the drugs of choice for mild to moderate acute pain.[4]

Acetaminophen is most often recommended for people with hemophilia because it doesn't affect the blood's clotting ability, as do some other pain medications. Brand names of acetaminophen include Tylenol and FeverAll®. Although acetaminophen is relatively safe, high doses and long-term use may cause liver damage—an especially serious concern for people infected with hepatitis C.[5] *Warning:* Acetaminophen is also found in many OTC drugs, including some cold medications, sold for purposes other than pain relief, but this may not be displayed prominently on the label. Acetaminophen may also be combined with other painkillers (for example, opioids) and sold under a brand name, such as Vicodin®

and Darvocet®. But be careful: the inclusion of acetaminophen in these drugs may not be obvious if you don't read the label carefully. Accidental overdose can occur if you give your child acetaminophen plus another drug that you don't realize also contains acetaminophen. To prevent overdosing with acetaminophen, read the label carefully and consult your physician or pharmacist for the correct dosage. And remember, when it comes to acetaminophen dosing, more is not better.

> *For acute pain caused by bleeding, Reuben normally takes Tylenol.*
> *— Wendy Sass, New York*

NSAIDs include common OTC pain medications such as aspirin, ibuprofen (Motrin®), naproxen (Naprosyn®), and ketroprofen (Orovail®). Many other NSAIDs are available by prescription only. No two NSAIDs work in exactly the same way. Each has slightly different side effects and effectiveness, and each lasts for a different length of time. Unlike opioids (see next section), all NSAIDs have a *ceiling dose*, the maximum safe or effective dose of a drug. Taking doses above the ceiling dose offers no additional therapeutic benefits, yet it significantly increases the risk of serious or life-threatening side effects such as kidney failure, liver failure, or gastrointestinal bleeding.

NSAIDs reduce pain, but unlike acetaminophen, they also have an anti-inflammatory effect. They help reduce swelling and inflammation in joints, often providing more relief than acetaminophen. But NSAIDs have drawbacks for people with bleeding disorders:

- Most NSAIDs reduce the blood's ability to clot, by inhibiting platelet adhesion.
- NSAIDs can cause gastrointestinal bleeding and ulcers.
- NSAIDs can harm the kidneys and liver.

Although many people with hemophilia report taking OTC NSAIDs for pain, physicians don't often prescribe high-dose NSAIDs for people with hemophilia. If used, NSAIDs should be taken at the lowest effective dose, for a limited time, and in limited circumstances. Never give your child NSAIDs without consulting your HTC staff!

Some NSAIDs are simply dangerous for people with bleeding disorders. Aspirin (acetylsalicylic acid or ASA) deserves a special warning: *Aspirin should never be used by anyone with hemophilia* because it forms an irreversible chemical bond with COX-1 (an enzyme in the blood involved in the clotting process). The bond prevents platelets from adhering to each other to form a platelet plug—the first step in the blood-clotting process. This effect on platelets is irreversible and lasts for the life of the platelet, about seven to ten days. A person with hemophilia who takes aspirin risks gastrointestinal bleeding and uncontrolled spontaneous bleeding. Aspirin is found in several dozen OTC medications, including many, like Pepto-Bismol™, not indicated for pain relief. Carefully check any OTC medication for the presence of acetylsalicylic acid or ASA—and don't use it![6]

All NSAIDs are not equal in effectiveness and side effects, and some are more dangerous than others for people with bleeding disorders. Some NSAIDs, such as ketorolac (prescription-only, brand name Toradol®), have a potent effect on platelet adhesion and are more likely than other NSAIDs to cause gastrointestinal bleeding. Check with your hematologist about the tendency of a particular NSAID to cause gastrointestinal bleeding, and about its effect on clotting.

Low-dose ibuprofen (Motrin) is commonly used to treat pain and inflammation. Ibuprofen also inhibits platelet activation, but much less so than aspirin, and the effect is temporary, lasting only about four hours. While taking ibuprofen, people with hemophilia may have no excessive bleeding problems, but they should *not* take it when a bleed is in progress. High-dose ibuprofen (600 or 800 mg tablets) is a prescription-only medication that poses a greater risk of gastrointestinal bleeding and should be used only under a doctor's direct supervision. And of course, no one should take another person's prescription pain medication!

Selective COX-2 inhibitors (*coxibs*) are a different class of NSAIDs, developed to reduce the risk of gastrointestinal bleeding and ulcers for people taking the drug for an extended time. By targeting only the enzyme COX-2 and not COX-1, these drugs theoretically shouldn't affect platelet activation, as do other NSAIDs. But MASAC recommendation #162[7] reports some incidences of bleeding, and recommends using coxibs at the lowest effective dose, for short duration. Currently only one coxib, celecoxib (Celebrex®), is available in the United States. Although NHF recommends this drug for short-term use, many people with hemophilia use it long term to treat mild to moderate chronic joint pain. *Always consult your HTC about NSAID use.*

Treating mild to moderate acute pain is almost always manageable with OTC or prescription-strength acetaminophen or NSAIDs. To treat severe acute pain, for a short time you may need to use an opioid, or an opioid plus an NSAID or acetaminophen. For example, the prescription drugs Darvocet, Percodan®, Percocet®, and Vicodin all contain both an opioid and a non-opioid analgesic, such as acetaminophen or aspirin.[8] *Note:* Percodan contains both an opioid and aspirin, and should not be taken by people with hemophilia.

Of my three sons with inhibitors, only Nathan ever needed pain meds, and only for acute pain. He toughs out chronic pain. He's been on aggressive pain therapies since he was four. Now when he has an acute bleed, he starts with Tylenol, and then uses Percocet if Tylenol alone doesn't work. He judges what he needs himself. He takes one dose usually, when he goes to bed.
—*Kerry Fatula, Pennsylvania*

As part of an overall pain management plan, your physician may also prescribe adjuvant analgesics, drugs with no direct pain-relieving properties: medications to treat insomnia, anxiety, depression, and muscle spasms can significantly help some patients. Opioids and adjuvant analgesics are usually reserved for severe acute pain and chronic pain.

Managing Chronic Pain

Unlike acute pain, chronic pain often doesn't respond to OTC medications. Even high-dose, prescription-only NSAIDs may not reduce the pain; and when used for extended periods, they pose a significant risk of bleeding complications and other serious side effects. So for moderate to severe chronic pain, opioids (narcotics such as morphine and codeine) are the drugs of choice. Unlike NSAIDs, opioids have no ceiling dose. They don't damage the kidneys or liver, don't cause gastrointestinal bleeding, don't increase the risk of heart attack, and don't interfere with the clotting cascade.

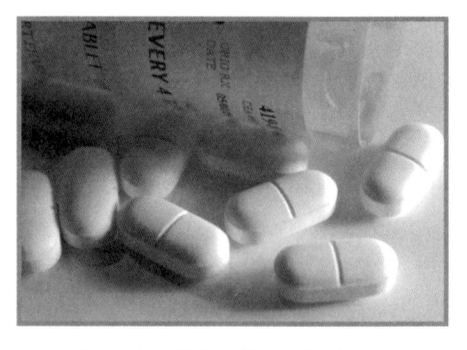

Noah is only three, and his ankle has caused chronic pain for months. He can't sleep, and we see many behavioral and personality issues. We always have Tylenol with codeine at home for when he has severe pain. It's hard to watch when your child is in severe pain. —*Cicely Evans, Massachusetts*

For very severe joint bleeds, Reuben has sometimes taken morphine while in the hospital. We have used morphine only for the most severe bleeds, and even then we haven't used it for more than a few days. —*Wendy Sass, New York*

Opioids do have side effects, including nausea, dizziness, drowsiness, twitching, constipation, urinary retention, bladder spasm, and itching. Many people using opioids for long periods report becoming tolerized to these side effects—that is, the side effects go away. Some side effects that don't go away, such as constipation, can be treated with various medications. Constipation may require a change in diet and the proactive use of stool softeners and stimulant laxatives. In rare cases, high-dose opioids can cause potentially dangerous respiratory depression, to the point where breathing stops. Respiratory depression occurs more often in the elderly and young children. That's why opioids are rarely prescribed for young children.[9] In spite of their side effects, opioids are safe and effective for treating moderate to severe chronic pain.

You may worry, perhaps needlessly, about the long-term effects of opioids on your child. And your physician may also have fears—or even incorrect information—about the risks of addiction. Unfortunately, many physicians are poorly informed about treating chronic pain.

Addiction, Tolerance, Dependency: What's the Difference?

Most physicians have no qualms about prescribing necessary pain medications for acute pain. But opioids carry the stigma of addiction: *everyone* has seen the scary portrayal of narcotics abuse in the movies or on television, yet most people don't know that many of these portrayals are inaccurate. In fact, misinformation about opioids abounds in the lay media and even medical journals. Both you and your physician might have fears, or outdated and incorrect information, concerning the risk of addiction.

Misunderstanding about opioids often centers on the meaning of three terms:

- tolerance
- physical dependence
- addiction

Tolerance

Tolerance occurs when the same dose of a drug becomes less effective over time. Normally, opioids are prescribed at the lowest possible effective dose to start. Then, as the patient becomes tolerized and the drug becomes less effective at reducing pain, the dose is increased to maintain effectiveness. This can be done several times because unlike NSAIDs and acetaminophen, opioids have no ceiling dose. But if a patient continues to develop a tolerance to higher and higher levels, then the physician will need to switch to another opioid. Why? Because high levels of opioids increase the risk of side effects like respiratory depression. *Note:* A patient who is tolerized to an opioid may be taking a dose that could be lethal to someone who is new to the drug. *Never take another person's prescription pain medication!* Narcotics can and should be used when needed. When used under proper supervision, studies have shown that they can be effective, with limited addiction issues. Developing a tolerance to the narcotic is normal and does not indicate addiction.

> Eshton has probably always been in pain. His chronic pain runs around 4. He has acute pain weekly that runs between 6 and 8, and that lasts from one to seven days. —Joyce Hewitt, Michigan

Physical dependence

When the body has become dependent on a drug, withdrawal symptoms (sweating, rapid heart rate, nausea, diarrhea, anxiety) will occur if the drug is suddenly stopped or the dose is lowered too quickly. Physical dependence is often confused with addiction, but *dependence is not addiction*. Physical dependence is considered a normal reaction to opioids and to many other drugs. Indeed, anyone on opioids for more than several days is usually considered dependent. To avoid withdrawal symptoms, the dosage must be decreased slowly over time, a process called *tapering*. Suddenly stopping a medication that causes dependency (going "cold turkey") can be life-threatening. Always consult your healthcare professional before stopping any opioid.

> I've used Contin® [timed-release morphine drug] for twelve years. When I forget to take it, I feel like I've got the flu. Your stomach does flip-flops; you get diarrhea. Once when I forgot to take the drug, and I had those symptoms, I took the pill, sat down, and within an hour those feelings disappeared. My doctor says that if I want to quit, I'd have to spend a week in hospital, and they would slowly take me off it. —Fred Horlas, Iowa

Addiction

Addiction is characterized by behaviors that include impaired control over drug use, compulsive use, continued use despite harm, and craving. According to the American Pain Society, addiction is a medical diagnosis: "a primary, chronic, neurobiological disease, with genetic, psychosocial, and environmental factors influencing its development and expression."[10] Addiction causes quality of life to deteriorate. Addiction often leads to increasing functional impairment and a state of persistent sedation or intoxication from overusing the drug. The addicted patient may also show psychological symptoms of addiction, including increased irritability, anxiety, depression, and apathy.

In some cases, what *appears* to be addiction may not be addiction. When pain is undertreated, a patient may show "drug-seeking" behaviors that look like signs of addiction. He may groan and moan, watch the clock, or ask repeatedly for medication before the prescribed dose is due. His complaints may seem excessive given the cause of the pain. This behavior is called *pseudoaddiction*.

How can you distinguish pseudoaddiction from true addiction? In pseudoaddiction, the behavior disappears when the pain is adequately treated. But for people who are truly addicted to opioids, the behavior *worsens* when the drugs are administered. The "treatment" for pseudoaddiction is simple: treat the pain effectively. This means (1) assessing whether the pain is a type that typically responds to opioids, and (2) evaluating whether the dose, scheduling, and route of administration are appropriate. If the pain responds to opioids, then escalating the dose aggressively until the pain is relieved should resolve the problem and eliminate pseudoaddictive behavior.

> There are not too many options for the type of pain Matthew has experienced. He has chronic pain in his knee and ankle joints. He also suffers from migraine-type headaches due to the effects of superior vena cava syndrome [an obstructed vein inside the chest that leads into the heart] he developed from a central line and blood clots. Matthew's chronic pain is managed by taking [the narcotic] methadone daily. Acute pain is harder to manage. He takes Tramadol and uses lots of ice and distraction techniques. Matthew has used narcotics long-term since he was eight years old and is considered by his doctors to be physically dependent on narcotics. Unfortunately, they now do not work well for acute, short-term use because of his continuous exposure.
> —Debbie Porter, California

Because most people with hemophilia will suffer from chronic pain later in life, it's essential to understand the difference between tolerance, physical dependence, and addiction. Dependence is not addiction! Use of opioids does not automatically lead to addiction. Don't let misinformation or fear prevent you from getting adequate pain treatment for your child. Studies show that opioid addiction is rare among chronic pain sufferers: around 1% to 2%. Remember, good pain management is the key to taking any medication safely.

Managing Chronic Pain: The Multi-Modality Approach

Pain management is an ongoing process. Your child's response to a medication may change over time; what works at one stage of life may not work in another. Chronic pain is best managed by a combination of medication and non-medication treatments. The *multi-modality* or multidisciplinary approach allows you to control pain with less medication.

You'll need the expertise of specialists in pain management. If you're lucky, your HTC will have a pain clinic with physicians who understand chronic pain and can help develop a *pain management plan*. If not, you can request a referral to a pain clinic at a nearby teaching hospital.

Every pain management plan should include exercise. Exercise has many benefits:

- strengthens muscles, which protects joints, reducing joint bleeds
- increases flexibility and range of motion (ROM)
- improves sleep quality
- releases natural painkillers, or *endorphins*
- helps maintain healthy weight, which decreases stress on joints, reducing joint bleeds
- improves mood

Your HTC physical therapist can design an exercise program to meet your child's needs. People with inhibitors and significant joint damage may not be able to participate in typical exercise routines. In this case, hydrotherapy (aquatic or pool therapy) is often recommended. Hydrotherapy lets the patient swim, walk, or do specific ROM exercises in warm water. Warm water cushions stiff joints, relaxes muscles, increases flexibility, and provides gentle resistance. Through its buoyancy, water also reduces stress on weight-bearing joints.

One of the goals of pain management is to use the lowest possible dose of drugs to control pain. Non-medication methods can help control pain so you can reduce the dose of prescription painkillers your child needs. You and your HTC can—and should—explore adjunct therapies to reduce pain, help control bleeding, and speed healing.

Non-Medication Therapy: CAM

CAM (Complementary and Alternative Medicine) is any adjunct therapy, like massage, used *along with* conventional medicine.[11] Here are some of the most common CAM therapies:

Relaxation Therapy. Pain often causes muscles to tense and anxiety to increase. Relaxation therapy teaches you to relieve tense muscles, reduce anxiety, and alter your mental state. *Mindfulness meditation* helps you focus attention on a specific object or on your breathing patterns to induce relaxation. *Guided imagery* is a conscious meditation technique of relaxation, practiced in a peaceful setting, using sights, sounds, or a combination of sensations to help you visualize a soothing mental image, like walking on a beach at sunset.

Biofeedback Training. This method reduces stress by teaching you to how to recognize and change your biological reaction to stress and pain. In biofeedback, you use electronic equipment to monitor your physical responses: you can lean to decrease your heart rate, slow your breathing rate, or reduce your muscle tension, thus reducing your pain level.

Behavioral Modification. Some people with severe chronic pain may become anxious, depressed, homebound, dependent, or even bedridden. Behavioral modification helps you create a step-by-step approach for confronting challenges by changing your behavior and shifting your attitude.

Stress Management Training. When your pain level is high, then your stress and anxiety levels probably are, too. This training helps you maintain a routine schedule for activity, rest, and medication. It incorporates exercise or PT into your daily routine, and trains you to keep a positive outlook.

Hypnotherapy. Therapeutic or medical hypnosis directs your focus inward to induce an altered state of consciousness or "trance state" to help you relax and reduce pain and anxiety.

Counseling. Individual, family, or group counseling with a professional trained in pain management can provide emotional support and guidance.

Acupuncture. This ancient Chinese technique involves inserting and manipulating very thin needles into specific points on the body known to control pain pathways. When inserted, the disposable sterile needles are believed to interfere with nerve transmission of pain signals. Studies have shown the effectiveness of acupuncture in treating pain in people with hemophilia, with no reported risk of bleeding from the needle insertion sites.[12, 13] Nonetheless, some physicians believe that bleeding after acupuncture is a concern for people with hemophilia, and may advise against the procedure. Before beginning this therapy, consult with your HTC team. Also make sure the acupuncturist does not reuse needles, has experience using acupuncture on people with hemophilia, and practices aseptic technique to prevent infections (especially important for people with ports or artificial joints).

I was on twelve different meds to control pain. Tom Tam, my acupuncturist, already knows where I am hurting before I tell him. He sends his chi to me, and I feel tingling. He told me the L5 and T7 vertebrae were pinched from sitting in the wheelchair for so long. He puts needles in my head, back and leg. Over an eighteen-month treatment period, I decreased the methadone from 150 to 35 mg a day. I was able to decrease the amount of Neurontin and Lyrica, because the pain wasn't as bad anymore. My HTC had told me that I would never walk again, and now I walk fine. The HTC pain management center was happy but very surprised! — Richard Pezzillo, Rhode Island

Therapeutic Massage. This technique involves the manipulation of soft tissue by a trained therapist. The goal is to increase blood flow to the painful area, reduce muscle tension, and induce relaxation. Consult your HTC before beginning any massage therapy: improper massage techniques can cause or aggravate bleeds.

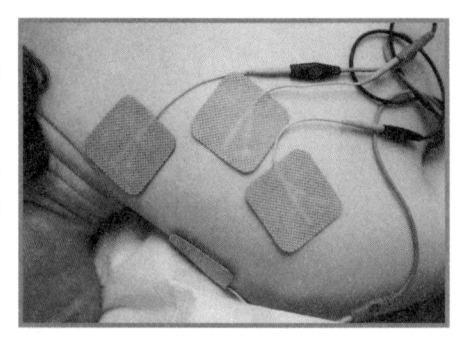

Transcutaneous Electrical Nerve Stimulation (TENS). TENS is a user-controlled device that delivers electrical impulses of varying intensity to the muscles via electrodes. The goal is to interfere with or inhibit pain transmission along nerves. TENS has proved useful in reducing some types of pain. The unit is portable and can be worn under clothing to provide pain relief all day.

■ ■ ■

Many other therapies may also help control pain, including acupressure, chiropractic manipulation, aromatherapy, ultrasound, and laser treatments. Ultrasound therapy warms joints internally to provide pain relief. Laser treatments may provide pain relief in a similar way, although the exact mechanism is unknown. Some patients even report feeling benefits from magnet therapy, although most medical professionals ridicule this. Some patients use herbal therapy for pain relief. Most physicians do not recommend herbal therapies or botanicals ("holistic care") because many inhibit platelet adhesion, which prolongs bleeding. And such therapies may interact or interfere with other medications. Don't take any herbal remedy without consulting your HTC.

The number one method of alternative pain relief for children that was reported effective by almost all parents interviewed for this book? Distraction. Refocusing the mind on something meaningful and fun can be a great strategy. In his book *Anatomy of an Illness*, Norman Cousins wrote that after being diagnosed with terminal cancer in 1964, along with his conventional therapy, he watched comedy movies over and over. He discovered that laughter gave him some relief from his terrible pain. And he survived.[14] Always have some amusing distraction available for those long nights: music, movies, board games, video games—whatever works.

The medication can only do so much to take the edge off, and Leland understands the benefit of meditation, but video gaming has become the

*pain management tool. He has control for once over what's going on.
—Jane, Massachusetts*

Our son does have his comfort things, like a teddy bear. Or he'll get clingy with me, and we'll sing songs as a distraction. And there's TV. We have unlimited membership to Blockbuster! —Derek Nelson, Utah

Matthew has tried anti-anxiety medications, antidepressants, and biofeedback. None have worked. The most successful alternative therapies are ice and distraction. Video games, TV, board games . . . you name it! —Debbie Porter, California

Neurogenic Pain

For some patients, there is little relief from one kind of chronic pain: neurogenic (or neuropathic) pain. This pain is caused by damage to the nerves themselves. Phantom limb pain is one example: long after a limb has been amputated, a patient may still feel pain from the toes or ankles of the missing limb. Though the peripheral nerves of the extremity are gone, the central nervous system still "remembers" the nerve signals and transmits them to the brain. Why this happens is unknown. For some patients, drugs or TENS may successfully reduce the pain, but for more than half of patients with neurogenic pain, nothing seems to offer relief.

Neurogenic pain feels like you are on fire. The burning is unbelievable, and it feels like there are sharp knives up and down. You can't sit, or have anything touch you. It's different than a bleed. It's not tingly, like a bleed, where if I don't move, the pain is not so bad. Neurogenic pain just doesn't stop. —Richard Pezzillo, Rhode Island

Neurogenic pain continues long after bleeds have resolved, and it's difficult to treat.

Neurogenic pain is our biggest challenge. For years, Leland had acute pain, associated with bleeds, which was manageable with Tylenol. Then, just before he turned eleven, we noticed that the bleeds were more painful; this was first time he had neurogenic pain. Leland can now tell the difference between bleed pain, arthritic pain, and neurogenic pain. He was in pain every day, twenty-four hours a day, with neurogenic pain for eighteen months. Now we are always on edge, wondering, is this bleed going to last for a week or two, or will it lead to neurogenic pain for a couple of months? —Jane, Massachusetts

Watching your child suffer from neurogenic pain is the most helpless feeling in the world, and sometimes there's little you can do about it. In some cases, even conventional medicine is limited in its effectiveness. When your child experiences neurogenic pain, you need to consult pain management specialists and investigate CAM. And make sure you provide support for the rest of your family, as you'll face many sleepless nights and long days. But even through this type of pain, your child can persevere, mature, and adapt.

How Pain Affects Your Child

Pain, especially chronic pain, is far more than physical discomfort. It affects every aspect of your child's life.

Many studies have found that sleep disturbance is one of the main problems for patients with chronic pain. Sleeping well refreshes the mind and body. But being in pain makes it hard to sleep well; pain often feels worse at night. Pain causes stress, which worsens the pain, and also causes the release of hormones such as adrenaline. That makes sleeping difficult. This is one reason that you must address stress and anxiety before pain management can be really effective. Not only is it tough to get to sleep or fall into a deep sleep, but your child may also wake repeatedly during the night when he rolls over on a painful limb. Lack of sleep affects your child's mental sharpness and his daily activities.

> *There have been many nights without sleep because Tristan literally screams and cries in pain. We are all so tired during these episodes.* —Jessica Herren, Pennsylvania

Pain may affect your child's appetite, causing it to increase or decrease. People in pain often avoid social activities or relationships. Hobbies, sports, or music may lose their appeal. The emotional impact of pain can cause anxiety, depression, fear, and anger. Pain makes it hard to be productive at school or work. Pain saps your child's energy and makes daily life less enjoyable. Pain significantly decreases quality of life.

How can you avoid these negative consequences? *Treat all pain early and effectively!* Because your child knows his pain better than anyone, he can tell you what works and what doesn't. With his direction and your HTC's expert advice, you can help him make decisions about pain management that he will one day make on his own as an independent adult.

How Pain Affects the Family

Pain puts tremendous stress on families, especially when it happens to children. Your child may delay reporting bleeds. And if parents downplay pain and a disruptive bleed occurs, the result may be sorrow, guilt, frustration, blame, or anger. For some families, especially those with inhibitors, pain seems to control their lives.

> The main complication is the extreme heartache it brings to see your child in so much pain, and the emotions you feel at the lack of control you have—the fact that you can't take it away. —Sasha Cheatham, Oklahoma

> I sometimes think, I can't listen to this anymore, but my mothering instinct says, stay with him, rub his back. But I'm thinking, I need to get out of here! Listening to him moan, I almost snap. —Jane, Massachusetts

> Pain issues have been especially hard on every aspect of our lives, from the emotional toll it takes to the physical demands it places on every member of the family. Pain controls the mood of the household sometimes, and dictates where we will vacation. Or if there will be a vacation at all. Pain eats away at intimate relationships and blurs the lines between sibling responsibilities. Behind every thought or action lies the realization that this may cause our son to hurt and eventually be physically crippled. —Joyce Hewitt, Michigan

You can help your family deal with pain when you learn about pain management treatments, both conventional and alternative. Encourage your child to report pain promptly. Help him develop a way to describe his pain. Treat bleeds immediately and treat pain immediately.

To reduce the risk of chronic pain from permanent joint damage, infuse early and aggressively, and consider prophylaxis. When necessary, consult pain management specialists and investigate CAM. Develop a pain management plan with the help of pain specialists at your HTC. If this option is unavailable at your HTC, or if you feel your pain is not being adequately managed, then advocate for a referral to a hospital with a pain center and expertise in dealing with chronic pain. It may take many months of trial and error to arrive at a successful pain management plan that addresses your needs. Regardless of how long it takes, don't resign yourself to toughing it out. Show your child that he has options for handling pain. ■

> Colton has been through so much, he is amazing to me. He doesn't complain. If something is hurting him, he takes Tylenol—maybe. These kids have developed a high tolerance for pain. He never complains about the pain in his joints, and yet he must feel pain. —Debbie Branch, Kansas

■ NOTES

1. You may also want to consider preventing bleeds by using prophylaxis with bypassing agents. This means daily infusions with NovoSeven, or infusions every day to every other day with FEIBA. Until further studies confirm the benefits, prophylaxis with bypassing agents should be considered experimental, though many hematologists are beginning to talk about prophylaxis. Discuss this approach to pain management with your HTC team to help you make the best decision.
2. Use shorter time periods for hands and feet because they have smaller muscles and little fat; use longer time periods for larger muscles like the thigh.
3. This is not recommended for bleeds in the forearm or calf, as reduced blood flow or progressive swelling from an untreated bleed may cause pressure on a nerve, leading to compartment syndrome, a critical complication that may lead to nerve damage. If the extremity becomes "tingly," loosen the wrap. Be mindful of how long you leave on the compression dressing. Remove the dressing at least once daily to inspect the area.
4. In one study, 196 people with hemophilia were surveyed about how they experience and treat pain. Approximately 34% of respondents used acetaminophen (Tylenol) to treat pain, and approximately 39% used NSAIDs. Sponsored by Novo Nordisk and four HTCs, this study was conducted by the Munson Medical Center in Traverse City, Michigan, and the Henry Ford Health System in Detroit. Witkop M, Lambing A. Pain assessment. *HemAware.* 2007 May/June;12:91. This pain study may be found at www.henryford.com/painstudy.
5. The maximum daily adult dose of acetaminophen is 4 g with a recommended dosage of 352–650 mg every 4–6 hours, or 1 g every 6 hours. For children younger than 12 years and/or less than 50 kg in weight, the maximum daily dosage of acetaminophen is 80 mg/kg (not to exceed a cumulative daily dose of 2.6 g). Therapeutic weight-based oral dosing for children is 10–15 mg/kg every 4–6 hours, with a maximum of 5 doses per 24-hour period. Weight-based rectal suppository dosing for children is higher at 15–20 mg/kg per dose.

    For adults, the minimum toxic dose of acetaminophen for a single ingestion is 7.5–10 g. Single ingestions of 12 g or higher have high potential for liver damage.

    Children who have ingested 250 mg/kg or more of acetaminophen within 24 hours are in danger of acetaminophen-induced hepatotoxicity; the minimum *toxic* dose in children is 150 mg/kg.

    Patients who ingest more than 350 mg/kg develop severe hepatotoxicity, if they are not appropriately treated. Defendi GL, Tucker JR. Toxicity acetaminophen [Internet]. [place unknown]: Medscape; 1994–2010. Updated 2009 Aug 25 [cited 2010 Feb 16]. 1 screen. Available from: http://emedicine.medscape.com/article/1008683-overview
6. Although most aspirin-related compounds containing salicylic acid also affect platelet adhesion, two do not: salsalate (Disalcid®) and choline magnesium trisalicylate (Trilisate®). These are sometime prescribed for children with hemophilia.

7. MASAC document #162: MASC recommendations on use of Cox-2 inhibitors in persons [Internet]. New York: National Hemophilia Foundation; 2003 [cited 2010 Feb 16]. 1screen. Available from: http://www.hemophilia.org/NHFWeb/MainPgs/MainNHF.aspx?menuid=57&contentid=175
8. People with hemophilia should never take any drug containing aspirin, such as Percodan, which contains aspirin and oxycodone. People with hemophilia should not take other NSAIDs or acetaminophen while taking combination painkillers, as this may result in an overdose, causing kidney or liver damage.
9. Respiratory depression may also result from an overdose or use of other depressant drugs, such as alcohol, while taking an opioid. Patients have been known to accidentally overdose on some slow-acting opioids that may not take effect for several hours. Patients who take a dose of a slow-acting opioid and feel no relief may mistakenly believe the dose is too low, or think they forgot the dose, and take another, resulting in an overdose when the slow-acting drug takes effect several hours later.
10. American Pain Foundation. Treatment options: a guide for people living with pain [Internet]. [place unknown]: Scribd [cited 2010 Feb 16]. Available from: http://www.scribd.com/doc/5709854
11. If you choose a CAM therapy not specifically recommended by your HTC, please tell your HTC pain management team. Some therapies can increase your risk of bleeding or have serious side effects.
12. Wallny TA, Brackmann HH, Gunia G. Successful pain treatment in arthropathic lower extremities by acupuncture in haemophilia patients. *Haemophilia.* 2006 Sep;12(5):500–502.
13. Rosted P, Jergensen V. Acupuncture used in the management of pain due to arthropathy in a patient with haemophilia. *Acupuncture in Medicine.* 2002;20(4):193–95.
14. Cousins N. Anatomy of an illness as perceived by the patient: reflections on healing and regeneration. New York: W. W. Norton; 1979.

SUMMARY 6
Managing Pain

- Pain is purely subjective. There is no scientific way to measure type, level, or intensity of pain.

- Teach your child to acknowledge, report, and respond to pain promptly.

- Pain is either acute or chronic. Acute pain lasts for hours, days, or even months. Chronic pain is ongoing, and lasts six months or longer. Acute pain is usually caused by bleeding into joints and muscles. Chronic pain is usually caused by arthritis.

- Chronic pain is often underdiagnosed and undertreated.

- RICE (Rest, Ice, Compression, Elevation) helps reduce pain from bleeds and speeds healing.

- Pain medications to treat acute and chronic pain are often divided into three groups: non-opioids, opioids, and adjuvant analgesics.

- Non-opioids include acetaminophen and non-steroidal anti-inflammatory drugs (NSAIDs). Never take NSAIDs without consulting your HTC.

- Opioids are narcotics, and include hydrocodone and morphine. Opioids may also be combined with non-opioid analgesics such as acetaminophen or aspirin. People with hemophilia should not use aspirin. Carefully check any OTC medication for the presence of aspirin, acetylsalicylic acid, or ASA. Common brand names of combination opioids with non-opioid analgesics include Darvocet, Percodan, Percocet, and Vicodin.

- Know the differences between drug addiction, tolerance, and dependency.

- CAM (Complementary and Alternative Medicine) includes relaxation, biofeedback, behavioral modification, stress management, hypnotherapy, counseling, acupuncture, massage, and transcutaneous electrical nerve stimulation (TENS).

- Distraction with television or video gaming may help your child manage his pain.

- Neurogenic pain is caused by damage to the nerves themselves, and often is not alleviated with treatment.

- Pain management is an ongoing process. Your child's response to a pain medication may change over time.

7 Ports, PICCs, and Pokes

Your child with hemophilia and inhibitors will need many needlesticks—also called "sticks" or "pokes."[1] Whether you are treating bleeds with bypassing agents every two hours or twelve hours, administering daily infusions for ITI, undertaking prophylaxis, or even doing prophylaxis with bypassing agents while on ITI, you'll be inserting many needles into your child's veins.

During the long ITI regimen, some children with prominent, resilient veins can continue receiving infusions through *peripheral* veins. These are distant from the heart, as in the hands, arms, or legs. Peripheral veins are often visible just below the skin and are usually easily accessed directly through the skin. But if your child has only one good vein, has hard-to-find veins or veins that "roll," or if he is very young and facing prophylaxis or ITI, repeated sticks can be traumatic for him and you. To make infusions easier and to preserve his delicate veins, your HTC staff may recommend a *central venous access device* (CVAD).[2] These are typically recommended as a temporary measure—usually no more than three to five years—with the goal of using peripheral veins as soon as possible.

> Living so far from the clinic, having a CVAD has made a world of difference. It allows for prompt treatment, fewer hospital trips, and shorter hospital stays because we can treat at home. —Chasity, Mississippi

Central Venous Access Devices

The idea behind a CVAD, also called a *central line*, is simple. Instead of directly infusing into a peripheral vein, you infuse through a device that has a large "target" for the needle on one end, and a length of tubing (a catheter) at the other end, which is placed inside a big, central vein within the neck or chest.

There are two general kinds of CVAD: *internal* and *external*. Both must be surgically implanted; the surgery for an internal CVAD is slightly more involved than for an external CVAD. External and internal CVADs each have advantages and disadvantages. Your choice of

CVAD will depend on how long you need venous access, and on what limitations in activities you're willing to accept.

External CVADs have one end of the catheter positioned outside the body. Infusions are given through the external portion of the catheter and not directly through the skin. The catheter is accessed via a syringe, through a cap or hub attached to the catheter.

Internal CVADs, known as *ports*, have no external parts. They are implanted beneath the skin and are accessed by a needlestick through the skin directly into a part of the port called the *reservoir*.

In both kinds of CVAD, one end of the catheter is positioned within one of the large central veins near the heart, often the superior vena cava.

> *Venous access has been a very difficult for us. Andrew had a Hickman line placed when he was five days old. This was removed at ten months due to infection. Then we had eight ports. He has also had a few PICC lines between his ports. His final port, which has been in two years, has been infection-free, which coincides with being free of his inhibitor.* —Richard and Lynley Scott, New Zealand

External CVADs: Peripheral, Tunneled, Nontunneled

A *peripherally inserted central catheter*, or PICC line, is inserted directly into a peripheral vein, such as the one on the inner arm near the elbow. The catheter is threaded through the length of the vein in the arm, coming to rest in a large vein near the heart. Generally, PICC lines are temporary, lasting at most about six months. They can be surgically inserted in an outpatient procedure. Common brand names of PICC lines include Per-Q-Cath® and Groshong® PICC.

Nontunneled CVADs are short, large-bore catheters inserted through the skin and directly into one of the deep veins of the body, normally the subclavian or the jugular. These catheters are not used for long-term infusion therapy; your child probably wouldn't be using this device for factor infusions. Nontunneled CVADs are most often used in emergency situations for critically ill patients.

A *tunneled* CVAD, unlike a PICC, does not directly enter a vein at the location where it is inserted. Instead, it's tunneled under the skin, entering a vein at another location. This reduces the risk of infection and allows the catheter to be used longer than PICC lines and nontunneled CVADs. Tunneled CVADs may be used for months to years. They require surgical placement, usually under general anesthesia. Examples of brand names of tunneled catheters include Broviac®, Hickman®, and Leonard®.

Internal CVADs: Ports

A port is a CVAD that is surgically implanted completely under the skin. It consists of a catheter threaded into a vein at one end, with a reservoir attached at the opposite end. The reservoir is a quarter-sized hollow disk made of plastic, stainless steel, or titanium. The top of the reservoir is covered by a silicone *septum* through which a special non-coring Huber needle is inserted.

You'll need to push a needle through your child's skin to access the port, and use only a Huber needle to avoid damaging the septum. Common brand names of ports include Port-a-Cath®, BardPort™, Mediport®, and PassPort®.

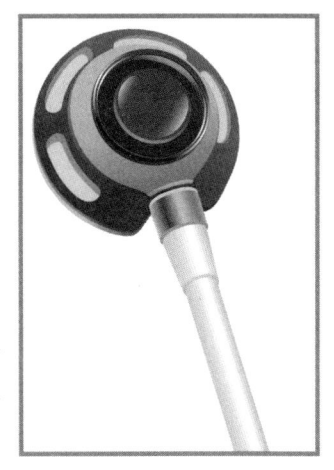

Port implantation surgery usually involves two small incisions. Most ports are implanted in the chest, but they can be placed almost anywhere, including in the upper arm or near the waist. The port is usually sutured, or sewn, to underlying connective tissues to support it and prevent it from rolling over. Ports have no direct opening to the outside of the body; all you might see is a bump under the skin. Ports may be accessed up to 2,000 times before the septum breaks down and they must be replaced.

CVADs: Advantages and Disadvantages

Each CVAD has advantages and disadvantages, and one device may be more practical than another for your child's needs.

Externally accessed CVADs

Advantages: Insertion isn't complicated. It can be done either under general anesthesia or using a local anesthetic. A short hospital stay might be needed to monitor the site for complications like prolonged bleeding. Accessing the CVAD won't require a needlestick through the skin.

The Broviac worked well when our son was a baby because we didn't have to poke him every time we needed to use it, but the nightly bandage changes and inability to get it wet made it impractical as he got older. —Joyce Hewitt, Michigan

Disadvantages: These devices may function for as few as six months. Because the catheter tip extends outside the body, there is a higher risk of infection. A dressing must be kept over the exit site so it remains sterile and dry, and must be changed frequently. The catheter's hub, or end, must be kept clean. You'll have to restrict your child's activities: no baths or swimming because they increase the infection risk, and no roughhousing or contact sports. Each HTC and surgeon's recommendations may differ for these activities, and it's important to understand what you can and can't do with an external catheter. The catheter or dressings may also attract stares and attention.

Both the Broviac and PICC lines were easy to use, but needed a significant amount of maintenance to prevent infection. It was difficult to bathe our son: we didn't submerse him in water, so swimming was out. Since both devices came out of the body, the risk of infection was higher. Other kids were sometimes interested in them and stared or wanted to explore them. —Shari Luckey, Michigan

Internally accessed ports

Advantages: Compared to external CVADs, a port will allow your child to participate in more activities, with no restrictions on bathing or swimming. When the port is not accessed, there is no direct line into the body for bacteria to enter. Physicians often recommend ports for ITI because of the convenience and lower risk of infection.

We had a Port-a-Cath implanted when Lee was six. He's had no problems—not sore, not tender, no infections. Lee was okay with it and adjusted well. —Eleth Ridenhour, Kansas

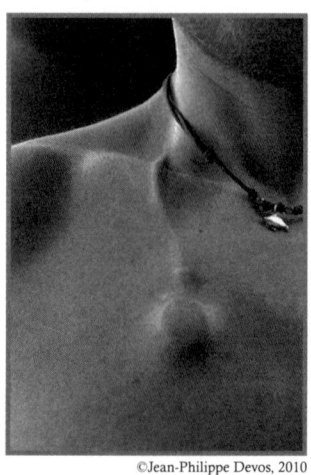

©Jean-Philippe Devos, 2010

Disadvantages: Surgical insertion and removal of a port is more involved than for an externally accessed catheter. Ports may look noticeably odd. If your child is thin, a lump will be visible on his chest when he is shirtless. Be prepared for comments and stares! You might opt to have the port placed on the upper arm, where a lump may be less obvious. As your child grows and accumulates more muscle and body fat, his port may become less visible. Many HTCs do not use a port immediately after surgically implanting it, to allow the skin to heal at the insertion site. This means that for the first one to two weeks after the port is placed, factor is infused using a peripheral vein. Other HTCs leave the port accessed for a week or longer after the surgery, which means that they leave a needle in the new port.

Even when you've selected a CVAD, you must be on guard against one risk that is common to them all: blood infection.

Complications of CVADs: Blood Infection

Of the several complications that can happen, the most common is a blood infection. If not promptly diagnosed and aggressively treated, blood infections can be life-threatening.

> *Blood infections are serious. We got home from having Beau's port placement surgery, and the next morning he had a high fever and was shaking. The on-call surgeon told us it was too soon for a wound infection. We visited our pediatrician, who ran a culture but found nothing. When we got home, we saw that the on-call hematologist had left a message to return immediately. We argued that Beau was fine (the Tylenol was working) but he insisted we be admitted. When we arrived, Beau's fever spiked to 105.5 degrees, and he was shaking. The HTC put him on IV antibiotics immediately. In hindsight, we should have used an ambulance. One of the scariest days of our lives.* —Kari Atkinson, Iowa

Several studies have found that almost everyone with hemophilia and inhibitors who uses ports or external CVADs will eventually develop a blood infection. The reason? A CVAD provides a direct route into the bloodstream—for both medicine *and* bacteria. Bacteria introduced into the bloodstream through the port can cause *sepsis*, a serious blood infection.[3] Symptoms of sepsis may include high fever, chills, lethargy, irritability, resting heart rate greater than ninety beats per minute, high respiratory rate, elevated white blood cell count, and sometimes redness around the port or catheter site. Children under age six are more likely to get port infections. There is a direct relationship between port use and infection risk: the more you infuse, the higher the risk of infection.[4] The risk of infection also increases when several people access the CVAD.

> *We had to stop ITI because Jonathan's ports were getting infected.* —Jackie, Massachusetts

Catheter and port infections can be hard to resolve with antibiotics. This is because the catheter and reservoir—the foreign material in the body—provide a surface on which bacteria can colonize, creating a thin layer called a *biofilm*. The bacteria in the biofilm secrete a slime layer over themselves, protecting them from the effects of the antibiotic and from attack by the body's immune system. These infections often do not respond well to antibiotics, so the CVAD must be removed to completely clear the infection.[5]

> *Jonathan has had a Broviac, two ports, and two PICC lines. They all worked great, but all except one PICC line got infected. He's been hospitalized ten*

times, all for infections! Once he was in the hospital for one month for a port infection. I was devastated! We stayed with him the whole time; he was never alone. —Jackie, Massachusetts

In some cases, a child may develop a fever or chills every time he receives an infusion through the port. This happens because bacteria can live within the CVAD itself. When an infusion is given through the CVAD, the bacteria are pushed into the bloodstream along with the factor, causing fever or chills. Diagnosing a blood infection involves a blood test. Twenty-four hours after the test, a physician can make a preliminary diagnosis. But it may take up to forty-eight hours to completely rule out an infection. Because a blood infection is serious and can be life-threatening, physicians usually treat the patient with antibiotics while the blood samples are being cultured. You should insist on blood cultures *immediately* if your child develops a fever or has any other signs of infection.

Bacteria can also cause infection around the central line insertion site. If bacteria travel along the outside of the catheter, a *tract infection* can develop, which may be painful and require antibiotics. To clear this type of infection, the catheter will probably have to be removed.

Report a Fever!

When your child has a CVAD, you must report all fevers over 101 degrees to your HTC. Even if other symptoms are present, including flu-like symptoms, medical staff will assume that there is a port infection and take precautions until the exact cause of the fever is determined. *Delay in treating a fever can result in serious, life-threatening complications.* Always call your HTC when your child with a CVAD has a fever!

Preventing Infections: Aseptic Technique

The best way to reduce the risk of infection while accessing the CVAD is to use strict *aseptic technique*:

1. Wash your hands thoroughly and use sterile gloves.

2. Carefully clean the infusion site with topical antiseptics, such as chlorhexidine or alcohol and povidone-iodine (PVP-I or Betadine®).

3. Use only sterile equipment (syringes, gloves, needles, dressings).

The procedure for prepping a port differs slightly at each HTC, so learn the procedures supported by your HTC. Learning aseptic technique takes time, practice, and patience. At first, the steps may seem cumbersome and difficult, but in time the procedure will become second nature. Remember: to reduce the risk of infection, always be very careful and never take shortcuts, even when you're a pro at infusions.

With a port, you push the Huber needle through the skin, through the silicone septum, and into the reservoir of the port. After you've infused the factor, you flush with saline followed by heparin, and then remove the needle.[6] But you can also leave the port accessed by leaving in the needle and taping it to the chest. Check with your HTC to see if that is recommended, and under what circumstances. Many HTCs have strict policies about leaving the port accessed. An accessed port increases the chance of infection, so many HTCs don't allow the needle to stay in place, especially if treatments are only once or twice a day. But most HTCs will allow a port to remain accessed if infusions are every two hours, for example.

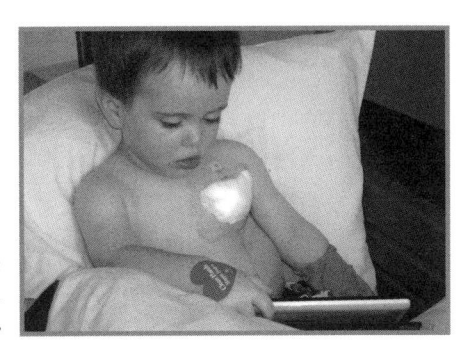

Whenever the port is accessed, the area must be covered by a sterile dressing and must not get wet or dirty. Besides the patient or caregiver, only specially trained doctors and nurses should access the port. Medical staff untrained in the use of ports may fail to thoroughly prep the site, increasing the risk of infection. Or they may use an incorrect needle, damaging the septum. Or they may use too much force in pushing the factor, which can separate the catheter from the reservoir or burst the catheter.

Believe it or not, good dental care is also important in preventing CVAD infections and for overall health, because bacteria can enter the bloodstream from the gums. Regular flossing and brushing promotes healthy gums, reducing the risk of port infections. Some doctors also recommend prophylactic antibiotics for dental work in patients with CVADs to avoid introducing infections during dental procedures.[7]

Complications of CVADs: Obstruction

Obstruction, or *line occlusion*, occurs when something disrupts the flow of factor into or out of the catheter or line. You or your HTC staff may suspect a line occlusion if it's hard to pull back on the syringe when checking for a blood return, or if it's hard to push medicine into the device. Several scenarios can cause line blockage, and depending on the circumstance, you may need to visit the hospital to resolve a line occlusion.

If you suspect a line occlusion, the needle position is the first thing to check: improper needle position can block or impede flow through the needle. When accessing a port, you must insert the needle through the septum to the back wall of the port, and insert it *straight*. If you insert the needle at an angle—a squirming child can make a straight shot tough—and feel resistance when infusing, you need to remove the needle and reinsert a new one to solve the problem. If you have trouble reaching the back of the port with the needle, you can request a longer needle. This is a common scenario for caregivers first learning to infuse through a port. Fortunately, it's an easy problem to fix.

In another scenario, the position of the catheter within the vein may cause a temporary blockage. This happens especially when the catheter lies against the vein wall rather than in the center of the vein. Depending on where it was placed, the catheter can also get pinched or kinked, often between the clavicle and the first rib, partially obstructing the catheter. Having your child turn his head or raise his arm may temporarily unkink the catheter long enough to administer factor. Contact your physician immediately if the catheter shows signs of obstruction: for example, if you have trouble pulling back on the syringe when checking for blood return. This scenario can lead to the catheter breaking.

An obstruction common to all CVADs is the formation of a *fibrin sheath* along the catheter. This happens when a foreign object, such as a CVAD, is placed in the body. Foreign material tends to activate the clotting cascade, causing fibrin and sometimes clots to form on and around the device. Too much fibrin can block the end of the catheter, creating a sheath that acts like the paper wrapper on a straw. A fibrin sheath can block the passage of fluids through the catheter. Sometimes it's possible to push fluids through the catheter if a fibrin sheath is present, but checking for a blood return is difficult. In this case, the sheath acts like a one-way valve.

A blockage can also be caused by a blood clot. Some clots form within the catheter or the port. If it's possible to push fluids through, but difficult to get a blood return from the port, a *ball-valve clot* may exist. Here's what happens: when you flush fluids through the port, the clot is pushed away from the opening of the catheter, allowing the factor to flow out of it; but when you try to get a blood return, the ball-valve clot acts like a one-way valve or cork, plugging the entrance to the catheter when you check for return by pulling back on the syringe plunger. Blood clots and fibrin sheaths may be resolved with special clot-busting medicine, administered through the line. This medicine, called *tissue plasminogen activator* (tPA), is safe and widely used on all kinds of patients. Brand names include Activase® and Cathflo™.

To reduce the possibility of a clot forming in the line, ports and most catheters are flushed with 10 to 20 mL of saline followed by 3 to 5 mL of heparin after factor infusions. Some HTCs prefer heparin/saline flushes, using a pulsing action to push out any proteins that may be left after the factor is infused.[8]

If it's hard to push factor into the line, *do not use more force to push the factor!* This can rupture the line or cause the catheter to disconnect from the reservoir.[9] Use 10 mL or larger syringes when infusing through a central line, because smaller-diameter syringes deliver a greater force with the same amount of plunger pressure. If the factor is hard to push, push *slowly over a longer period of time* and call your HTC immediately to have the problem diagnosed and corrected.

Complications of CVADs: Deep Vein Thrombosis

Another common complication associated with CVADs is the formation of a deep vein thrombosis, or blood clot. A DVT may sometimes develop with no signs or symptoms, and go undiagnosed unless the physician specifically looks for it with a Doppler ultrasound, MRI, or CT scan. DVT occurs when a blood clot forms in one of the large veins. Such clots may be initiated by fibrin sheaths on the CVAD, which attract and collect other proteins passing through the vein, causing a clot to develop. Over time, the body compensates for decreased blood flow in a vein by developing collateral, or secondary, veins to reroute the flow of blood around the clot.

A child's body can develop these collateral veins relatively quickly—in just months—and experience few or no side effects from the DVT. The longer the catheter is in place, the greater the risk of developing DVT. Most DVTs occur after catheters have been in place for at least four years. Some studies report a 22% to 50% rate of DVT in hemophilia patients with ports.[10] In some cases, there are no signs or symptoms of a DVT. In other cases, a DVT may cause pain in the shoulder, neck, or arm; aching discomfort; swelling; enlarged surface veins; or discoloration on the side of the body where the thrombosis exists. Notify your HTC immediately if you observe any of these signs or symptoms because a DVT can have serious consequences. If a clot breaks loose, it may travel to the lungs, causing lung damage and possibly death.

Complications of CVADs and Ports: Skin Breakdown

Infections, line occlusions, and DVT are the most common complications of CVADs, but they aren't the only ones. Other complications may be minor, or they may be catastrophic, requiring emergency surgery to remove the CVAD. One minor complication is skin irritation from the constant tape and dressing changes. The port itself may be fine, but the skin nearby is red, scaly, itchy, and sometimes scabbed over.

One relatively rare complication is *skin erosion*, or the thinning and breakdown of the skin over the site of the port reservoir. This can also happen at the site of the Broviac where medical tape is frequently applied. You can recognize skin erosion by the thinning, bright red skin at the port site. Skin erosion has multiple causes: a reservoir placed too close to the surface of the skin; bleeding within the port pocket (a hole made in the fat or pectoral muscle for the port); infection in the port pocket; friction between the port and the skin; and sometimes, irritation from accessing the port repeatedly at the same site. In severe cases, the port may make its way through the skin and become partly exposed. At times, the port can be rescued by using peripheral venous access or another external catheter temporarily, to give the port site a rest. At other times, and in all cases of persistent infection, the port must be removed to allow the site to heal.

> *A major tragic event was when the port site broke open. We were accessing it every day, and the skin broke down, and it was gushing blood. We called the HTC and drove there at once. They took the port out and put a Hickman in. The Hickman kept bleeding from the incision site. It lasted a week. The HTC put a port back in. Now we leave the port accessed four days at a time.*
> *—Ashley Druckenmiller, Iowa*

> *We've had one port, which had to be removed. The port caused a constant bleed in our son's chest. It was painful and constantly bleeding internally. It was replaced with a Broviac. This Broviac worked great until one morning, when it just began slipping slowly out of his body. It was replaced with another Broviac, which is still working great. —Cicely Evans, Massachusetts*

Complications of CVADs: Mechanical Failure

Ports are also subject to mechanical failure, which can cause a host of problems. Catheters can burst or separate from the reservoir, and the septum of the reservoir can rupture. If that's not enough, the reservoir can flip over, preventing the port from being accessed. Catheters can break from repeated pinching between the shoulder blade and the first rib. More commonly, catheters are damaged by high pressure from forceful pushing on the syringe plunger, especially when using smaller-diameter syringes (less than 10 mL). Mechanical failure can cause heart damage if the catheter breaks, migrates to the heart, and interferes with the action of the heart valves. The loose catheter may also travel to the lungs, blocking blood flow to the lungs and possibly causing lung damage. The septum may fail, allowing *extravasation*, or leakage of drugs or fluids from the reservoir into the surrounding tissues. When a port fails mechanically, it must be removed, and the broken catheter must be "fished out" of the central vein or wherever it's lodged.

Whenever possible, the best way to infuse factor into the veins is through peripheral access. When frequent venous access is necessary and becomes difficult, a CVAD is often the best choice for easy venous access, especially in very young children.

Because of the risk of complications, most HTCs recommend that CVADs be used as temporary measures until it's possible to use peripheral venous access. CVADs should not be considered permanent. Of course, the timing depends on your specific situation. Some children need a CVAD in place for several years, while others can successfully transition to peripheral access after a year or two. Work with your HTC to determine what's best for your child.

Alternative to Ports: Arterio-Venous Fistula (AVF)

The arterio-venous fistula is *not* an implanted port, catheter, or other synthetic device.[11] It's not a device at all, but a surgical procedure that causes the enlargement of a vein, usually in a child's arm, so that parents can gain easy venous access by a regular needlestick. No tourniquets are needed during infusions. To create an AVF, the surgeon short-circuits the circulatory system by making a direct connection between an artery and a vein.

Veins are not designed to carry the high-pressure blood carried by arteries. When a vein is connected to an artery, the high-pressure arterial blood causes the vein to expand and the vein's wall to thicken. The enlarged vein is now a much easier target for a peripheral needlestick, and the stressful search for a suitable vein is over. Once an AVF is created, it takes about six to eight weeks or longer for the vein to "mature," or become enlarged and suitable for infusions. During this time, factor is often infused through a PICC line.

AVFs have two major advantages over ports: (1) a lower risk of infection, and (2) a lower risk of thrombosis. The risk of infection is lower with an AVF mainly because no foreign materials, such as plastic or metal, are used inside the body. Without synthetic material, it's harder for bacteria to gain a foothold and form a biofilm. The same holds true for thrombosis: synthetic materials activate the clotting cascade and cause thrombosis. Without synthetic materials, the risk of thrombosis is much lower. And while all CVADs are considered temporary and eventually must be removed, AVFs are considered permanent but can be reversed with another surgery. AVFs are less likely to clot off, and unlike CVADs, they aren't susceptible to mechanical failure. The AVF can be dismantled if there are complications, or for cosmetic reasons. But if the vein fails to mature, no surgery is required.

> *When Chris was two, his two CVADs were removed because of infection. I decided to go with an AVF because at that time, Chris was receiving factor every day, and I didn't want to just stop cold. It's now matured to where I can use the actual vein. He's had his fistula for ten years.* —Kelly Millette, Illinois

Despite their advantages, AVFs have potential complications. Surgery to create an

AVF isn't always successful. About 5% of them clot off and are not usable. Another 5% to 10% fail to mature. AVFs may also cause the vein to enlarge, not only at the site of the fistula, but possibly up the entire length of the arm—in some cases looking like a giant varicose vein. And because an AVF short-circuits the normal flow of blood, it's also possible that the AVF may "steal" some of the blood flow from the extremity below the AVF. This can result in cold hands, cramping, and in severe cases, tissue damage caused by lack of blood flow. Although AVFs have been used for decades in hemodialysis, relatively few have been created in people with hemophilia in the United States. We don't know for sure yet about any long-term complications.

The AVF procedure requires a skilled surgeon with experience in fistula creation.[12] Your surgeon should carefully explain all the risks, benefits, and alternatives. The entire process takes about three hours in the operating room with anesthesia.

> My father was the first in the United States to use an AVF for hemophilia. My husband and I were desperate to use one because our son had clotted off both subclavian veins, and people told us we could not do peripherals with the amount of factor we needed to give him. —Debbie Porter, California

CVAD or AVF?

It may seem inevitable that a child with an inhibitor will have a CVAD, at least at some point in his life. But if your child can't keep a line in place, or if he has too many infections, he might not be able to use a CVAD. And without one, he might not be able to tolerate the constant peripheral venous access needed for ITI. In this case, your child may be a good candidate for an AVF.

So, AVF or CVAD? If CVAD, what kind? These are decisions to make with your HTC team. If you choose a CVAD, you'll need to accept the significant risks of infection and DVT, and understand the time investment required to perform proper aseptic technique during infusions. You may need to try several options before finding the device or procedure that works best for your child.

> We were worried about scars, and about canceling swim lessons. It was an emotional rollercoaster. You can't measure all of the tears. It sucks. But part of your brain says, this is good for him, he needs this. You fear the unknown, but as a parent, you must do the best for your child. You even get jealous of others with hemophilia at times, because everything is going so well for them! —Kari Atkinson, Iowa

Learning about the available and appropriate devices and procedures will make your decision easier. Try to hear both sides, positive and negative, from other parents and HTC staff. Then weigh the pros and cons, consult your HTC team, and make a choice that will be comfortable and effective. Ask your HTC to introduce you to families with boys who have one or more of these devices or an AVF so you can see what they're all about. ■

> *I have been accessing Tristan's port since he was eighteen months old. It's like second nature to me. I use aseptic technique, and Tristan has never had a port infection. A benefit of having the port is the convenience. Because we infuse at home, quality of life has been so much better for the whole family.*
> *—Jessica Herren, Pennsylvania*

Comparison of Venous Access Options

Method	Advantages	Disadvantages
Peripheral veins (external needlesticks)	Avoids all problems of CVADs	Small veins may be hard to access and may require frequent HTC visits for child and parent; ITI requires many needlesticks, which could damage veins
CVAD (implanted port device)	Easy to access, low visibility, reliable	Infections, blood clots, device failure; following proper aseptic technique takes 20 minutes or more
CVAD (external central venous catheter)	Easy to access, no needlestick through the skin, reliable	Infections, blood clots, altered body image, restricted activities
AVF (arterio-venous fistula)	Easy to access, quick, reliable, low visibility, low risk of infection	May reduce blood flow to hand, clot off, fail to mature, or cause enlargement of vein running up the arm

■ NOTES

1. Some material in this chapter taken from "Which Central Venous Access Device to Use? Weighing the Options" by Jill Lathrop, PEN, May 2001, and "Another Option for Venous Access in Children with Hemophilia: The Arterio-Venous Fistula," by Leonard Valentino et al. PEN, May 2003.
2. MASAC Recommendation #115 states that CVADs may be used to facilitate venous access in patients with hemophilia. MASAC recommendation #115: MASAC recommendations regarding central venous access [Internet]. New York: National Hemophilia Foundation; 2006 [cited 2010 Feb 16]. 1 screen. Available from:
   http://www.hemophilia.org/NHFWeb/MainPgs/MainNHF.aspx?menuid=57&contentid=297
3. Approximately 33% of people with hemophilia who use a port develop a blood infection known as bacteremia during the life of the port. Bacteremia may lead to sepsis, commonly called blood poisoning, which can be fatal.
4. To determine the extent of the infection, blood may be drawn from both the CVAD and another site on the body. In this way, the physician can determine if the infection is in the device, or if it has spread throughout the body.
5. If you are using immunosuppressive drugs and have a port, the risk of port infections is higher. Parents must maintain a heightened level of awareness about fevers and illness. Give prompt treatment before your child develops serious signs of infection.
6. Some parents use a numbing cream, such as EMLA, when they access their child's port. Using a numbing agent before inserting the needle makes the process pain-free. Even without the cream, accessing the port involves a simple needlestick. In time, the area over the port becomes desensitized, and pokes are less painful. Note that EMLA is a petroleum-based medication; it may increase the risk of infection because it may trap skin bacteria over the site despite appropriate cleansing procedures. Ask your HTC about EMLA and other numbing creams.
7. As a precaution for people with CVADs, it's always advisable to take a prophylactic dose of an antibiotic before having any dental work done, including teeth cleaning. Contact your dentist for an antibiotic prescription before your appointment.
8. Groshong catheters are only flushed with normal saline.
9. Catheters are typically rated at 25–40 lb per square inch of pressure (psi). With "normal" hand pressure, you can easily generate up to 80 psi using a 10 cc syringe.
10. Dr. Marion Koerper reported a 22% rate of DVT in people with hemophilia and ports. Another study involving people without hemophilia found a 50% rate of DVT with ports. DVT is more common than local port infections, which one study found occurred at a rate of 3%.
    Koerper MA, Ester S, Cobb L. Asymptomatic thrombosis of innominate vein in hemophilic children with subcutaneous venous access devices (ports). National Hemophilia Foundation 48th Annual Meeting; Oct 17–20,1996; San Diego. Abstract.

Ewenstein et al. Consensus recommendations for use of central venous access devices in hemophilia. *Haemophilia.* 2004;10:629–48.
11. The AVFs used in hemophilia differ from those used in hemodialysis, which sometimes involves a synthetic graft, in which a tube of synthetic material is sewn between the vein and the artery.
12. Most American HTCs do not do AVF surgery. Rush University Medical Center in Chicago, Illinois, performs the vast majority of the AVF surgeries in the United States.

SUMMARY 7
Ports, PICCs, and Pokes

- Your child with hemophilia and an inhibitor will endure a tremendous number of needlesticks. With prominent, resilient veins, your child can receive infusions peripherally, directly through the skin.

- A central venous access device makes infusions easier. CVADs are either internal or external.

- A peripherally inserted central catheter, or PICC line, is inserted directly into a peripheral vein, and lasts about six months.

- A tunneled CVAD does not directly enter a vein at the location where it is inserted. Instead, it's tunneled under the skin, entering a vein at another location, and may be used for months to years.

- A port is an internal CVAD that is surgically implanted under the skin. It consists of a catheter threaded into a vein at one end, with a reservoir attached at the opposite end. A needlestick through the skin is required to access the port. Before they need replacing, ports may be accessed 1,000 to 2,000 times.

- Each type of CVAD has advantages and disadvantages.

- Up to 85% to 100% of people with hemophilia and inhibitors who use ports will eventually develop a port infection.

- The best way to reduce the risk of infection is to use strict aseptic technique.

- The CVAD may need to be removed to completely clear the body of a CVAD infection. Report all fevers over 101 degrees to your HTC.

- Line occlusion, or obstruction, occurs when something disrupts the flow of factor into or out of the catheter or line. You must visit the hospital to resolve a line occlusion.

- The formation of a DVT, or blood clot, is a common complication of CVADs. Most DVTs occur after catheters have been in place for at least four years. If your child has pain in the shoulder, neck, or arm; aching discomfort; swelling; enlarged surface veins; or discoloration on one side of the body, notify your HTC immediately.

- The AVF is a surgical procedure that causes the enlargement of a vein, usually in a child's arm, so that parents can gain easy venous access by a regular needlestick.

8 Surgery and Inhibitors

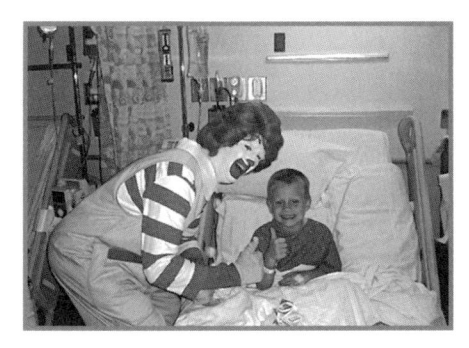

As recently as 1994, distinguished orthopedic surgeon Robert Duthie wrote that elective surgery is "absolutely contraindicated" in the presence of significant levels of factor VIII antibodies.[1] How far we've come in such a short time! With the availability of new bypassing agents, it's now possible to perform surgery on most inhibitor patients. Patients with inhibitors can be treated successfully for a variety of conditions with surgeries that include dental procedures, joint replacements, and even heart surgery.

When considering surgery, the primary concern is controlling bleeding during and after the procedure.

Because it is difficult to control bleeding, inhibitor patients should carefully consider the potential risks and benefits of a surgery. This could involve getting the opinion of several doctors about whether the surgery is necessary and possible. —Wendy Sass, New York

Early Surgeries

Your child may already have had surgery: circumcision. This is a common way that parents with no family history of hemophilia suddenly learn that their child has hemophilia.

Another common early surgery for people with hemophilia, and especially with inhibitors, is port placement. This is because ITI might be recommended soon after the inhibitor is discovered, and ITI requires frequent infusions. We discussed the placement of ports in chapter 7, and generally there are few complications with port surgery, though they can happen.

Andrew had to have surgery once to remove an infected port. It was done by a junior doctor, and vessels were not tied off properly. He was on huge doses of NovoSeven but continued to bleed. He required two further trips to the oper-

> ating room, the last one with a very experienced surgeon who finally managed to control the bleeding. Further factor concentrate wasn't going to resolve this; it was a surgical issue where the vessels needed to be sealed properly. —Richard and Lynley Scott, New Zealand

> Before Tristan's port surgery, the surgeon sat down with us and went over the whole procedure: where it would be placed and how it worked. It was great to know there were no surprises. The day of surgery, the doctor explained again what they would be doing and approximately how long it would take. Tristan's upcoming dental surgery will be carefully planned. Communication between the dentist and hematologist is key. They will work together to make sure that everyone is on the same page and we know exactly what will take place during the procedure. —Jessica Herren, Pennsylvania

Other childhood developmental milestones may include ear tubes or dental surgery, especially if wisdom teeth must be pulled.

> Our son's surgeries since using NovoSeven have been relatively uncomplicated, with the exception that after our son had bilateral ear tubes placed, he continued to bleed on and off out of his right ear for a year postoperatively. —Joyce Hewitt, Michigan

But the most serious of elective surgeries a person with hemophilia and inhibitors may face is joint replacement.

Joints

Joint disease is the most common complication in severe hemophilia, and it's more common and severe in people with inhibitors. It's also one of the most common reasons for major surgery in hemophilia. Repeated bleeding into joints causes degenerative joint disease, which eventually leads to hemophilic arthropathy, a painful and debilitating form of arthritis.

Because of frequent bleeds and difficulty controlling bleeds, people with inhibitors are at high risk of developing joint disease. But joint disease is not inevitable, and if a patient develops it, there are options. Several surgical procedures can slow or halt the progression of joint disease or, for people with severe joint disease, can make the limb functional again and eliminate or reduce pain.

> Elective orthopedic surgery made a tremendous difference. I could hardly walk before surgery. —R. H., Connecticut

I spent most of my life on crutches until my double knee replacement surgery. I couldn't walk without rebleeding, and surgery permitted me to walk again.
—Eric Lowe, Indiana

To make the best decisions about your child's joints if they require treatment or surgery, you'll need to understand what joints are and how they function.

Anatomy of a Joint

A joint is a place where two bones meet. Joints allow the skeleton to move. There are several types of joints in the body (see appendix D). Some joints don't move much, and some move a lot. The freely movable *synovial* joints are where most of the action takes place, because these joints allow lots of movement. The joints in your limbs—knee, ankle, fingers, toes, elbow—are synovial joints.

Not surprisingly, the synovial joints are also where most of the bleeding occurs. These joints share four main features, which you should know in order to understand surgery options later:

Joint capsule: a thin sheet of fibrous connective tissue that encases the joint.

Synovial membrane or synovium: the innermost lining of the joint capsule, which secretes a lubricant called *synovial fluid*. The synovium contains many small blood vessels that supply oxygen and nutrients for the cartilage covering the ends of the bones; the cartilage has no blood vessels of its own. The synovium also helps remove unwanted substances from the joint cavity. The surface of the synovium may be flat, or covered with tiny finger-like projections called *villi*.

Synovial fluid: the slimy, viscous lubricant secreted by the synovium. Synovial fluid fills the joint or *articular* cavity—the space in the joint between the bone ends—and serves as a lubricant to prevent friction between the bones. Typically, there is little synovial fluid in a joint, with the cartilage on the ends of the bones covered by only a thin layer of the fluid.

Hyaline (articular) cartilage: a layer of smooth, rubbery cartilage covering the ends of the bones. Along with synovial fluid, the hyaline cartilage allows frictionless movement of the bones. No friction means no pain.

Synovial joints can also be classified by their structure and by the kind of movement they allow. Three classifications are important for you to know because these joints tend to bleed more than other joints:

Hinge joints: allow movement of approximately 180 degrees in one direction only, like a door hinge. Examples: knee and elbow.

Ball-and-socket joints: allow circular movement and provide the greatest ROM. Examples: hip and shoulder.

Gliding joints: relatively flat surfaces that slide past each other and are held in position by ligaments; allow a fairly limited ROM.[2] Examples: ankle and wrist.

What Happens When a Joint Bleeds?

A joint bleed, or *hemarthrosis*, happens when one of the many blood vessels of the synovium ruptures, leaking blood into the joint cavity. The rupture may result from injury or trauma, or may happen spontaneously for no apparent reason. For people with hemophilia, an untreated joint bleed can rapidly fill the joint cavity with blood, causing pressure within the joint capsule and pain. Without treatment, pressure from the pooled blood in the joint will eventually cause the bleeding to slow or stop.

The body doesn't like having blood in a joint cavity. Blood is irritating to the joint. So after a joint bleed, cells in the synovium secrete proteins (enzymes) that break down the blood, allowing it to be absorbed.[3] But in this process, the synovium and cartilage are irritated by the breakdown products of these blood cells. This causes an inflammatory response: more blood flows to the area, causing tissues to swell, and allowing cells of the immune system to more easily move into the joint to help break down and remove the blood cells. It takes about four to six weeks for the pooled blood to be fully absorbed from the joint. Still, some breakdown products, such as *hemosiderin* (water-insoluble iron deposits), released from the red blood cells, may remain in the joint. Hemosiderin stains the normally white synovium a rusty brown color, and is thought to contribute to the death of cartilage cells. Hemosiderin also irritates the synovium, increasing inflammation.

When the synovium is inflamed, its finger-like villi become engorged with blood. This makes the villi more likely to rupture, causing the joint to rebleed. Repeated bleeding continues to irritate the synovium; it thickens, grows more blood vessels, and develops longer villi. The longer villi give the synovium the appearance of a shag carpet instead of a smooth sheet.[4]

Now the stage is set for a vicious cycle: the thickened, inflamed synovium bleeds more easily, causing more irritation and inflammation, and more frequent bleeds. The end result? A chronically inflamed synovium and a joint that bleeds easily, often spontaneously, with no apparent trauma—a target joint.[5]

> *I wanted fewer bleeds in my knee. I wanted to move and exercise my joint with less pain and swelling. I wanted to walk again . . . without crutches.* —Anonymous

Synovitis and Arthritis

Chronic inflammation of the synovium, common in target joints, is called *synovitis*. Synovitis leaves the joint swollen, giving it a "spongy" feeling, even after infusions of factor. If left untreated, chronic synovitis eventually leads to destruction of the cartilage in the joint and a debilitating form of arthritis called hemophilic arthropathy.

Arthropathy is characterized by the overgrowth of some parts of the bone in the joint, the *erosion* (destruction) of joint cartilage, and the loss of space between the ends of the bones in the joint. This condition eventually results in bone rubbing against bone, which causes excruciating pain. Without treatment, the bones may eventually grow together, or fuse, preventing any movement of the joint.

By the time a joint begins showing signs of arthropathy, the synovial membrane is often partially destroyed and replaced with scar tissue, in a process called *fibrosis*. As fibrosis progresses, bleeding into the joint becomes less and less common, but joint destruction continues.

Ankles and knees are most often affected by bleeds because they are large, weight-bearing joints, which are more likely than small joints to bleed. Hinge joints, such as the knee and elbow, and gliding joints like the ankle, bleed more frequently than ball-and-socket joints, such as the hip and shoulder. Pain and damage in one joint can affect other joints in the same limb. For example, if a knee joint isn't working properly, this may cause loss of ROM. If your child can't stretch out or bend his leg completely, his gait will be abnormal, causing more stress on his ankle and hip, and increasing the chance that they will bleed.

Synovectomy: Cure for Chronic Synovitis

If your child develops synovitis, your hematologist may recommend a *synovectomy*, the surgical removal of the overgrown synovium.[6] The goal of synovectomy is to decrease the number of bleeds in a joint. If synovitis is caught early, this procedure may short-circuit the vicious cycle of bleeds and joint destruction. *Note:* Although a synovectomy will reduce the frequency of bleeds, it may or may not stop the progression of joint disease.

The great news is that after the synovium is removed, the joint capsule produces a new, "clean" synovium, usually within sixty days.[7] When performed in the early stages of synovitis, synovectomies often effectively stop the progression of joint disease. Synovectomies performed at a later stage of synovitis, after joint damage has begun, can reduce the frequency of bleeding but may not halt the progression of joint disease.

Synovectomies can be surgical, radioactive, or chemical.

Surgical synovectomy

There are two kinds of surgical synovectomy:

- open (also called a *radical* synovectomy)
- closed (also called an *arthroscopic* synovectomy)

An open or radical synovectomy is a major surgical procedure involving a large frontal incision on the joint to remove the synovial lining. With this procedure, the surgeon can remove more synovium than with arthroscopic synovectomies. It's expensive and requires general anesthesia, a few days' hospitalization, prolonged factor replacement, and a long and painful course of physical therapy. PT is needed to break up or prevent adhesions (scar tissue that forms between two body parts where there should be no bond) and to prevent loss of ROM.[8] Even with PT, open synovectomies often cause some loss of ROM. Although this procedure has an 80% success rate in preventing further bleeds, it isn't usually performed today on patients with hemophilia because we now have arthroscopic procedures.

> Leland had a bad hamstring bleed, and as he recovered, his unusual gait stressed out his knee. Within two months, his knee went from healthy to bleeding constantly, even when he was on bed rest. Within two months, there was so much synovium that his HTC did an open synovectomy to clean it out. After surgery, Leland was in the hospital for ten days, on bed rest for a month, and on a continuous physical motion machine [CPM] twenty-four hours a day. We wanted to start PT, but he was in excruciating pain and having other bleeds. It was six to nine months' recovery before he was really able to walk. —Jane, Massachusetts

The closed or arthroscopic synovectomy requires a skilled orthopedic surgeon with meticulous technique. Under local or general anesthesia, the surgeon makes a quarter-inch incision and inserts a narrow fiber optic camera (arthroscope) into the joint. The arthroscope produces magnified images of the joint's interior to guide the surgeon. Sometimes the patient is also allowed to watch the surgery! Another small incision allows the surgeon to insert a motorized shaver, used to cut out the synovium. The debris is then suctioned out. A few of these small incisions may be needed to gain access to all parts of the joint.

PT often begins the day after surgery and may continue for six to twelve weeks, to help patients regain ROM and limb strength. Compared to open synovectomies, arthroscopic synovectomies have a faster recovery time (the patient can move the joint immediately), shorter hospital stay, lower cost, less factor usage, less pain, and less loss of ROM. Arthroscopic synovectomies are more easily performed on large

Surgery and Inhibitors

Arthropathy: How Bleeding Damages Joints over Time

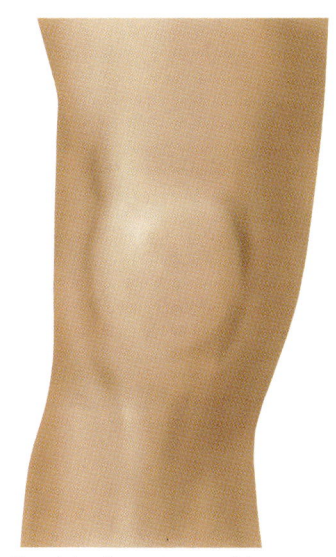

1. Outside view of normal knee

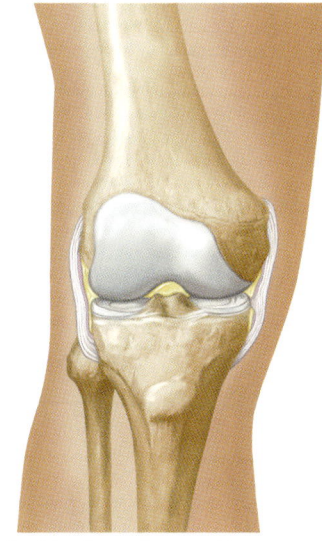

2. Inside view of normal knee

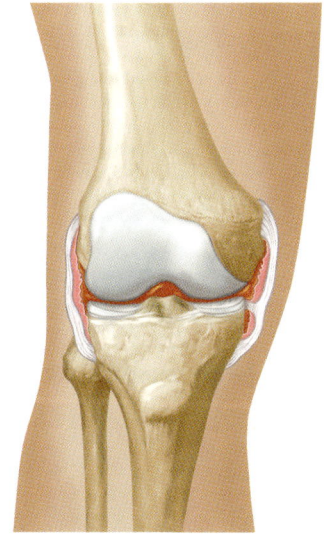

3. Onset of a knee bleed

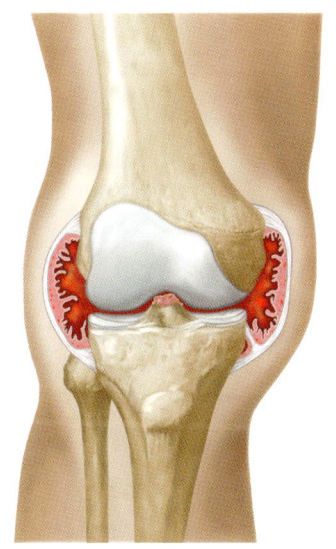

4. The synovium becomes inflamed

Reprinted with permission. Illustrations by Robert Margulies. www.robertmargulies.com

Managing Your Child's Inhibitor

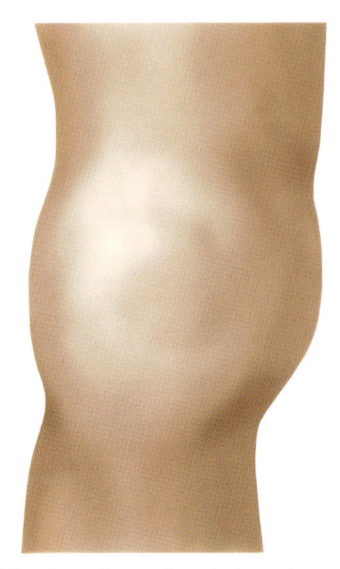

5. The knee is swollen, hot, and painful

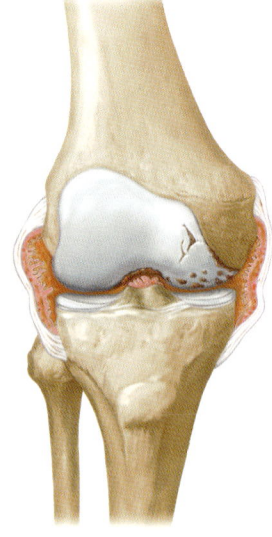

6. With repeated bleeds over time, the joint deteriorates

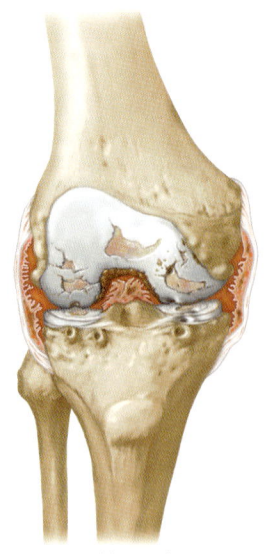

7. Chronic synovitis and arthropathy

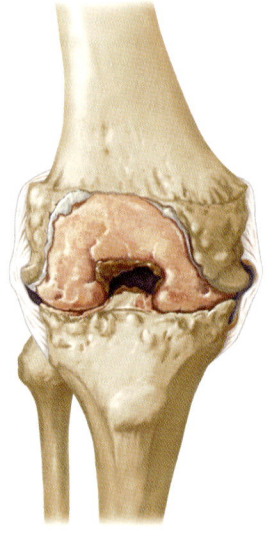

8. Advanced arthritis: bone against bone; the knee can no longer bend

joints like the knee than on small joints like the elbow. As with any surgery, there are risks. Even with a skilled surgeon, a closed synovectomy carries a small risk of bleeding, infection, and damage to nerves or blood vessels.

Radioactive synovectomy

Radioactive synovectomy (also called *radionuclide synovectomy* or *synoviorthesis*) involves injecting a small amount of radioactive material (an isotope) into the joint. Radiation emitted by the isotope slowly kills the cells of the synovium,[9] causing it to dissolve. New, healthy synovium replaces the dying synovium. A radioactive synovectomy does not produce instant results: because the synovial cells die slowly, your child may not see the benefits for a few months.

The good news is that this outpatient procedure is fast, relatively painless, and requires less factor than any other kind of synovectomy. Your child can go home shortly after the isotope is injected. He may need to wear a splint for two to three days to immobilize the joint and help prevent the isotope from leaving the joint capsule. There's less need for PT after a radioactive synovectomy, and the procedure can be repeated up to three times, if needed. Radioactive synovectomies have a success rate of 70% to 85%, or higher when the procedure is performed in the early stages of synovitis.

Drawbacks? In some cases, the new synovium may overgrow again (especially when the joint has a thick synovium) and another procedure may be needed within a few years. A radioactive synovectomy works best to treat synovitis in its early stages, because it can destroy only about one-quarter to one-third of an inch of synovium, and it may not be 100% effective if the synovial membrane is very thick. There's also a small potential for the radiation to cause cancer in the joint or cancer of the blood (leukemia).[10] This procedure is not usually performed on young children because of the unknown risk of damage to the growth plate[11] and the potentially higher risk of cancer.[12]

Chemical synovectomy

A chemical synovectomy is similar to a radioactive synovectomy. But instead of an isotope, a caustic chemical such as *osmic acid* or *rifampicin* is injected into the joint. Although these chemicals destroy the synovium, this procedure is generally considered less effective than a radioactive synovectomy.[13] But on the plus side, a chemical synovectomy doesn't carry the risk of cancer for young patients, and it may be preferable for children under age ten.

■■■

No matter which synovectomy is chosen for your child, keep in mind that it won't make a joint like new or correct joint damage that has already occurred. Nor can it restore lost ROM. In fact, in open synovectomies, there is often a *loss* of some ROM. The major benefit of these procedures is a decreased number of bleeds, which reduces pain and makes the joint more functional. If joint disease is caught early, a synovectomy can stop or slow its progression. As with all procedures, a synovectomy is more challenging for a child with an inhibitor. Undertake it with caution, and develop a good plan with input from your HTC team and an experienced surgeon.

Joint Replacement

Sometimes a joint is so irreversibly damaged that it no longer functions and causes severe, chronic pain. At this point, many hemophilia patients opt for total joint replacement, also called *arthroplasty*. The goal of joint replacement is to restore functionality to the limb and reduce or eliminate pain. Joint replacement surgery is *not* done on children because it will result in uneven bone growth between the affected limb and the normal limb.

In total joint replacement, the ends of the bones at the joint are cut off to accept an artificial joint made of metal and ceramic or plastic parts. The artificial joint is called a *prosthesis*. Joint replacement surgery normally takes one to two hours and requires prolonged, extensive PT to restore ROM.

In people with hemophilia, joint replacement is often done on hips and knees, occasionally on shoulders, and rarely on elbows or ankles (see "Radial Head Excision" and "Ankle Fusion" sections that follow). Knee and hip replacements have high success rates in people with hemophilia and have been performed since 1975. Once implanted, a prosthesis should last ten to fifteen years before it wears out and needs replacement. Your HTC will probably discourage high-impact sports, such as running, basketball, and tennis, because they may increase wear and cause the prosthesis to fail prematurely.

Joint Replacement Surgery: Complications

The major risk of joint replacement surgery in people with inhibitors is bleeding. But another complication is infection of the joint. People with high-titer inhibitors have a higher risk of bleeding during and after the procedure, and also an increased risk of prosthesis infection. Because of this, they are considered poor candidates for joint replacement surgery. Some HTCs refuse to perform joint replacements on patients with high-titer inhibitors because of the lower long-term prognosis.

Deep prosthesis infections can cause pain, loosening of the prosthesis, bone destruction, and systemic infection. Early infections, within weeks of surgery, can be successfully cured with a surgical "washout" of the joint together with IV antibiotics.

Late infections, developing months to years after surgery, are another matter. As with any artificial material inside the body, artificial joints are subject to biofilm infections (see chapter 7), which are resistant to antibiotic treatment. To cure these infections, the joint usually must be removed and an antibiotic spacer must be inserted.[14] Then, at least six weeks of IV antibiotics are prescribed before a new replacement joint can be implanted. If bone destruction from the infection is extensive, a new prosthesis may not be an option. In this case, it may be necessary to fuse the bones (see "Ankle Fusion" section that follows), eliminating movement of the joint. In rare cases, the limb may have to be amputated.

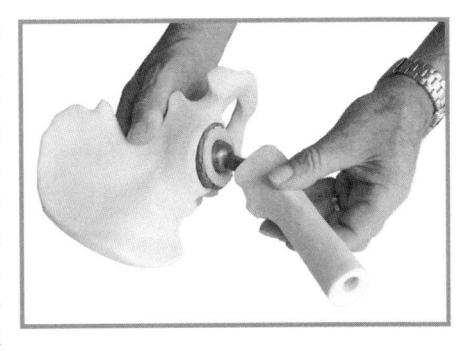

Over the life of the replacement joint, the risk of deep prosthesis infections in people with hemophilia may be as high as 9%, significantly higher than the 1% to 4% infection rate in people without hemophilia. Why? It's thought that factor infusions and dental procedures may introduce bacteria into the bloodstream and eventually into the joint. To reduce the risk of infection, patients receive antibiotics before, and for days to weeks after, surgery. After a joint replacement, your physician probably will want to give prophylactic doses of antibiotics before any invasive procedures, such as dental work or colonoscopy, that may introduce bacteria into the bloodstream. Other factors during surgery may help reduce infection rates: strict sterile technique; shorter operating time; less tourniquet time; reduced foot traffic in the operating room; and specialized operating theaters with ultra-clean air flow.[15]

The most common complications after knee replacement are blood clots in the leg or pelvis, or deep vein thrombosis (see chapter 7 for more on DVT). To minimize the risk of DVT, a hematologist may prescribe blood-thinning medication, such as heparin, for several weeks postsurgery.[16] And patients may need to wear compression stockings or an intermittent compression device (ICD; similar to a blood-pressure cuff that alternately inflates and deflates) to keep the blood circulating in the legs. Moving around after surgery also helps prevent blood clot formation. The day after surgery, most patients are moving their legs in PT.

Radial Head Excision

Although joint replacement is often performed with good results on knees and hips, other joints are replaced less often because replacements don't fare as well. For example, about 50% of elbow replacements fail because of infection, and they also have a high rate of mechanical failures, such as the prosthesis pulling loose from the bone.[17] But there are other options: the preferred surgery to treat hemophilic arthropathy of an elbow involves removing the end of one of the bones in the forearm. This is called a *radial head excision*.

The elbow is created by the meeting of three different bones:

> ***humerus:*** large upper-arm bone
>
> ***ulna:*** larger bone of the forearm, on opposite side of thumb
>
> ***radius:*** smaller bone of the forearm, on same side as thumb

Overall, the elbow acts like a hinge joint, but it really contains three different types of joints within a single joint capsule. These three joints allow the arm to pivot and twist. The disk-shaped end of the radius at the elbow is called the radial head. It allows the forearm to rotate, so you can turn your palms up and down. The radial head slides against the end of the humerus when the elbow bends and straightens, and it rotates against the ulna when the forearm twists.

Your child may be a candidate for radial head excision if . . .

- he bleeds repeatedly into his elbow despite prophylaxis,
- his elbow causes constant pain, or
- his radial head is enlarged and eroded, preventing his forearm from rotating.

Radial head excision involves cutting off the end of the radius. Sounds gruesome, but surprisingly, when done properly this procedure doesn't cause joint instability. An open synovectomy is usually performed at the same time as a radial head excision. This surgery very successfully restores forearm rotation and reduces pain and bleeding. But take note: radial head excision is less successful at restoring ROM and reducing pain if the joint damage has progressed so that the joint between the humerus and ulna is damaged; this joint controls flexion (bending the arm) and extension (extending the arm). Radial head excision is not usually performed on children. If performed before children have achieved most of their growth, this surgery can cause uneven bone growth.

Ankle Fusion

Because of high failure rates, the ankle is rarely replaced. So to reduce the number of bleeding episodes and lessen or eliminate pain, your physician may recommend a joint fusion, or *arthrodesis*. Unlike radial head excision, this surgery does not restore function. Instead, the ankle loses some function and is made less bendable. Yet people with ankle fusions can easily walk, with a near-normal gait.

The ankle joint is another place where three bones meet:

tibia: large bone of the lower leg (shin bone)

fibula: small bone of the lower leg

talus: between the heel bone and lower leg bones

The ankle joint is a gliding joint, part of which acts like a hinge joint that allows motion in only two directions: toward and away from the body.

In a typical ankle fusion, called a *tibiotalar fusion*, the talus is fused to the tibia and the fibula. If the arthropathy is severe, the talus may also be fused to the heel bone below it; this is called a *subtalar fusion*. A tibiotalar fusion may be done arthroscopically or open. The surgeon removes all cartilage from the ends of the bones, and then uses screws to join the bones. At the point of contact between the raw bone ends, the body starts the healing process by growing new bone, "fusing" the bones together. After surgery, the ankle is in a cast for about six weeks, with no weight bearing allowed. After the cast is removed, the patient usually wears a weight-bearing ankle brace or boot for another six weeks. Ankle fusions often take at least twelve weeks to heal, and may take as long as nine months for full recovery and return to normal activities.

To avoid uneven growth in both legs, ankle fusion is usually performed after age twenty, when the skeleton has matured and stops growing. As with other orthopedic surgeries, blood clots and infections are potential complications. About 20% of ankle fusions are *nonunions*, meaning they don't result in a complete fusion. In these cases, surgery must be repeated to achieve total fusion. After an ankle fusion, most people with hemophilic arthropathy of the ankle report no pain and a greatly improved quality of life.

Good Advice for Any Surgery

If your child suffers from a target joint or synovitis, it's best to consult with your HTC team: the physical therapist, hematologist, and nurse; and an orthopedic surgeon, experienced with hemophilia, who works closely with your HTC. Your team will monitor your child's joints and identify potential problems to help prevent, stop, or slow the progression toward hemophilic arthropathy. If your child develops arthropathy, consult with your team to determine the best surgical option. For better results, most surgeons choose to perform surgery as early as possible. For example, once *contractures* have developed (see page 187), surgery may reduce pain but not restore ROM.

Every day I deal with joint pain and stiffness, even in the joints that were replaced. I thought it meant replacing like for like. No one ever said, "This will hurt like Hades, and at best this new joint will be 85% effective. And it could get infected." No one said, "This is not a panacea. This is not a total solution. You won't get 100% flexion." No one set my expectations too high, but no one presented the full picture either. —Anonymous

If surgery is recommended for your child with an inhibitor, learn as much as possible about it: what's required before, and what to expect during and after. Get clear instructions about eating and drinking before and after surgery, what medicines to take, how much exercise or activity to do, and where to go on the day of surgery. Know the plan for managing bleeding during surgery, and understand the risk of infection afterward. Know your options for controlling pain (see chapter 6). Arrange to have help from a family member or a caregiver. See page 133 for a list of questions to ask the hematologist, surgeon, anesthesiologist, nurse, and entire HTC team.

And don't forget to look into the insurance side of surgeries. Which surgeries are covered? Which procedures are covered? What kind of out-of-pocket costs will you face? How will this surgery impact your lifetime cap?

Before any surgery, have your child's inhibitor level tested again. If he is factor IX deficient, be sure to ask about the probability of an anamnestic response: will the inhibitor titer rise when factor IX is infused?

All joint surgeries require a tremendous commitment to proper follow-up and rehabilitation. Don't schedule your child's surgery at a time when you can't fully commit to the work needed for the best outcome. Have a clear understanding of what's involved, and make your decision with that commitment in mind.

With any surgery, there are risks. And some risks are higher for people with inhibitors. You can help reduce risks by asking lots of questions before you agree to surgery, and by working closely with your team afterward to ensure compliance and recovery. ■

Questions to Ask Your HTC Team and Surgeon

- What surgical procedures are you recommending, and why?
- What is the goal of the surgery?
- How common is this procedure?
- Are there other ways to treat this condition without having this procedure?
- What are the risks of having this procedure?
- Are the potential benefits of surgery worth the potential risks?
- What is the success rate of this procedure for people with hemophilia and inhibitors?
- Where will the procedure be done?
- Is the surgeon experienced in operating on people with hemophilia and inhibitors?
- How will bleeding be controlled?
- What is the plan if bleeding is not easily controlled during surgery?
- How long will my child be in the hospital?
- Can I stay overnight with my child?
- Can I use my child's own factor for the surgery? If not, how much will it cost (per IU, per mg) if my child uses factor from the hospital?
- Does my insurance cover the procedure? The PT?
- How long will it take to recover from the anesthesia?
- Will my child have side effects from the anesthesia?
- How will postoperative pain be controlled?
- How long will it take to rehabilitate and return to normal activities?
- How often will my child need PT?
- What outcome can I expect for my child?
- What will my child's quality of life be like if he doesn't have surgery? If he does have surgery?
- Could my child lose any present ROM as a result of the surgery?
- Can the surgery help my child regain any lost ROM?

NOTES

1. Duthie R, Dodd C, Giangrande P. The management of musculoskeletal problems in the haemophilias. New York: Oxford University Press; 1994. p. 193.
2. Ligaments are bands of connective tissue that hold bones together.
3. Immune cells called phagocytes engulf and break down red blood cells.
4. Overgrowth of the synovial membrane is called *synovial hyperplasia*.
5. According the Centers for Disease Control and Prevention Universal Data Collection System, a target joint is defined as a joint in which recurrent bleeding has occurred on four or more occasions during the previous six months or one in which twenty lifetime bleeding episodes have occurred. U.S. Department of Health and Human Services, Public Health Service. Report on the Universal Data Collection System (UDC) [Internet]. Atlanta: Centers for Disease Control and Prevention, National Center for Infectious Diseases; 1999 Mar;1(1):16 [cited 2010 Feb 16]. Available from:
http://www.cdc.gov/ncbddd/hbd/documents/UDCReport3-99.pdf
6. Some reports in medical literature suggest that prophylaxis, combined with PT or home exercises designed to gain motion and strength in the affected area, may help reduce the frequency of bleeds, which may help decrease joint inflammation. Talk to your HTC physician about this possibility if your child is having frequent joint bleeds. Stephensen D. Rehabilitation of patients with haemophilia after orthopaedic surgery: a case study. *Haemophilia*. 2005 Oct 7;11(Sup 1):26–29.
7. Siegel H, Luck J, Siegel M, Quines C, Anderson E. Hemarthrosis and synovitis associated with hemophilia: clinical use of P 32 chromic phosphate synoviorthesis for treatment. *Therapeutic Radiology*. 1994 Jan;190:257–61.
8. Adhesions start forming two to three days after surgery and, if not broken up or prevented by PT, may significantly reduce ROM after a synovectomy.
9. Radiation usually kills the most superficial layers of the synovium, depending on the depth of penetration of the radiation.
10. At NHF's 61st Annual Meeting, October 29–31, 2009, Dr. James Luck, an orthopedic surgeon who had been performing radioactive synovectomies at Orthopaedic Hospital of Los Angeles for ten years, reported that only two cases of tumor formation had been observed in over 8,000 procedures done worldwide.
11. The growth plate is an area of active cell division near the ends of bones in young children.
12. Rapidly dividing cells, such as those in young, growing children, are more susceptible to radiation damage than are cells of adults and thus have a higher risk of cancer due to radiation. In August 2008, NHF reported that two children with hemophilia, ages nine and fourteen, developed acute lymphocytic leukemia about ten months after receiving Phosphocol® P 32 injections used for radioactive synovectomy. Dunn A, Manco-Johnson M, Busch M, Balark K, Abshire T. Leukemia and P32 radionuclide synovectomy for hemophilic arthropathy. *J Thromb Haemost*. 2005;3(7):1541–42.

13. Rivard G, Acute I. Chemical synovectomy in haemophilia: status and challenges. *Haemophilia*. July 2001;7(Sup 2):16–19(4).
14. An antibiotic spacer is typically made of antibiotic-impregnated bone cement and may be articulated or non-articulated. It is designed to span the gap between the two bones until the infection is cleared and a new prosthesis can be inserted.
15. To reduce blood loss, all or part of a total knee replacement may be done with a tourniquet on the thigh. Tourniquet times of longer than 120 minutes have been associated with higher infection rates. Horlocker T, Hebl J, Gali B, Jankowski C, Burkle C, Berry D, Zepeda F, Stevens S, Schroeder D. Anesthetic, patient, and surgical risk factors for neurologic complications after prolonged total tourniquet time during total knee arthroplasty. *Anesth Analg*. 2006 Mar;102(3):950–55.
16. The major concern with DVT is the potentially fatal possibility that the clot will travel to the lungs (called a pulmonary embolism). If your doctor finds evidence of blood clot formation, your child will probably get a higher dose of blood-thinning medication for a longer time.
17. Kasper C. Hemophilia Bulletin [Internet]. Los Angeles: Orthopaedic Hospital; 2006 Jul 2 [cited 2010 Feb 16]. Available from: http://www.carolkasper.com/Hemophilia/Bull%20July%202006.pdf

SUMMARY 8
Surgery and Inhibitors

- Patients with inhibitors can successfully be treated for a variety of conditions with surgeries that include dental procedures, joint replacements, and even heart surgery.

- In surgery, the primary concern is controlling bleeding during and after the procedure.

- Joint disease (arthropathy) is the most common complication in severe hemophilia, and is more common and severe in people with inhibitors.

- There are several types of joints in the body. Most bleeds occur in synovial joints. Synovial joints are movable, and include the knee, ankle, and elbow.

- The synovium is the innermost lining of the joint capsule. It secretes synovial fluid, which prevents friction between the bones.

- Joint bleeds, or acute hemarthrosis, occur when one of the many blood vessels of the synovium is ruptured, leaking blood into the joint cavity. Chronic inflammation of the synovium is called synovitis. If left untreated, chronic synovitis eventually leads to destruction of the cartilage in the joint, and to arthropathy.

- A synovectomy is the surgical removal of the overgrown synovium. It will reduce the frequency of bleeds, but it may or may not stop the progression of joint disease.

- Synovectomies can be surgical, radioactive, or chemical.

- When joint disease is advanced and pain is chronic, many hemophilia patients opt for surgical total joint replacement.

- To treat arthropathy of an elbow, the preferred surgery is radial head excision, which involves removing the end of one of the bones in the forearm.

- The ankle is rarely replaced, and instead may be surgically fused (arthrodesis). People with ankle fusions can easily walk, with a near-normal gait.

- Before surgery, have your child's inhibitor level tested again. If he is factor IX deficient, be sure to ask about the probability of an anamnestic response.

Part 2

■■■

Daily Life with Inhibitors

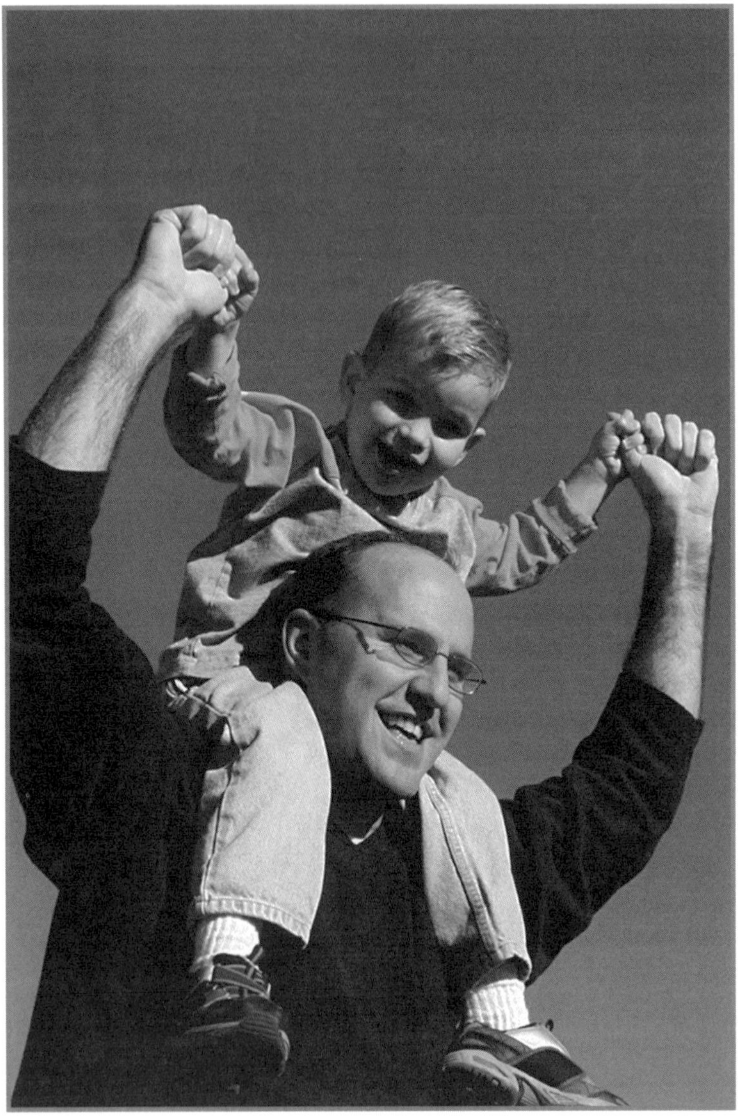

9 Caring for Your Child Emotionally and Physically

Raising a kid with an inhibitor—it's a lot about preplanning. —Sonji Wilkes, Colorado

When your child is diagnosed with an inhibitor, you must focus immediately on learning new medical terms, managing a new dosing regimen, and making critical treatment decisions. Basically, you'll need to address all of the subjects covered in the first half of this book.

After the initial feelings you experience when you first learn of the inhibitor diagnosis, you may be apprehensive about coping at home. At the hospital or clinic, you may feel secure and supported. But once you get home on your own, you may feel vulnerable, and frightened of the immense responsibilities you now face. The number one fear is bleeding: What will happen when he bleeds? How will it differ from bleeding before the inhibitor diagnosis? How will you respond? Despite being instructed in handling bleeds with an inhibitor, most parents don't fear a bleed as much as they fear failing or falling apart.

Coming home from the hospital, my biggest fear was, am I emotionally going to be able to cope with this? I work, and my son needs factor twice daily. —Eleth Ridenhour, Kansas

I was afraid that Jonathan would have a lot of bleeding episodes, and I drove myself crazy trying to make sure he didn't fall and get hurt—impossible to do with a baby learning to walk. I realized that he would fall and that I needed to deal with it. —Jackie, Massachusetts

My fear was that my son would have uncontrolled bleeding and could die. People always ask me, "How do you do it?" Well, how do you not do it? I have no choice. I spent a lot of time crying in my bedroom at night. But I was raised to do what you must do. —Debbie Porter, California

Eventually, you'll turn your attention to the impact inhibitors will have on your daily life as a parent, employee, and family member. For some families, inhibitors change everything. For others, inhibitors change very little. Much depends on matters within your control: your own perception of what might happen, your confidence level about handling it, and your preparation. And much depends on matters outside your control: how your child bleeds, and how he responds to treatment.

> *Looking back, we can see how much more complicated the inhibitor made our lives: increased hospital stays, infections, increased recovery times from bleeds, increased rebleeds, and stress on family life. As we focused on Andrew's needs, this left less time for us as a family and a couple, and less time with family and friends. —Richard and Lynley Scott, New Zealand*

Common Feelings at Home

The inhibitor diagnosis brings many practical and emotional challenges into your home. Every child with an inhibitor experiences hemophilia differently, in its effect on everything from lifestyle to pain level to treatment response. It's understandable, then, that every family also experiences the impact on home life differently. What is a frustrating experience for one family may be simply a nuisance for another.

Every family must ultimately develop its own method of dealing with these challenges. Yet sometimes, the intensity of our emotions can hamper our ability to deal effectively with practical issues. So you may need to take care of the emotional side first, before you feel you can manage the practical side.

> *The first ten years were hell. We had many visits to the HTC. We were worried, angry, and frustrated; that affected my ability to relate to my husband and my other child. I was nervous all the time, couldn't sleep at night, and felt that life was going to be awful. It's better now. —Debbie Porter, California*

> *Nothing was different as a result of inhibitors. We knew our son couldn't play baseball or tee-ball, so instead we use a tee-ball stand with tennis balls, which don't hurt him. He cuts grass, goes hunting with his daddy. Nothing stops him. We've known people who have kept their kids from living, but Ethan is not going to grow up like that. —Kim Stubbs, Mississippi*

For children who develop an inhibitor a few years after the hemophilia diagnosis, home life changes can seem radical and worrisome. The family has gotten used to a certain way of living, and has "conquered" hemophilia, only to be hit by a curve ball: inhibitors. The result can be an increase in the emotions and concerns that you've already experienced while processing the hemophilia diagnosis.

> *Inhibitors changed our life. We had lived with just hemophilia: our kids rollerbladed, rode bikes, played baseball, fencing, archery. We infused first, and then life was normal. Once our son had an inhibitor, everything changed.*

It was terrifying. We had no safety net. Factor had been our safety net, and now there were no assurances. —Janet Brewer, Massachusetts

Having a child with hemophilia is hard; having one with an inhibitor is even harder. For the first few years, I had no choice but to deal with it. I couldn't be depressed or cry all the time—I had to take care of my son. When he was about four, I completely broke down because I didn't have any type of release. —Julie Baker, Nevada

Though hemophilia is rare, inhibitors are even more so. Families who once found comfort and support in the hemophilia community may now feel completely alone, and may risk becoming isolated.

As parents, we became even more protective and reclusive, due to shiners and goose eggs while living in a very small town. —Chasity, Mississippi

Being "on your own" can be challenging, even overwhelming. And though many of these worries are understandable, many parents focus on worst-case scenarios because they fear the unexpected. But little by little, you will find solutions. You'll begin to understand inhibitors in a practical way, in your home with your child. And just as you'll find solutions to the many challenges you now face, you'll find new ways of thinking that can empower you. Begin right now, with a change in attitude.

I reminded myself that "what if" doesn't rule the world. What if a meteor fell from the sky? What if the train derailed? Logan didn't care about "what if," so why should I? So I always try to prepare for an unexpected bleed. I always take at least one dose of factor and supplies with me. It's just being responsible for your child, regardless of any medical condition. A life of "what if" is no life at all. —Anonymous

Although you may feel alone at first, remember that help and support do exist. Find a good outside source of support: your HTC, a parents' group of people with inhibitors, or good literature about inhibitors.

We feared that the inhibitor wouldn't go; that Andrew wouldn't be able to be on prophylaxis; that we'd be unable to control a bleed. We spent time talking with our hematologist and nurse, and reading information on inhibitors. This helped us to get on with living. —Richard and Lynley Scott, New Zealand

One of your goals as a parent is to try to make life as normal as possible for your child, even when he has a medical complication like inhibitors. How to do that? First, take steps to alleviate your fears by making small environmental changes, such as removing sharp-edged furniture and deciding whether to use protective gear. Next, you'll need to weave higher frequency of infusions into your daily routine. Finally, observe and note your child's specific bleeding issues. With these actions, you can smooth the bumps in your daily agenda and ease your harried mind to better enjoy your child and family, despite the diagnosis.

Common Bleeds and Milestones

A child with hemophilia, regardless of inhibitors, is going to bleed. A child with an inhibitor is not prone to bleed more often than a child without an inhibitor, but how he responds to treatment will determine how hard it is to resolve his bleeds. So although it may seem that your child bleeds more often, he may just be bleeding longer as you try to resolve *each* bleed.

> *Austin bled more as he became more active. The bottoms of his feet bled from walking. If he bit his tongue or a tooth came in, he would drool blood for three weeks.* —Julie Baker, Nevada

As an infant, a child with hemophilia may have bleeds when he learns to walk: his ankles, knees, and even buttocks may bleed when he falls.

> *There were a lot of bottom bleeds. We encouraged our daughter Nora to walk, but with Thomas not so much. We double diapered him—it's the best trick! He'd still get bleeds where the diaper didn't cover him. Sometimes I put the diapers on too tight and gave him a bleed.* —Sonji Wilkes, Colorado

Every child with hemophilia—with or without inhibitors—has his own bleeding pattern. You'll need to learn your child's pattern: for example, does he tend to bleed more often from one part of his body? Before your child becomes verbal, you'll have to figure out where he's bleeding. As he learns to speak, encourage him to recognize his own bleeds. Eventually, he'll be able to report to you where he is bleeding.

> *He gets soft tissue bleeds, mostly on his arm above his elbow—from the high chair, his playpen, and his walker—but he doesn't bleed much in his legs.* —Chasity, Mississippi

> *Soft tissue and muscle bleeds in the knees, legs, and buttocks occurred most of the time when Tristan started to crawl and walk. We also had a lot of head injuries requiring CT scans because he tended to bang his head on the floor whenever he got frustrated or mad.* —Jessica Herren, Pennsylvania

He tends to bleed into his big toes in both feet. We're not sure what's causing the bleeds, so we're experimenting with different shoe and slipper styles.
—*Derek Nelson, Utah*

While you try to determine your child's individual bleeding pattern and tendency to bleed, you can expect some common hemophilia bleeds as he matures. Joint bleeds, nose bleeds, gum bleeds, urinary tract (UT) bleeds, and gastrointestinal (GI) bleeds are all possible. Your child may never get these bleeds, but it helps to be prepared, just in case. If he is on prophylaxis following ITI, these common bleeds may rarely or never happen.

Head trauma is a constant concern for toddlers, who are naturally inclined to climb and run around—and often fall. Head bumps are always an urgent situation. Call your HTC at *every* instance of head trauma, even if you can't see a bump or bruise. Remember that even when you can't see evidence of a bleed, an internal bleed could be occurring. When in doubt, infuse.

Expect certain bleeds at specific developmental stages. For example, it's common for preschoolers to pick their noses, causing nose bleeds. These are usually harmless, but messy. An infusion might be needed, followed by doses of Amicar or Lysteda, to stabilize a clot. Mouth bleeds are among the most frequent bleeding episodes in toddlers.

As a young child, my son had many mouth bleeds. They were hard to treat and often resulted in hospitalizations of several weeks. We were able to partially manage them with Amicar. As he grew older, he had more frequent joint and muscle bleeds. —*Wendy Sass, New York*

Just growing presents challenges! Some parents believe that growth spurts trigger bleeds: uncoordinated muscles may cause a child to fall, muscles may tear, and stress may affect joints.

As he grew, every time he got a new pair of shoes it was always accompanied by an ankle bleed. —*Joyce Hewitt, Michigan*

To track your child's bleeds, keep a log. This can help you uncover tendencies and patterns in his bleeding. It also helps your HTC to individualize your treatment plan. Whether your log is a spreadsheet file on your computer or handwritten pages in a notebook, be sure to record these details for each bleed or infusion:

- Date
- Cause of bleed (if known or suspected)
- Location of bleed

- Brand name of factor infused
- Lot number
- Assay size

Handling Frequent Dosing

Your child with hemophilia and an inhibitor may need frequent infusions, depending on your treatment plan. If you use FEIBA, treatment could be every eight to twelve hours. NovoSeven RT treatment may be as often as every two hours. If your child is undergoing ITI (see chapter 4), treatment could be daily, with regular hospital visits. All of this takes coordination and juggling, and when treatment changes, your entire infusion strategy may change. Families need to plan how and when to infuse, so that home life isn't too disrupted.

> *Our daily routine didn't change much except that once ITI began, Coty started receiving factor daily via CVAD. Hard? Not really. We found nightly infusions worked best.* — Chasity, Mississippi

> *Finding time for the daily infusions wasn't so bad. I tried to think of it as a few more minutes of "quality time" with Logan, though I don't think he would agree!* — Anonymous

Although some parents find it easiest to infuse at night when their child is calm and tired, the ideal time medically to infuse is early in the morning, before your child starts his routine activities. Factor breaks down in the blood over time, and an infusion first thing in the morning will give him the factor he needs when he is most active.

ITI disrupts home life the most, because you need to visit the hospital repeatedly for infusions and blood tests. You must adjust your schedule to accommodate treatment, but you can prevent ITI from running your life. How? With careful planning and family or community support. Some HTCs seek the support of home care nurses to minimize family disruption. As the treatment plan evolves, your HTC eventually will allow you to administer factor for ITI at home. Find out if your insurance plan covers home nursing services to provide extra help.

> *Our home routines changed entirely. After our son was diagnosed with an inhibitor, I took a leave from my job to care for him. We were driving to the hospital three times a week for ITI, not to mention treatment for his other bleeds.* — Wendy Sass, New York

Be sure to plan for support. One single mother, whose child needed dosing every two hours for three days, was completely exhausted. As a single parent, all responsibilities fell on her. Her hematologist wisely hospitalized this child until the treatment was finished, so the mother could care for herself!

> Andrew would need NovoSeven every two hours for a number of doses, and then we would slowly increase the time between doses. Often he needed it for up to two weeks following a bleed to reduce the risk of rebleeds. The rebleeds (not the bleeds) were hardest to control. —Richard and Lynley Scott, New Zealand

> Bleeds took anywhere from one to three days of treatment with NovoSeven every three hours, three or four times a day—instead of once, as you do with just hemophilia. But our son hasn't had a significant bleed. —Jackie, Massachusetts

Environmental Changes at Home

To help alleviate anxiety about being home with a child with an inhibitor, many parents decide to alter their home environment to provide extra safety, reduce injuries, and promote peace of mind. Environmental changes range from adding pillows around the fireplace to carpeting floors to lowering crib heights. A "safer" environment, even if it adds little to his real safety, sometimes provides just the right amount of psychological support for parents, encouraging them to relax with their child.

> I went bubble-paper crazy! The house looked ridiculous! In retrospect, the bubble paper was a comfort to me. It made me feel I could sit and relax, and let him relax and explore. —Kari Atkinson, Iowa

Many parents suggest these environmental changes:

- Remove coffee tables.
- Replace any tables that have sharp corners or edges, or pad the corners.
- Invest in childproof gates.
- Increase household cleanliness if your child has a CVAD (see chapter 7).
- Pad the crib and fireplace hearth.
- Install baby gates to block stairs.
- Carpet hardwood floors.
- Remove throw rugs.

Managing Your Child's Inhibitor

> *Most furniture came out of our son's room. His mattress went straight to the floor for a while, so he wouldn't fall far if he fell off the bed. —Chasity, Mississippi*

> *We totally changed our environment. We were living in an older home with hardwood floors and decided to carpet our entire house—at no small expense! We removed hard furniture, including the coffee table, and used foam pullout chairs in our living room; our son used them for climbing. —Wendy Sass, New York*

But many parents change nothing at home!

> *We wanted him to learn how to live in a typical environment, so we changed nothing. He had lots of supervision to keep him out of trouble. —Shari Luckey, Michigan*

As you can see, there are no right or wrong answers. You'll need to find your own comfort level within your own home environment. Remember the key: don't overprotect your child or restrict him from playing and exploring, which is so vital for his normal development.

Helmets and Knee Pads, or Nothing?

Using protective gear on your child is controversial among parents and HTC staff. As with environmental changes, this is a personal decision, based on how comfortable you feel allowing your child to play and explore. Most parents recognize that hovering over their child is not ideal and can make him anxious and insecure. A helmet and knee or elbow pads can give reassurance and extra protection, especially during the toddler years. Usually helmets are recommended only for a short time while the child is learning to walk or is very active. Most children won't be wearing helmets to kindergarten.

> *We required Tristan to wear a helmet at all times, along with knee and elbow pads. It was difficult for us because he didn't like to wear anything on his head, knees, or elbows. I think we were rather paranoid at the time! —Jessica Herren, Pennsylvania*

> *Reuben's early years were fraught with anxiety, but he was a very active toddler. Our primary fear was head bleeds, but his helmet seemed to provide a lot of protection. —Wendy Sass, New York*

Austin always had a helmet on when learning to walk and when playing. I also had him wear knee and elbow pads. The best ones were for adults with wrist injuries—they worked great on his knees. —Julie Baker, Nevada

In rare cases, your HTC may strongly recommend a helmet: for example, if a child has suffered a brain bleed. And of course, your child must wear protective gear when he is old enough to bike, play ball, and rollerskate. But lots of families don't use helmets regularly, at home or at school. Some believe a helmet draws negative attention or makes their child look different. And some children simply may not need a helmet, perhaps if they have never had a head bleed and aren't prone to falling. Or their treatment may not be too complicated; they may respond well to infusions and have few if any rebleeds. There's nothing wrong or right about using protective gear daily. It's a matter of what's best for your child and for you.

We've never used a helmet, though for some HTCs and parents, it's an automatic decision. —Sonji Wilkes, Colorado

Finding Daycare and Sitters

One of your first practical concerns at home might be to find a trusted person to care for your child, especially if you work outside the home, but also just to give you a break. Dealing with inhibitors can be intense, and using your spouse or partner as a constant sitter isn't always a good alternative, as you both are emotionally connected to each other and to your child. You might want to spend some time together with your partner, or even alone, without partner or children. Try to find a good third party you know and trust to care for your child even for a short time: your parents, in-laws, other relatives, neighbors, or a professional daycare center. It's not easy, even with a trusted sitter: the best plans can go awry when you must be with your child for medical reasons.

After the diagnosis, we didn't feel comfortable leaving our son with anyone but family. It took a long time before we felt comfortable taking him to a drop-in daycare periodically. Once we enrolled him, we had to deal with his getting sick often; so we wouldn't take him when he had certain tests or surgeries scheduled, because we didn't want him catching something. —Sasha Cheatham, Oklahoma

I've never been able to put Matthew in daycare or have any babysitters who weren't registered nurses. I put Matthew in a daycare once when he was three years old and I was attending nursing school. He had constant bleeds and got hurt almost every day. —Debbie Porter, California

Some families decide to have one parent stay home with the child all the time. This might mean that one parent has to put a career on hold, or that one income will be lost. But for many parents, it's worth the peace of mind.

> *Tristan used to go to a daycare center, but we took him out—he was left in a crib with his leg caught between the slats and crying for forty-five minutes. My husband decided to stay home with him at that point. It gave us some peace of mind. —Jessica Herren, Pennsylvania*

> *I decided it would be difficult to put our son in daycare. It was hard to know when he had a bleed. I decided to stay home with him. That was comforting. —Anonymous*

But many parents work outside the home and successfully place their child in daycare or with a sitter. Some parents simply must work outside the home (especially to maintain insurance coverage), and others feel it's the best decision for their family's emotional health. Even a "bad" experience in one daycare, or with one sitter, doesn't deter many parents from searching for the right environment and staff for their child. Of course, when your child has a complication like an inhibitor, it might be challenging to find the right place or caregiver. Refer to chapter 14 on school issues to learn ways to approach staff, to model a positive, confident attitude, and to explain how inhibitors are handled.

> *When dealing with daycare or babysitting issues, much depends on how you, as a parent, introduce and explain a bleeding disorder. How you handle it can help the caregiver feel more at ease with your child and offer a huge sense of security. —Cazandra Campos-MacDonald, New Mexico*

> *We couldn't find a sitter and had to phone around for weeks to discover a place that would be willing to talk to us about having Esh attend preschool. —Joyce Hewitt, Michigan*

If you find a good daycare or preschool that will enroll your child, consider yourself lucky and blessed!

> *Our babysitter Shelley was calm with everything, and she was there for us, wanting to learn everything about inhibitors. It helped me to stay calm. She was our son's primary caregiver each day. —Ashley Druckenmiller, Iowa*

Safety Away from Home

One of the best things you can do for your child, and for your own peace of mind, is to get out sometimes. Visit a museum, zoo, or park, or go for a stroll with the carriage. But be smart! Above all, bring your factor and supplies with you, whether you are going out for a quick errand, like shopping, or having an all-day trip. You can even order handy travel packs from the manufacturer especially made for your brand of factor.

Always follow basic child safety rules.

When riding in a car, strap your child safely in an approved child car seat or booster seat—always in the back seat, away from airbags. Be sure the car seat is properly installed: highway statistics show that eight out of ten are improperly installed. Your local firefighters or police can professionally install child safety seats for free. *No child should ever be allowed to ride unrestrained in a moving car*, even if you're just going around the block. Most accidents occur within a few miles of home, and even a "small" accident can have dire consequences. Car accidents are the leading cause of death in children under age five. All fifty states have laws about using seatbelts, but state laws concerning car seats vary state to state. Regardless of what your state mandates, always use a car seat or booster seat, and always restrain your child inside the car.[1]

If your child goes on an outing with you, another family member, or a sitter, make sure he has medical identification tags. This is especially important if you are in an accident and unable to communicate with others, or when your child is in daycare or away from home without you. MedicAlert®[2] is one of the most popular brands of medical identification: your child's medical condition is inscribed on a bracelet, anklet, or necklace, with the phone number of MedicAlert Foundation. Any physician or ER staff member can call this 24-hour number to get your child's specific medical information. While your child is an infant, don't use a necklace. Instead, attach the medical identification bracelet to his ankle, or clip it to his jacket. Place a medical identification sticker on your car window. Consider marking your stroller and child safety seats with tags providing medical information.

Dental Care: Vital to Health

It's critically important to track your child's dental development, not just for inhibitor treatment, but for overall health. Never neglect your child's dental care. We tend to seriously underestimate the importance of proper gum and tooth care. Good dental care is more than just having a good smile. It ensures that

- your child's bite is even, decreasing chewing pain and promoting good speech;
- cavities are reduced, resulting in fewer invasive procedures; and
- the gums are pink and resilient.

Healthy gums bleed less and—*please read this carefully if your child has a CVAD*—help keep germs from entering the blood during dental procedures and causing a CVAD infection (see chapter 7).

Your introduction to dental care begins when your infant starts teething, at age three to seven months. Babies sometimes teethe on sharp or hard items that can cause small cuts on the gums, a nip on the tongue, or a tear in the frenulum (the skin that attaches the upper lip to the gums). Mouth bleeds are fairly messy and take a long time to heal. You'll want to use bibs, and you'll be washing sheets and shirts more often. Consult your hematologist: cold ice pops, cold drinks, frozen teething toys, and Amicar or Lysteda can usually help.

> *Teething was never a problem. We started Amicar immediately and used pressure—we had our son bite on a cold, wet washcloth.* —Shari Luckey, Michigan

Amicar should be your first line of defense against mouth bleeds. Amicar *does not clot blood*. It neutralizes enzymes in the blood and saliva that help break down food and blood clots, allowing a clot to stay in place longer to control bleeding. Amicar is typically used following an infusion of factor, and once a clot is in place, it may be used alone for a mouth or nose bleed.

Begin brushing your child's teeth as soon as they erupt, and help him learn to brush his own teeth by about age two. By age three, he should be brushing his teeth regularly with your supervision and seeing the dentist every six months. Start flossing too, because this is just as important as brushing—maybe more. Flossing removes bacteria and debris, buried in the gums next to the teeth, that regular brushing can't reach.

Tooth brushing occasionally causes some gum bleeding. This usually isn't serious. If gum tissue oozes blood for a while, you may give Amicar after an infusion of factor. Following any mouth or tongue bleed, and with the advice of your doctor, reintroduce tooth brushing carefully, using ultra-gentle toothbrushes. Your HTC may recommend giving Amicar for five days or more.

At around age six, your child will start to lose his baby teeth. Tooth loss may be uneventful, with no bleeding, or it may produce mild to excessive bleeding, requiring an infusion and Amicar. Mouth bleeds often look more serious than they are because the blood mixes with saliva, giving the appearance of a lot of blood. Your child may be anxious when he sees blood oozing from his mouth; even if he bleeds often, he usually doesn't see his own blood. Be sensitive to his fears about external bleeding from his nose or gums. Reassure him that it's okay, and that you have treatment to care for him.

Our son had a lot of bleeding when he lost teeth, especially on upper gums. He had to be hospitalized when he lost his two front teeth. One wouldn't stop bleeding, so they sent us to dental surgeons, who put fibrin glue on his gums.
—*Molly A. Eppenbach, Nebraska*

Home is where the heart is—and also where the action is. Parenting a child with an inhibitor means developing a plan for childcare, work, frequent infusions, and the occasional upset. Every child with an inhibitor is different, and every household is different. Figure out what works best for your situation, knowing that it's all trial and error. A good strategy is to make sure that everyone is informed, on board, and flexible. Things will change, your strategy will need adjusting, but eventually you will run a tight ship again! ∎

I've faced harder emotional changes than environmental. I had to change my work hours, because we had to give our son factor early in the morning. My husband and I just dealt with it; we didn't need family help or counseling. But we only handle it day by day. Our doctor said, "We'll see how it is in six months, then maybe we'll do more adjustments." We've learned we must be flexible. —*Eleth Ridenhour, Kansas*

We don't make inhibitors a big deal. You just do your medicine, and on you go. Our son has inhibitors, but we don't focus on that. —*Joyce Hewitt, Michigan*

■NOTES

1. For more information, visit www.saferchild.org/carseat.
2. For more information, visit www.medicalert.org.

SUMMARY 9
Caring for Your Child Emotionally and Physically

- Many parents worry about coping with bleeds when they return home from the hospital following the inhibitor diagnosis.

- An important goal is to find daycare or sitters for your child. It's essential to have a support system for emergencies, work, and just relaxing.

- Some families alter the home environment to provide extra safety and peace of mind: placing pillows around the fireplace, carpeting floors, and lowering crib heights.

- Some families decide to use helmets and knee and elbow pads to help reduce injuries and possibly decrease the number of infusions.

- Always follow basic safety rules for children. Use child safety seats in the car, and attach a medical identification tag to the seat or pin it to your child's clothes when you leave home.

- Regular home routines are often interrupted by frequent dosing.

- Certain bleeds, such as nose bleeds and bleeding during tooth loss, are common at specific developmental stages. Your child will have these common bleeds, but he'll also have his own unique bleeding pattern.

- Dental care is crucial to preserving overall good health. Your child needs healthy teeth and gums, not only to help prevent tooth and gum infections, but to also reduce the risk of germs entering the blood from the gums and infecting your child's CVAD.

10 Fostering Healthy Self-Esteem

Self-esteem refers to our feelings and thoughts about our personal value and capabilities: in other words, our self-worth. Having healthy self-esteem means that we can realistically assess our abilities, strengths, failures, and limitations—and still accept ourselves as worthy. One of the chief components of healthy self-esteem is the amount of mastery we feel, both internally over our thoughts and emotions, and externally over our environment and choices. People with healthy self-esteem often feel they have the personal power to change their lives and overcome difficult challenges.

> *Our son is a happy, healthy, outgoing, energetic child with a zest for life! —Sasha Cheatham, Oklahoma*

Self-esteem forms early. Part of a parent's role is to help foster positive self-esteem through unconditional love, age-appropriate feedback and education, discipline, and nurturing guidance. Parents must also encourage their children to be independent emotionally, and eventually, physically.

Independence is often challenged or delayed for children with hemophilia and an inhibitor. Frequent infusions, pain, interruptions in family and social plans, high expenses, physical limitations . . . so many things we take for granted when we live without inhibitors deeply affect daily life and self-esteem for families with inhibitors. When inhibitors constantly disrupt life with pain, needlesticks, or failed treatment, some children have trouble learning to master their environment, and they may develop anxiety, anger, or depression.

> *Stephen lost control over his own life. The medical care invaded our lives. Has he come to grips with it? He's better now. I've seen a tremendous change now that his knee is better. —Janet Brewer, Massachusetts*

> *Due to joint problems, Esh can't tie his own shoes well or open his own doors when he's in public. He hasn't been diagnosed formally, but I know he has bouts of depression. —Joyce Hewitt, Michigan*

There are many things you can do to help your child develop healthy self-esteem, despite inhibitors or other challenges that life may have in store.

Expressing Emotions

Everyone has feelings. Like you, your child may feel overwhelmed and powerless because of hemophilia and frequent inhibitor treatments. When others listen to you, and you feel supported, then you can help your child cope, too. Encourage your child to express his feelings openly, without judgment from you. When you know what he's feeling, you can help him learn to manage his emotions.

> *If I make Austin talk about having hemophilia, asthma, and autoimmune disease, he sometimes says he's fine with it, but I see in his eyes that he is hurting inside. —Julie Baker, Nevada*

In this chapter we'll discuss some techniques you can use to help your child express and manage his emotions:

- Acknowledge your child's feelings.
- Teach appropriate ways to vent emotions.
- Model appropriate responses to feelings.
- Let your child decide how he feels before you react.

Managing emotions can mean different things in different cultures. Some cultures place a high value on stoicism, or the ability to contain emotions, particularly negative ones like fear or anger. We also call this a "stiff upper lip," a high tolerance for pain (including emotional pain), or *compartmentalizing*. The expression of feelings tends to be ignored, while detachment and not complaining are rewarded. Other cultures encourage emotional expression and interpersonal connection when someone is in pain. Whatever your beliefs or cultural traditions, it's always a good idea to at least acknowledge your child's feelings: "I know you feel a lot of pain right now." And it helps to encourage him to acknowledge for himself what he feels, too. Once feelings are acknowledged, you can each explore how to express them—or decide not to express them—and then determine how best to manage them.

Acknowledge feelings

Acknowledging feelings isn't the same as agreeing with them or approving undesirable behavior. Your child might be angry or scared about having a shot, so he may scream. Lecturing him, scolding him, diverting his attention, ignoring him, or ordering him to stop may work in the short term, but it won't teach him mastery in the long term. So along with those short-term methods, also help him to *identify* his feelings and then *accept* them.

For example, preschool children often lack the names for feelings. Give his feeling a name by describing what you see: "You look angry." "You're crying. Are you sad?" "You're holding your teddy bear tightly. Are you scared?" This technique has incredible power to diffuse tension and calm your child.

> Stephen gets so angry that he won't talk about it. His brother's inhibitor went away, and Stephen's has not. How can you not feel angry with that? —Janet Brewer, Massachusetts

Vent emotions appropriately

Toddlers rarely verbalize their feelings. Instead, they may breathe rapidly or act out physically—throwing objects, biting, spitting, kicking, or head banging.

> We've had some problems with our son acting out due to constant painful joint bleeds, being inactive for two months, and having casts on and off, along with the pain. He is three and unable to totally communicate how he feels. —Cicely Evans, Massachusetts

Try these techniques to help your child express or vent his emotions appropriately:

- Give him a choice. Say, "I know you feel angry. You can squeeze my arm tightly, or you can punch this pillow. But kicking is not allowed." With these brief words, you've acknowledged his feelings, offered him a choice, and set appropriate limits.
- Give him a physical outlet. He can punch a pillow, tear up paper, cry, or draw a picture.
- Teach him to verbalize his feelings. Offer names for his emotions: joy, fear, pride, anger, sadness, hurt, fear, shyness, happiness.

It may happen one day: your child may say, "I hate you" or "I wish you weren't my mother [or father]!" If your child expresses negative feelings toward you, try to remember that he's probably not attacking you personally. It's hard to hear outbursts, but they are normal. Try to acknowledge what he *feels*, not what he says. And acknowledge your own feelings: "I know you don't like having needles, but it hurts my feelings when you say that to me. In our family, you can say, 'I hate having needles' instead of 'I hate the person giving me the needle.'"

> The day the doctor said, "It's no longer safe for you to play baseball," was the beginning of an ugly period in our son's life. He was angry that he couldn't do

the things he loved to do. He directed his anger toward me, and toward his sister. —Janet Brewer, Massachusetts

Model appropriate responses

How do you usually respond to challenges and obstacles in your life? Do you punch walls? Do you simmer silently? Do you complain? Swear? Blame others? Look for solutions? How you respond to life's challenges will influence your child's responses and affect his self-esteem. The influential pediatrician Dr. Benjamin Spock wrote that children are natural mimics, automatically modeling their parents' behavior and values. Spock called this *identification*.[1] Model for your children the best ways to handle frustration, stress, and emotions.

Begin by giving your own emotions a name: "Boy, waiting for three hours makes me feel frustrated!" or "It makes me sad when I see you hurt." Try adding some humor: "When I miss a vein in your hand, I feel so angry at myself that steam might blow out my ears like this: *whoosh!*" Show your child how you seek solutions: "I'm going to tell this nurse how I feel so I don't keep it all inside me," or "I'm going to leave the room and get a drink of water so I can calm down."

> *When a bleed is persistent, Jay has gotten frustrated with the constant pokes and had some outbursts. He'll yell, "I hate hemophilia!" or bang his hand on the table. He asks, "Why me?" I try to listen, and I tell him that sometimes I hate hemophilia too. I also tell him that if he hadn't gone through all these things, he wouldn't be the great person he is. —Shari Luckey, Michigan*

Model happy responses too! "I am *so* proud right now. You sat very still for that shot," or "Can I give you a big hug?" or "I'm glad you remembered to walk, not run, down the stairs. Nice job!"

Model ways to encourage others to express feelings: "Would you like to give your sister a hug because she was so helpful?" And model ways to show empathy: "I feel so sorry for that little boy who is crying. I wish I could make him feel better." Invite your child to tell you how he feels about his accomplishment or disappointment. Let him verbalize his feelings, both positive and negative. And listen to what he says, without judgment.

Let him decide

Do you gasp when your child trips? Do you give kisses and hugs as soon as he falls? Do you cry before he cries, or cry harder than he does when he's hurt? It can be so difficult for parents to let their child decide how *he* feels first, independently of how they feel. They tend to enmesh, or fuse, their emotions with their child's emotions, especially when he has a medical challenge. Enmeshing means that boundaries become blurred: where do the parents' feelings end, and where do the child's feelings begin?

> *I used to gasp every time he'd fall, and when I realized he'd started to cry, I'd get more upset. I was making him think something was wrong. Now I stay calm, I see how he reacts, and I let him decide his response. Then I check him casually while playing with him.* —Jackie, Massachusetts

When your child tries to express his feelings, especially negative ones, do you rush in to stifle or deny? "Don't say that!" "Don't cry!" "Be a big boy." Do you project your own feelings of fear or anxiety? "Oh, you poor thing!" Projecting your own feelings is different from showing *empathy*. The statement "I feel sorry for that little boy who is crying" describes how *you* feel about something. The statement "You poor thing" puts, or projects, your feelings onto someone who may or may not share them. You can usually avoid projection by starting your statements with "I feel . . ."

When the parent's and child's feelings become enmeshed, the child begins to lose confidence in his ability to identify and understand his own feelings. He loses some "ownership" of his emotions. In the long run, enmeshment causes emotional dependency, which weakens self-esteem. Let your child express his own feelings about hemophilia and injuries first. Withhold your own reaction for a moment—count to ten! Give your child the emotional space to first explore and verbalize his own feelings.

Blaming and Overprotecting

One major blow to healthy self-esteem is unjustified guilt, or the feeling that we are responsible for some misfortune we couldn't control. Some guilt is natural—even good—because it serves as a compass to guide us morally and ethically. Guilt lets us know when we have violated our own moral guidelines and helps us accept responsibility for our own behavior.

But when an unexpected situation happens—accident, bleed, illness—and things get intense, parents may blame each other or blame their child, instilling feelings of unjustified guilt. Your child should *never* be blamed for his bleeds, his hemophilia, his inhibitor, your insurance situation, or your unhappiness. In general, blaming is not a healthy or effective way to teach.

Nonetheless, when parents avoid blaming, yet fear for their child's safety, they may overprotect him. With hemophilia and inhibitors, overprotecting means trying to prevent *any* kind of injury—even to the point of interfering with normal development: "Don't run! You could get a bleed!"

How can you effectively teach your child about bleeds and safety without blaming or overprotecting?

- Realize that you can't prevent all bleeds, even serious ones. Bleeds happen.
- Understand that you may naturally be overprotective, just as he may naturally need to be rambunctious and active.
- Focus on specific behaviors and their consequences, not on your child's character. Talk about people in general, or rules in general, but not about him specifically. "When people run with their shoelaces untied, they can trip and get hurt" is much better than "I told you not to run with those shoelaces untied!"
- Emphasize the present, objectively: the bleed and how to treat it. "This looks like it needs factor," not "How did this happen?" Later, when things are calm, discuss objectively how such a bleed or injury can be prevented in the future. "What can we do next time this happens?"
- Teach your child about safety first, when he is old enough to learn, before letting him explore and play. Safety can start as early as age one. This helps him control consequences through *choice*. When he can choose to accept or ignore the rules, he'll learn the consequences.

A well-adjusted child wants to become more independent—and will learn to understand his limitations. A confident parent encourages independence, and helps him explore his limitations. Healthy self-esteem will carry your child farther in life than perfect joints.

Am I Different?

One day your child will surely realize that he is different: he has hemophilia and an inhibitor. If you acknowledge that he is different, will you help or hurt your child's self-esteem? This probably depends on how you present it. Children understand concepts in different ways at different ages, so it's best to advise him according to his age. How will you answer when your child asks, "Why me?" "Why am I different?" "Why did God give me this but didn't give it to him?"[2]

> Austin has gone through the stages: "I don't want to have hemophilia anymore," and "Why me?" He hoards food in his room to deal with his depression. He feels alone having an inhibitor. Although he goes to camp and stays in contact with his friends with hemophilia, none of them has an inhibitor or knows what it's like to deal with one. Austin goes to camp to be "normal" for the week, but he is still different. —Julie Baker, Nevada

For preschoolers, the best explanations have no cause attached: "You were just born that way," or "Nobody really knows why you have it." For school-age children, offer a simple scientific explanation: "Your body is just confused. For some reason, and we don't know why, it can't recognize factor when we infuse it." Teens can understand a more complete scientific explanation, which should include the terms *antibodies*, *immune system*, and *titer*.

Encourage him to notice how he is *not* different from others. Point out other kids who also have red hair, glasses or freckles, or who love music or karate. Arrange for him to spend time with other children who like to play checkers, collect marbles, or enjoy video games. Find out what he likes to do that is not affected by hemophilia, and encourage that activity with other kids.

At any age, a productive way to answer a question is to return the question: "Why do you think you were born like this?" or "Why do you think you have an inhibitor?" Then listen. Offer your child the chance to think aloud, work through his thoughts, and discover his feelings.

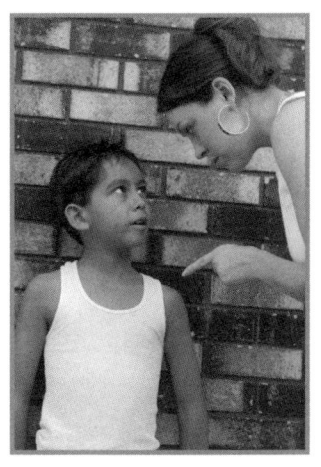

Discipline

How you teach discipline can impact your child's self-esteem, perhaps more than any other childrearing technique. Discipline doesn't mean spanking or punishment. Discipline means learning. The word comes from the Latin *discipulus*, meaning "student." For childrearing, discipline means learning self-control. And using self-control means making choices based on consequences. For example, people use self-control when they choose to obey the law rather than risk the consequence of fines or jail.

Self-control is closely related to self-esteem. People with healthy self-esteem tend to have strong internal methods of managing their own behavior and emotions, while understanding and accepting the consequences. They see themselves as actively influencing their personal destinies.

Use effective discipline at home by providing meaningful consequences. Consequences can take many forms. They may be positive: bestowing rewards, ignoring unwanted behavior, or giving praise. They may be negative: enforcing time out, removing privileges, or spanking. Before trying to shape your child's behavior, be sure to *explain in advance* the consequences of specific behaviors. When used consistently, meaningful consequences shape behavior and help children learn self-control by allowing them to make personal choices. And consequences will be key in helping your child make decisions about his hemophilia, his inhibitor, and all of his treatment. Consistency and consequences together will teach your child self-control. Here are some consequences you can use:

Ignoring is most effective for young, nonverbal children. Over time, your child's undesirable behavior will probably decrease if no one pays attention to him when he exhibits that behavior. Throwing a cup or cookie on the floor is one thing to ignore, but what if he head bangs or hits? Intervene with the least amount of attention. Place a foot under your child's head, but don't look at him. Or restrain him physically but gently, and don't talk to him.

Rewards promote a child's personal responsibility for earning a consequence—possibly a toy, special trip, or money. Rewards are not bribes. Bribes are under the parent's (not the child's) control, given before the desired behavior occurs: "Take this candy. Now behave!" Rewards are given after the desired behavior occurs, and give the child the chance to control his own behavior. They should be discussed ahead of time, or used as a surprise after "catching" your child showing good behavior. Remember that praise is also a reward: compliment him for calmly accepting cancelled plans, or congratulate him for cooperating with treatment.

Penalties cause physical or emotional pain or discomfort, and include corporal punishment (spanking), time out, logical consequences, and natural consequences. Penalties should be enforced calmly, without anger, and privately when possible.

- *Corporal punishment* includes spanking and hitting, which cause physical and emotional pain and can cause bleeds in a child with hemophilia. Use corporal punishment only as a last resort, if at all. *Never* use corporal punishment on an infant or toddler.

    While we have mostly refrained from smacking, on occasion we have chosen to use this, with no bleeds or bruising as a result. We've had more bruising from picking him up to give him a hug. —Richard and Lynley Scott, New Zealand

- *Time out* means having a child sit in a chair or room by himself, away from distractions. A general rule is one minute for each year of age, so a two-year-old should be timed out no longer than two minutes. Time out is not effective when unsupervised, when it lasts too long, or when it's enforced with rage or personal disgust. Time out is less effective for adolescents, who may see it as a reward!

We try to discipline Matthew just as we do our other children. It's sometimes tough to put a child in a wheelchair in time out, but we have done it many times. —Debbie Porter, California

Time out worked great when they were little, up to about age seven. —Shari Luckey, Michigan

Discipline is a main issue. Mostly we put him in time out or sit him down in the middle of the floor in his room and shut the door. When he comes out, we talk about what got him there in the first place. —Sasha Cheatham, Oklahoma

- *Logical consequences* are directly linked to the undesirable behavior. The penalty for hitting another child is to apologize to the victim. Throwing toys results in toys being removed for the rest of the day. Destroying property means replacing that property.

    Nothing worked with Austin for discipline. I'd put him in time out, and he would sit and talk to himself. I tried counting, and he laughed. I'd put him in his room, and he'd never come out. Once he went to touch the stove, and I slapped his hand and said, "Hot!" It left a bruise in the shape of my hand. So I couldn't use spankings. As he got older, I would take his favorite things away. I've found that making him earn back his playthings through good behavior works best for us. —Julie Baker, Nevada

- *Natural consequences* happen with no prompting. Leaving toys out in the driveway means that chalk gets ruined in the rain, or a toy truck gets run over by a car. The child alone is responsible for his own consequence. Of course, never use this technique when there is a risk of physical harm to your child.

Penalties and punishments are effective only when you choose a consequence that is meaningful to your child, and only when he knows ahead of time which consequence he'll receive for which behavior. Consider posting a sign listing family rules and consequences. To work effectively, consequences must be enforced immediately and consistently after each offense, without intense emotion and in an environment of love. Of all these, consistency is key, because it allows your child to quickly develop the connection between his action and the consequence, giving him more immediate control over his choices.

Self-Control through Participation

Let your child make some of his own decisions. It's a great way to foster self-control, and may help prevent behavior problems associated with treatments. However simple the choice—deciding which hand to use for an infusion, or which cartoon character bandage to wear—you are permitting him some control over his environment and body.

> *I learned to mix factor concentrate when I was five and to infuse myself when I was twelve. Then, I had to learn when to infuse. If I got hurt, I had to decide whether to treat or not. Infusing and making decisions about when to treat made me feel like I accomplished something important, and opened up a whole new world to me. I could go places on my own without my parents. At fourteen, I went out of state to basketball camp. —Anonymous*

What are some choices you can offer? Allow your child to participate in the infusion process. He can open the factor boxes, pop the caps off, clean the infusion site, pick a vein, help mix the factor, or hold the gauze on the infusion site. Or let your toddler decide which reward or treat he'll receive after an infusion is over. Letting him make decisions shows your confidence in him, and shows him that he is not powerless, even when he doesn't want an infusion. Making decisions gives him a positive focus, distracting him from more unpleasant things. The point is to give him a feeling of mastery: a child who feels some control over what's happening to him is less likely to resort to unwanted behavior, such as screaming or lashing out.

Coping with Anxiety and Depression

Children with inhibitors must deal with a tremendous number of medical procedures, disruption of normal activities, and a lot of pain. This may strip away feelings of control, and may lead to outbursts, anxiety, frustration, or depression. When a treatment fails, a child's feeling of mastery over his environment decreases, perhaps lowering his self-esteem.

> *Tristan was comfortable when he was getting infusions on ITI daily or every other day. We figured his skin was tough enough that he really didn't feel the initial needle insertion. Now that he's off ITI and we treat only as needed, he averages about two bleeds a month, if that. He hates to be stuck, and he cries. He works up great anxiety about being treated. We tell him each time why we have to do it. I think he gets more worked up about the initial stick than anything. —Jessica Herren, Pennsylvania*

Esh gets more frustrated by the pain and unpredictability than the bleeding.
—*Joyce Hewitt, Michigan*

One key to reducing anxiety is to provide some level of predictability. Help your child know what to expect, whenever possible. You can discuss upcoming clinic visits with him, and you can read age-appropriate books about hospitals, surgery, or treatment. In general, the more he can visualize or understand about what will take place, the more familiar it will seem, and the less anxious he'll feel.

You can greatly reduce your child's anxiety by a letting him make some decisions, regardless of his age. Even small decisions—which bandage to select, which treat following the hospital trip—can help your child believe that he has some control over his often-disrupted life.

No matter what you do as a parent to help your child cope, sometimes sad feelings are inevitable for both you and your child. Managing inhibitors is hard, and you're allowed the full range of human emotions, including sadness. But if sadness evolves into depression, make sure this is handled by your hemophilia team. You might want to speak to your HTC social worker, nurse, or a psychologist.

> *I think both Austin and I have some type of depression. It doesn't affect our daily lives, but I do notice that sometimes I want to be done dealing with his health issues. I have been taking Austin to see the psychologist and social workers at the local cancer foundation. Both of us are very outgoing, happy, social butterflies. But we both have bad days. When times are tough, it affects everyone.* —*Julie Baker, Nevada*

When possible, try to model appropriate, positive attitudes and behavior. Be mindful of your facial expressions, your breathing rate, even the words you use. If you act as if your child's treatment is a matter-of-fact part of life, he's likely to adopt that attitude, too. The best and simplest thing you can do is smile at him. Remember, your child is always watching you and learning from you!

Resilience: Unexpected Maturity Level

An unexpected outcome of experiencing pain and many medical treatments: your child may have stronger emotional resilience and greater maturity than most children his age.

> *Andrew is happy and outgoing. He's very comfortable in adult company. Ironically, we think this is due to his multiple hospital stays and adult interaction.*
> —*Richard and Lynley Scott, New Zealand*

> *Our son has had to come to terms with issues that no child should have to deal with. This has made him grow up much faster than he should have. So he is significantly more mature than is typical of his age.* —Joyce Hewitt, Michigan

If your child seems mature for his age, consider letting him actively participate in his treatment, if he's ready. Encourage him to speak directly with his medical providers when you have a clinic visit. Ask his HTC staff if he can participate at some level in important decisions involving his home treatment, physical activities, or infusion schedule. Help him take part in decisions and responsibilities that he's comfortable accepting.

> *Our son is very involved when we go to the clinic for appointments, and we discuss everything with him. He has input on all decisions that affect him.* —Shari Luckey, Michigan

Seeking Professional Help

Not all children rise to the challenges of inhibitors and emerge more mature than their years. Having an inhibitor can take its toll on your child—and you. Don't hesitate to enlist professional help. Your HTC has qualified nurses and social workers, and possibly psychologists, who can offer expert guidance. At some point your child may need to be evaluated for depression or pain medicine dependency. Being a responsible parent doesn't mean trying to solve everything on your own; it means knowing when and where to get help.

> *Seek out other people who are going through this. Don't be afraid to consider a counselor. We got Stephen to a psychiatrist at his HTC because he has terrible mood swings and lashes out. I try never to say "I understand," because I don't. How can I possibly understand what he's feeling and what he's going through?* —Janet Brewer, Massachusetts

> *There was a stage in Andrew's life, between ages two and four, when he was reluctant to participate in treatment and was less willing to follow instructions during hospital stays and clinic appointments. We were referred to a hospital-based child psychologist, who helped us develop skills to involve Andrew in all aspects of his hemophilia. She also helped us to understand his development and the impact his illness had on him. With consistency and acceptance, we worked through it all.* —Richard and Lynley Scott, New Zealand

Understanding and managing our own behavior and emotions is learned over a lifetime. Even in the best of circumstances, it's challenging. Children with inhibitors, like all children, don't always develop according to our parenting plans, despite all the support, attention, and love we give them. Don't be too hard on yourself when your child disappoints, when his grades slide, when he expresses hopelessness or frustration, when he refuses to self-infuse, when he's glued to the television or computer instead of reading good books! The keys to fostering healthy self-esteem are consistency, communication, love, and knowing when to seek professional help. Sometimes, children will simply be who they are going to be, despite your parenting. All in all, many children with inhibitors weather rough times, and not too surprisingly, most will emerge as sensitive, compassionate adults, disciplined and productive. ■

> *He's a realistic optimist with a touch of expected disappointment. Most of the time he's happy.* —Joyce Hewitt, Michigan

■NOTES

1. Spock B. Dr. Spock's baby and child care. 7th ed. New York: Pocket; 1998.
2. Read *Teach Your Child About Hemophilia* by Laureen A. Kelley (Georgetown, MA: LA Kelley Communications; 2007), available at www.kelleycom.com.

SUMMARY 10
Fostering Healthy Self-Esteem

- Perceived control over emotions, thoughts, environment, and destiny are key components of healthy self-esteem.

- Acknowledge your child's feelings, teach appropriate ways to vent emotions, model appropriate responses, and let him decide what he's feeling.

- Your child will realize he's different from others. Help him appreciate his differences—and similarities—by teaching and listening. Use words and concepts appropriate for his age.

- Encourage physical activity and play as much as is allowed. Teach limitations, too.

- Never blame your child for his bleeds. Guilt and blame damage self-esteem.

- Don't become overprotective in your effort to alleviate your feelings of guilt or fear.

- Let your child express his feelings independently from yours.

- Discipline is always a choice. Decide in advance how you want to discipline your child, develop a plan, and apply it consistently.

- Help your child cope with anxiety stemming from treatment changes by giving him the chance to make choices, however small.

- Acknowledge your child's maturity and resilience in overcoming so many challenges.

- Don't hesitate to seek professional help for managing feelings and thoughts.

11 Family, Friends, and Inhibitors

Self-esteem is shaped partly by our relationships with our families and with people in our community. Our parents, teachers, friends, and extended family all respond to us based on our behavior and the thoughts and feelings we express. In a way, they hold a mirror to us: they model and reflect attitudes, capability, and values.

After an inhibitor diagnosis, you may rely on your family and community for logistical and emotional support as never before. And most will rally to help. Grandparents, in-laws, siblings, your HTC, religious community, and neighbors can be your best allies to support you during tough times.

> My greatest source of support is my family. My sisters are always around for me when I can't cope. My mother-in-law is another great support. And friends who live out of state and have children without inhibitors are always around when I need them. —Julie Baker, Nevada

Although you may think of them as your support system, and of yourself as the person needing support, your family and friends probably need *your* support and guidance too. Because inhibitor management can be all-encompassing, not all family and friends will understand it—or stand it. Family members may distance themselves from you. Friends may avoid you. Some will pity you.

> Most people don't know why our son is in a wheelchair. If we tell people he has hemophilia, most don't know what that means. If anything, they think it means he will start bleeding all over the place. I think our children have been more reluctant to invite friends over because they are "embarrassed" by their brother. I think other people just feel sorry for us. —Debbie Porter, California

When you are just learning to cope, how can you also help friends and family understand? Fortunately, there are some things you can do to support them, enlist their help, and still nurture everyone—including yourself—through this challenging time.

Extended Family

Besides you and your child, the people most often affected by the inhibitor diagnosis are your own parents. It's hard to cope with your child's inhibitor, but you know you must do it. Who will if you don't? Grandparents aren't always so directly involved, but they love your child too. It may be hard for them to accept the diagnosis, medical treatments, and family lifestyle changes.

> *Ethan's grandmother, my mom, can't deal with infusions. She'll cry, "That's my baby! I can't take this." But Ethan says, "Grandmother, just get over it!" Still, he does not like to see his grandmother upset. —Kim Stubbs, Mississippi*

If you have a family history of inhibitors, your extended family may be more comfortable accepting the situation. The inhibitor might even be a cause to rally the family and bring them closer.

> *My family is very close to us. We had some family friction before Ty was born, but we all came together over him. —Anonymous*

> *The inhibitor has positively impacted relationships with our extended family, especially with my in-laws, where my relationship has been strained at times. It has allowed them to see what caring, conscientious parents we are. When we went through ITI, they finally saw their grandson feeling better, and came to appreciate what a brave and special grandson they have. Still, the family is a little apprehensive about caring for him, but I can't say I blame them. —Sasha Cheatham, Oklahoma*

If hemophilia and inhibitors are all new territory, your child's grandparents may have a hard time coping with the sudden changes in your life. If they live close to you, inhibitor care might become routine for them. If not, inhibitor care will probably be foreign, intense—and scary.

> *My extended family was okay, because I have a brother with hemophilia who understood the effects of the inhibitor. My husband's family was new to hemophilia and had a hard time understanding the inhibitor and treatments. —Cicely Evans, Massachusetts*

> *Some members of my father's family look at him as if he's a ghost: they won't talk to him. Some members of my husband's family talk to him but won't pick him up. My mom has gotten over it. She picks him up and enjoys being with him. —Chasity, Mississippi*

Sometimes the concern is psychological and fear-related: relatives are afraid of accidentally hurting your child. They may visit you, but not touch him. They may never ask about his condition. Sometimes the concern is logistical: the constant hospitalizations, infusions, and bleeding may be an imposition or inconvenience.

> *Relatives—now there's a hot button. When Esh was first diagnosed, everyone in the family stopped holding him and coming to see him. There's no family history, and although we went to three different clinic appointments with our families to explain what was happening, their support has been minimal at best. My family has even taken Esh's sibling to special events with the promise of taking Esh—which never happened. In one year, we made an average of 120 round trips to the clinic seventy miles away. He was admitted about every four to six weeks, for three to ten days, for almost six years. During that time, only his dad and sibling came to see him.* —Joyce Hewitt, Michigan

> *We have no family living close to us, so they see our son Noah only a few times a year; they don't see the everyday living with inhibitors and hemophilia. Noah needs daily port care. Taking care of a bleed means several doses a day over several days. Inhibitors do affect family connections. Noah can't spend much time alone with family members because I always need to be nearby.*
> —Cicely Evans, Massachusetts

After the inhibitor diagnosis, your relatives' reactions may closely mirror your own stages of acceptance: shock, denial, anger, and grief. Unfortunately, if they don't live with hemophilia daily, or live far away, some family members may never resolve these initial feelings. They may always seem stuck in a stage. When they are perpetually depressed or grieving over hemophilia, relatives can strain your relationship, constantly fearing bleeds or reminding you that you "gave" your child hemophilia.

> *Inhibitors run in the family. My mother knew the complications and was eager to learn more, as her brothers had hemophilia with inhibitors. But my grandmother cried because she felt it was her fault for passing along the gene.*
> —Jessica Herren, Pennsylvania

Any family member's undesirable reaction is probably founded in fear—fear that something terrible will happen, fear of the unknown, fear of being unable to prevent bleeds. Your relatives love your child and naturally fear for him. They also love you. But sometimes fear expresses itself in excessive control or visible anxiety, instead of gentle communication and honest feelings. Relatives may exhibit blame, shame, guilt, denial, overprotection, or rigidity. Fear may create an overbearing in-law who won't allow your child to act with normal spontaneity or energy, enforcing strict house rules when you visit. Fear may create an aunt who audibly gasps whenever your child runs or falls. Fear may be at the root of the interrogation you receive from your mother after an accident: "Why didn't you have a helmet on him? "Why do you let him jump off the bed?" "Why did you expose him to that unnecessary CT scan?"

Some families are proud of being from "healthy" stock. Hemophilia with inhibitors shatters this pride and creates a sense of vulnerability. These families sometimes respond by offering religious solutions in the hope of curing a child.

> My husband's mother thought that if she prayed enough, Matthew would be cured. She had a shrine in her kitchen for Matt. He almost died once, and she was there when he was resuscitated so she calls him "Miracle Matthew." She believes there will be a miracle some day and that God will protect Matt.
> —Debbie Porter, California

With time and experience, most family members will adapt to life with an inhibitor, just as you have.

How Siblings Are Affected

Brothers and sisters of a child with an inhibitor can be deeply affected by the diagnosis. For children, emotional stability and good self-esteem comes from trusting their family and their world. Trust is built on consistency, routine, and predictability. Imagine how an inhibitor can upend a sibling's world!

Birth order might matter. For a child without an inhibitor, daily routines are overturned when a new baby enters with the demanding needs of an inhibitor. By contrast, when a new sibling is born into an established environment of ports, ITI, and hospital trips, that's all he or she ever knows. Your other children's adjustments and behaviors will likely depend on whether hemophilia and inhibitors are the norm, or are a sudden interruption in the life they always knew.

> My twin daughters are five years younger than my son. They really don't know any difference in life without an inhibitor and seem to be handling things pretty well. They are protective of their brother and very compassionate when he has a bleed. —Shari Luckey, Michigan

Siblings can show great compassion when a brother has such a complicated and often painful medical condition.

The girls often go and get things for their brother when he is laid up. Sometimes they play with him or watch a movie with him. —Shari Luckey, Michigan

Still, it's normal for children to feel curious, jealous, ignored, or even hostile when a sibling has a chronic illness. Siblings see their parents' intense concern for the child with hemophilia: their brother may be allowed special privileges, such as skipping school or chores because of a bleed. He may get extra attention from relatives and neighbors. Perceiving discrepancies in attention and treatment, siblings without hemophilia may feel jealous, angry, or worried.

The siblings think they are being ignored, and that we only care about our son with the inhibitor. This is especially true of Matthew's older sister, who thinks that her life has been "ruined" by her brother. This has affected her relationship with him: she claims she hates him and believes we don't care about her. —Debbie Porter, California

How can you help your other children adjust to life with an inhibitor? Preschoolers often can't name or verbalize their feelings. They express their emotions as whines, complaints, tantrums, or misbehavior. Much of this is simply a cry for attention from Mom or Dad. Sibling rivalry is often a way of saying, "I need more attention."

There's a lot of competition for attention between my kids. You try to set aside equal amounts of time to spend with your children, but sometimes when there is a bleed or bump or bruise, it requires a good amount of your time focusing on that one child. It's difficult on us as parents, because we start to feel bad. —Jessica Herren, Pennsylvania

You can begin by verbalizing your children's feelings.[1] This often has a calming effect. Acknowledge feelings, even negative ones like anger or jealousy. When you ignore or downplay negative feelings, you *invalidate* them. You encourage your child to believe that her feelings aren't real or important—and neither is she. In truth, it's normal and acceptable not to like a family member at times! Remember, an acknowledgment is not an endorsement of the feeling; it's an endorsement of the child. You're not saying, "It's okay to hate your brother." You're saying, "It's okay to feel like you hate your brother sometimes." Acknowledgment tells children that their feelings are valid and important—they *matter*. Once you acknowledge feelings, you can move toward coping with them positively and expressing them appropriately.

Coty's sibling is two years older. She never seemed to resent Coty. She loves her brother and has always loved to help out. Sometimes, though, she has sought attention by faking sick. —Chasity, Mississippi

When children believe their needs are being met, their behavior usually calms down, and they regain emotional stability. You can help by meeting their unique needs, spending time alone with them, and acknowledging their feelings.

> Emily has felt some resentment. So Friday became our day. We would go shopping, take her doll and stroller, and just hang out. My mother would take my son. My children are real protective of each other. She knows he has hemophilia, but she's never been jealous much. The doctors and nurses were very sweet to Emily and I think that helped her a lot. —Kim Stubbs, Mississippi

You can also model good behavior and appropriate emotions for your children.

> I think I made my other son, Cameron, nervous. I was always telling him to be careful with his brother. Cameron was only four, so it was hard for him to understand. But no harm done: Cam is not careful with his brother at all now! —Jackie, Massachusetts

You can minimize perceived differences in the way your children are treated by trying to use the same discipline for all, and by being consistent with family rules, expectations, and consequences. You can also spotlight individual accomplishments by offering special treats, rewards, or attention to each sibling for unique talents, positive behavior, or special events like birthdays or school performances.

Involve your children without hemophilia in their sibling's care as far as they feel comfortable, but without making them feel responsible for his care. When children are involved, they feel useful and needed instead of helpless and unimportant. Give them a choice: "Would you like to help out? When?" Assign them specific responsibilities: "Can you please get the factor ready?" "Would you like to apply the tourniquet?" Siblings often feel less resentful when they know they are needed and appreciated. They can spend special time with you, doing a special job.

> We have taken Tristan's sister, Taylor, to clinic visits, and the social workers have educated her and helped her understand her brother's disorder. They have given her coloring books and even used a medical doll to help her understand about ports and infusions. I've taken Taylor to meet other children with hemophilia, their parents, and their siblings. We allow Taylor to help with

Tristan's infusions, which helps her feel included and important in her brother's treatments. —Jessica Herren, Pennsylvania

The Gasps and the Pity

It's almost impossible for anyone to truly understand the difficulties and pain faced by a family with inhibitors. But people will try to reach out and understand. Most often, you'll get appropriate sympathy from relatives, friends, and others: a warm touch, a generous gesture or gift, kind words. But an attempt at sympathy can also be expressed in gasps, *oohs*, *ahhs*, and comments like "Poor you!" At times, sympathy will feel uncomfortable to you, because without a deeper understanding, sympathy can highlight the distance or difference between you and the other person.

We do get the occasional gasp and anxiety. Most parents say, "Oh, my God, the poor thing, will he ever outgrow it?" We just explain what it is. —Jessica Herren, Pennsylvania

Sympathy may lead people to say and do what you consider the wrong things for your child. Unable to put themselves in your shoes, they may restrict your child's play, single him out, excessively worry over him, or treat him too differently. You may need to gently explain to others how you would like your child to be treated: what's helpful to say and do, and what is not.

We have asked aunts and uncles not to tell their kids, "Don't hit Jay." We have asked them to tell their kids, "Don't hit anyone!" —Shari Luckey, Michigan

Grandpa's real protective. He's always saying, "Be careful!" When Colton was five, he jumped and broke his arm. Grandpa thought the world was coming to an end. Grandpa was more worried than we were! —Debbie Branch, Kansas

To relatives and friends, a word of advice: show concern and appropriate sympathy, but not pity. Pity separates you from the family and makes a child feel self-conscious, aware that something is "wrong" with him. Pity emphasizes our differences. Try this: instead of reacting immediately, begin by asking questions, then listen deeply and nonjudgmentally, and try to put yourself in the family's shoes. Try to stress the positive, and put the self-esteem of your young relative first. Before you comment on a situation, ask yourself, *How will this impact the child with the inhibitor? How would I feel if I were the child and heard this?* Our good intentions and desire to show we care—sympathize—may lead us to say things or behave in ways that aren't helpful. When in doubt, simply ask the parents for feedback: "What would be most helpful for me to say or do?" That's real friendship and family!

As the parent of a child with an inhibitor, you can get things started by modeling the behavior you'd like to see from your friends and relatives. If they see you acting in a matter-of-fact way when a crisis hits, they'll take their cue from you. And so will your child!

Teach Them, and Include Them

As parents, you can strengthen family ties by offering to instruct family and friends. Teach them what an inhibitor is and how to infuse. Invite them to clinic visits or community hemophilia events. They may not want to be included and may reject your offers, but you can try. Offer every year or so; relationships change over time, and a distant relationship can get closer with a change of seasons.

> My mother attended an educational meeting where she could ask questions and get insight on Tristan's treatment and technology advances. Other family members have shown no interest in learning about Tristan's disorder, let alone his inhibitor. We gave our in-laws a booklet about hemophilia and inhibitors, but they haven't really tried to read or understand it. Sometimes that gets frustrating. I worry about my sister, who likely is a carrier, as she plans to have more children but hasn't taken an interest in learning about hemophilia with inhibitors. —Jessica Herren, Pennsylvania

> We have very supportive relationships with extended family, who have accepted all aspects of Reuben's diagnosis, and who try to understand. His grandparents, for example, have met our entire treatment team. —Wendy Sass, New York

Invite your relatives to an educational session or meeting with your HTC team so they can learn from neutral authority figures. The meeting can highlight concrete ways to help, dispel fears, and make relatives feel competent.

To involve relatives, perhaps the most accessible and concrete task is the actual infusion. Enlisting help with the infusion demystifies everything. Suddenly, others can see what's "normal" for your family. It's a chance for you to model calmness, and to teach them infusion steps that could be vital in a pinch.

> We have always treated Andrew in our living room so if people were there, they would see Andrew's courage and self-control, and the skills we've learned. We allow family members to learn as much of the treatment process as possible. It gives them an opportunity to see how we make our treatment decisions. —Richard and Lynley Scott, New Zealand

We've let the grandparents and other family members be involved in the infusion process, mostly by watching. But they don't feel comfortable accessing him, and I don't think he would go for it either! It has helped them see that he gets his infusion and goes about his day just like other children. —Sasha Cheatham, Oklahoma

Including siblings in the infusion helps them feel wanted, needed, valuable, and competent. It's probably the best activity for building self-esteem and fostering closeness between sibs.

Jay doesn't like his sisters around when he gets his treatment—it's even worse now that he's a teen! We are helping him understand that they need to be involved too. —Shari Luckey, Michigan

What can grandparents, in-laws, cousins, family, and friends do to help?

- Don't avoid the family.
- Watch and listen to the family before you react to a situation.
- Don't judge or give advice. Instead, ask for advice about how best to help.
- Be honest. If you can't watch an infusion, or don't have time to drive to the HTC often, just let the family know.
- Express concern and interest. Don't express pity, but do show compassion.
- Treat the child with hemophilia normally. Don't single him out.
- Learn about hemophilia and inhibitors. Attend a support group meeting with the parents.
- Learn to participate in the infusion process.

Relatives are in a unique position to help a family in need, and to promote and reinforce a child's healthy self-image. They play a role that no one else can play. The entire family can view the inhibitor diagnosis as an opportunity to build stronger bonds. When a favorite uncle, cousin, or grandparent reinforces the message "You are normal. You are loved unconditionally," the child's feeling of self-worth can help him overcome some of life's harshest trials.

Our wider family has become closer as a result of the demands placed on our nuclear family. We rely on extended family to get us through difficult times. Grandparents have stayed overnight at hospital with Andrew, which has cemented stronger bonds. —Richard and Lynley Scott, New Zealand

Your Community

Families can be tremendous sources of support, but don't use your family as your only means of support. You can find expert support in a less emotionally charged relationship at your HTC. Often HTC social workers volunteer to meet with extended family members to work through issues and form stronger families. If there is no social worker, your HTC nurse could be a great alternative.

> *I was a single mom and alone. Rachel, my HTC nurse, was my lifeline. I took up a lot of her time; she would talk to me for hours, as if she didn't have another patient or family to meet with. I couldn't believe how much time she spent with me. After speaking to Rachel, I felt comforted.* —Anonymous

Your local hemophilia organization may have support and educational meetings to help parents and families cope and get informed, and you may even meet another family with inhibitors. Don't get discouraged if you don't meet another family right away! Sometimes just being in a hemophilia community is enough to help you feel supported.

> *There has been no negative impact on our relationships, and our extended family has made sacrifices. With the added stress caused by inhibitors, we've had to learn to ask for and accept help from others. Pride and independence won't help you much. Interdependence and humility go a long way when you are in need.* —Richard and Lynley Scott, New Zealand

Until recently, no community resources existed for inhibitor families—no place for them to meet and share their unique concerns. Hemophilia meetings focused on the needs of the non-inhibitor community. Many inhibitor families had never met another family with inhibitors, unless by chance through an HTC or local hemophilia organization. Many felt like outcasts, isolated. They thought the wider community didn't want to hear their troubles or understand life with an inhibitor. While all the talk was about prophylaxis and having a normal life, families with inhibitors suffered in silence.

> *Having inhibitors is isolating. You can't necessarily relate to those who have just hemophilia. At times, your life is so much more complicated. Your experiences are so overwhelming, and you just try to get through the day, just try to make your child comfortable. I go through stages when I can reach out and talk to others, but during an acute episode, I shut down and I don't want to talk to anyone—not even another with an inhibitor. There are times when you can't talk about it. It floods you. You can't ask for help or get above it. You're too tired.* —Janet Brewer, Massachusetts

In 2005 the first Inhibitor Education Summit[2] was held, a visionary meeting that galvanized the inhibitor community. Families were flown in from all parts of the nation to meet, share, bond, and learn. For the first time, inhibitor families had a meeting of their own, a place to go for support. Aside from the development of bypassing agents, this summit was probably the most revolutionary event to date for the inhibitor community. It highlighted the need for emotional and educational support, and the need for a cohesive community.

The Inhibitor Education Summits have been a gold mine. —Joyce Hewitt, Michigan

We initiated the idea to change our son's treatment regime after we went to the first Inhibitor Education Summit, where we got a lot of knowledge and spoke to others with inhibitors. —Derek Nelson, Utah

Try to attend an educational meeting about inhibitors soon. And consider bringing your relatives, to open their eyes to your unique world. ■

Quick Ways to Connect to Siblings without Inhibitors

Every child needs attention from parents, often when we are least able to give it! Giving enough attention to meet a child's needs may require lots of time. This can be challenging when the child with hemophilia and an inhibitor needs even more time. But there are some things you can do for the sibling without an inhibitor:

- Give your child lots of hugs and kisses.
- Smile at your child more often.
- Create a special signal, unique to your child, to show affection.
- Call your child by a special nickname.
- Tell your child you've set aside time to spend together later.
- Let your child choose a favorite activity to share later.

■NOTES

1. Read *Teach Your Child About Hemophilia* by Laureen A. Kelley (Georgetown, MA: LA Kelley Communications; 2007), available at www.kelleycom.com.
2. To learn more about the inhibitor education meetings, contact your HTC or NHF.

SUMMARY 11
Family, Friends, and Inhibitors

- Relatives are in a unique position to help, and to reinforce a child's healthy self-image.

- Relatives are often afraid of the diagnosis. They may distance themselves, worry excessively, or be overly emotional.

- Relatives' reactions may differ according to whether hemophilia and inhibitors run in the family, and whether they have experienced them.

- It's normal for children to feel compassionate, curious, jealous, ignored, or even hostile when a sibling has a chronic illness.

- Siblings need routine and reassurance. Acknowledge their feelings, include them in daily care, and give them special time alone with you.

- Relatives and friends should try to show appropriate sympathy and compassion, not pity.

- Include family and friends in infusions and clinic visits.

- Find expert professional support at your HTC.

- Attend an inhibitor education meeting.

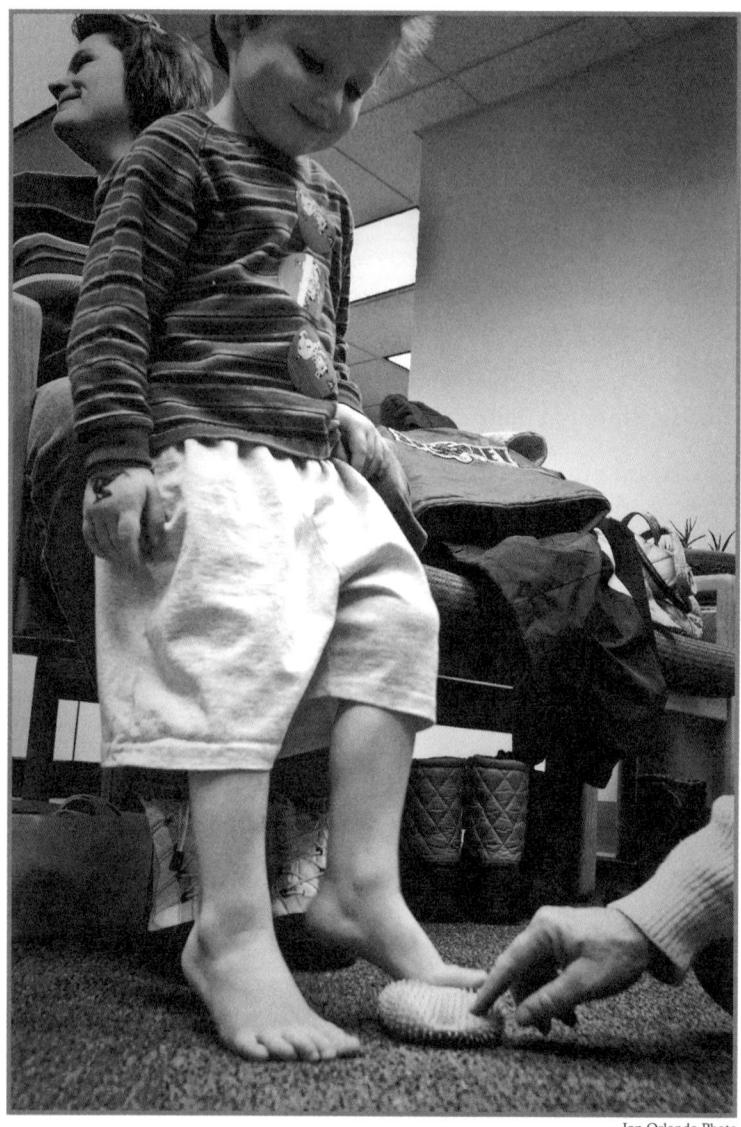

Jon Orlando Photo

12 Keeping Joints Healthy

Bleeding into joints is the most common medical problem for someone with hemophilia. And joint disease is the most common complication of hemophilia. Repeated joint bleeds can destroy cartilage and bone, leading to disability and chronic pain. Preventing joint damage is the focus of much of hemophilia treatment. It's more challenging if your child has an inhibitor, but there are steps you can take to minimize joint disease and promote healthy joints.

Joint health is key to overall good health and high quality of life. Your child will have less pain, greater mobility, better career options, and better quality of life when his joints are in good shape. Unfortunately, some joint damage is almost inevitable for people with inhibitors. You'll want to start early, in partnership with your HTC, to create a plan to minimize joint damage and keep your child's joints in good shape through his formative years.

> *We allow Tristan to run, jump, play, and ride his bike with a helmet. We encourage it for joint health and normality.* —Jessica Herren, Pennsylvania

> *I grew up watching my brother limp in pain from age thirteen because for half of his life, he had arthritis equivalent to that of an eighty-year-old. With the diagnosis of our son Noah's inhibitor, all the worries we had for his quality of life have returned. We take each day in stride and do everything in our power to use all the resources available.* —Cicely Evans, Massachusetts

A good preventive plan to preserve your child's joints will include an assessment of his current joint status, and will emphasize these key components:

- Treat early and adequately.
- Encourage physical activity.
- Keep weight under control.
- Include physical therapy when needed.
- When necessary, use supportive devices such as splints, crutches, and wheelchairs.

Treat Early and Adequately

If your child has successfully completed ITI (see chapter 4), he will probably be on prophylaxis, using standard factor concentrate. Receiving factor replacement regularly will help reduce the number of joint bleeds and prevent later joint damage.

If your child is on ITI but has not successfully completed it, your HTC team may instruct you to use bypassing agents in addition to factor when your child has breakthrough bleeding.[1] Prophylaxis with bypassing agents is in the early stages of study. Until this becomes a standard, approved treatment, you'll have to try to treat every joint bleed at its onset, or as early as possible, with adequate amounts of factor. For families using on-demand treatment, this means infusing *immediately* at the first hint of a bleed. To do this, you'll need to know the symptoms of various bleeds. It's tempting to "wait and see," especially when you're busy with household tasks, getting ready for school or work, or trying to catch a plane. But the sooner you infuse, the better your chances of minimizing joint damage. When in doubt, infuse!

But first ensure that you and your HTC have developed a plan for dosing. *It's imperative that you know the recommended dosing size and frequency and do not deviate from your HTC's recommendation.* This includes watching for thrombotic complications (see chapter 5). Remember that even when the bleed hasn't stopped, you can "overdose" when using bypassing agents (unlike with standard factor VIII), increasing your child's risk of unwanted blood clots. It's especially important to call the HTC if you are adhering to the plan, but it doesn't seem to be stopping a bleed.

> *I play tennis and signed up for basketball intramurals. When I was a high school junior and senior, I still played basketball. The bleeding was managed with FEIBA.* —John Salierno, New Jersey

It's best to treat immediately in the following situations:

- after any injury to the joint, or abnormal twisting or overextension
- when your child is limping, favoring a joint, or paying attention to a joint for no obvious reason
- when your child reports an unusual feeling that's hard to describe (an *aura*) in the joint
- when your child feels tingling or warmth in the joint
- when your child seems irritable or cranky for no reason, or your infant is excessively fussy and cries more when you move certain areas of his body

When a joint bleed has progressed without treatment, symptoms will include pain in the joint, stiffness, heat, swelling, and limited movement. If your child is still too young to verbalize that he has a bleed, watch for his refusal to use or straighten a limb or to bear weight on it; these are often the first signs of a bleed in a toddler. Always try to infuse factor *before* you see swelling, if possible. When a joint bleed has progressed to include pain and stiffness, your child may need many factor infusions, along with RICE, over a period of days or weeks to fully resolve the bleed.

It's important to recognize the time it takes for a joint bleed to fully resolve. Although swelling and pain may decrease rapidly, it may take weeks or even months for the joint structures to fully recover and for inflammation to dissipate. Synovitis, an inflammation of the membrane lining the joint, may occur with the first joint bleed, and the risk of synovitis increases greatly with repeated bleeds in the same joint. Early synovitis can usually be treated with anti-inflammatory medications or steroids and may take weeks or months to resolve, even with no additional bleeding! Advanced, chronic synovitis can be resolved only by a synovectomy, the surgical removal of the inflamed synovium. See chapter 8 for more on synovitis and joint care.

Prevent Joint Bleeds with Physical Activity

Along with aggressive treatment and/or prophylaxis to help reduce the frequency of joint bleeds, physical activity and fitness will benefit your child. Strong, flexible muscles help stabilize joints, decreasing the risk of joint and muscle bleeds. Physical fitness helps physically *and* psychologically by managing appetite and mood.

Physical activity also helps children feel skilled and accomplished. A lean body reduces stress on joints, and can even make finding veins easier. Good coordination improves your child's ability to avoid or handle trips, falls, and bumps.

> *Our son stops and thinks before he does something. He can't go up the slide, but he can go down it. He bikes, runs in the backyard, and jumps. He knows that running on grass is okay, but running on cement is not. He kicks a soccer ball, but I don't think he'll play an organized sport. We're encouraging swimming and golf.* —Sonji Wilkes, Colorado

Physical activity doesn't need to involve organized sports, many of which are off limits for lots of children with inhibitors. But all kids can and should participate in some form of regular physical activity. An activity program with long-lasting physical benefits should include *aerobic exercise* and *resistance* training.

Aerobic exercises include swimming, bicycling, walking, running, and dancing—

anything that works up a sweat and makes your heart pound for a while. Aerobic activities strengthen your most important muscle, the heart, for a more efficient body and longer life. If you worry that your child can't run, for example, there are alternatives. Hiking and walking are good. Many families have discovered the joys of Wii™ (including Wii™ Sports and Wii Fit™) to keep children safely active indoors and generate lots of sweat and family fun![2]

> We play with a Nerf football in the park. Our son can still do baseball and football, but in a different way. You can't take this away from them because they have a medical condition. Life still has to go on. He loves tennis, and we all play tennis. —Kim Stubbs, Mississippi

Resistance training includes lifting weights, using resistance bands, or using your own weight against itself—any activity that challenges your muscles so they tone and grow. Resistance training strengthens muscles; this is crucial to protect joints from stress, wear and tear. Your child can actually reduce his risk of joint bleeds when the muscles supporting the joint are strengthened. *Warning:* Pre-teens should not lift weights, and kids with some joint damage may harm their joints further by incorrectly lifting weights. For guidelines on developmentally safe ages for lifting, and for individualized instruction on safe resistance training, consult the physical therapist at your HTC. The therapist can guide you in setting appropriate limits, and can help your child learn the best way to achieve goals without harm.

Swimming is the hands-down winner for best overall sport for children with hemophilia, with or without inhibitors. It has no impact on joints, offers the highest aerobic benefit of any sport, and develops strong muscles that protect joints. Boys with hemophilia who swim regularly have the fewest joint bleeds, and fortunately, most children naturally love the water.

> Andrew has taken swimming lessons since he was about one. This has been fantastic for building strength and keeping him active. When we eradicated the inhibitor, we enrolled him in a gym and fitness class that focuses on confidence and increasing gross motor skills more than on skill and perfection. We've noticed a big improvement in his physical fitness, his willingness to give things a go, and his confidence. —Richard and Lynley Scott, New Zealand

Keep in mind that competition in physical activities will change as your child grows. Noncompetitive kickball can become a competitive, risky sport by high school. Tee-ball becomes baseball. Soccer with 60-lb eight-year-olds will become a contest between 140-lb teens. When a sport or activity becomes so competitive that your teen risks serious injury, it's time to reconsider. On the other hand, some individual sports, such as swimming or ping-pong, do not involve physical contact and can provide both physical and recreational benefits for a lifetime.

> We enrolled Lee in karate when he was four. It directed his energy to something positive. He loved it. It taught him to develop balance and take care of his body. Physical training helped. After age eight, Lee started baseball. Ultimately, when he was older, baseball was more intense, more competitive. In high school he made varsity as a freshman, so all this time he was building up his body more. We firmly believe his conditioning helped prevent bleeds. —Eleth Ridenhour, Kansas

Warming up and stretching correctly are as valuable as exercise. Proper warm-ups help prevent muscle tears and stress on joints. Stretching can be taught by your HTC, and should be done before all physical activity.

Remember that an injury or bleed doesn't mean failure. Your child might suffer a ligament or tendon tear, just like anyone else. Giving factor alone won't make these injuries improve. When your child is injured playing sports or doing any physical activity, take him to a hemophilia-related physical therapist or orthopedic surgeon.

Alternatives to Physical Activity

Sometimes you just can't find appropriate physical activities for your child. Inhibitors can be tough: frequent dosing, ITI, and bleed recovery may require long stretches when your child can't put his joints at risk through physical activity. This may mean limiting or eliminating these activities for a time, or even indefinitely. Although swimming is often touted as the best physical activity for people with hemophilia, some children just don't like swimming.

> Physical activity has been a big challenge. It's been difficult for Matthew to exercise in any way. We have a swimming pool at home and encourage him to swim, but he doesn't want to. —Debbie Porter, California

> Our son has had a continuous ankle bleed for three months. This has prohibited him from swimming and most of the activities he wants to do. —Cicely Evans, Massachusetts
>
> There was a time when I hated hemophilia because I couldn't play any sports. Then I discovered video games, and now I play guitar. —Nathan Fatula, Pennsylvania
>
> I got all my Boy Scout merit badges and became a senior leader. My father took me to ball games and race car exhibitions. In school, I became manager of the basketball team. I learned how to sit and watch, but I tried to stay involved as much as possible. —R. H., Connecticut

If physical activities need to be curtailed for a time, speak with your HTC about when your child can resume something physical. Without physical activity, your child may face more health complications from a sedentary lifestyle.

The Dangers of Obesity

Even children without inhibitors will risk joint problems if they don't maintain a healthy weight. It's a real risk in America: the CDC estimates that in 2009, a whopping 65% of American adults aged twenty and older were overweight. Overall, a shocking 33% were obese. We are the fattest country on earth, and this also applies to the hemophilia community. The CDC's Universal Data Collection (UDC) project data[3] show increased body mass index (BMI) for American boys with hemophilia in 2009.

There are many reasons for this dangerous trend. Advanced technology encourages lots of time in front of television and computers. Because of our top-speed lifestyle, we often rely on fast foods, mostly high in fats.

If your child with an inhibitor is gaining weight, ask your HTC team to recommend a nutritionist. Along with the contributors to obesity just mentioned, the inactivity caused by an inhibitor puts your child at risk of unhealthy weight gain. A nutritionist can review your family eating patterns and recommend good changes. Don't be surprised if you're asked to stop consuming soft drinks, usually a number one offender!

Excess weight leads to decreased physical activity, which leads to excess weight . . . and greater risk of joint damage. It's harder to find veins in an overweight child. Heavier children need more factor, which burns faster through your lifetime insurance limit, or cap. A responsible parent must assess the family's weight issues, create a plan with a physician, and guide the family to make positive, permanent lifestyle changes. Shut off the television and PlayStation®, or get a Wii. Get outside with your child daily. Just a little consistent activity, and fewer calories, may be all it takes to prevent weight gain.

Physical Therapy and Joint Contracture

When your child has a bleed, your HTC team will advise you about appropriate product choices, doses, and dosing schedule. If the bleed involves a muscle or joint, ask your HTC physical therapist and other team members whether you'll need to immobilize your child's limb and, if so, how and when he can resume normal activity. After a severe joint or muscle bleed, your child might need physical therapy to speed recovery and regain lost muscle strength, flexibility, and coordination. PT involves the supervised exercise and stretching of joints and muscles, and may include other therapeutic treatments such as heat/cold, electrical stimulation, splints, ultrasound, and manual therapy. The goals of PT:

- Restore strength and normal range of motion.
- Help children walk again or walk with a better gait.
- Keep muscles strong to protect joints.
- Identify and help resolve posture and flexibility problems that can lead to injuries and bleeds.
- Teach how to protect and support a bleeding or target joint.
- Use adaptive equipment like splints or crutches to ease daily activities.

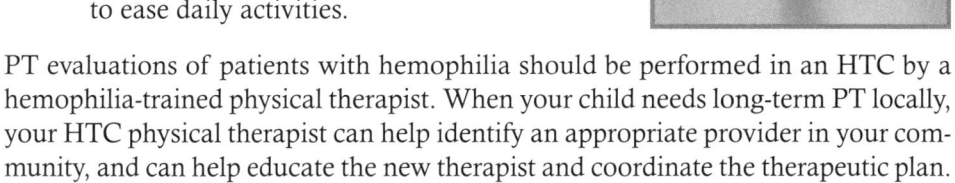

PT evaluations of patients with hemophilia should be performed in an HTC by a hemophilia-trained physical therapist. When your child needs long-term PT locally, your HTC physical therapist can help identify an appropriate provider in your community, and can help educate the new therapist and coordinate the therapeutic plan.

PT can also help prevent a common complication often associated with hemophilic arthropathy: a joint contracture. This happens when the soft tissues around the joint—muscles, ligaments, joint capsule—become tight and restrict the normal joint motion. In hemophilia, contractures can occur when the joint is immobilized after a serious joint or muscle bleed. For example, to reduce the pain of a knee bleed, your child may keep his knee flexed, or bent. This eventually causes muscles to shorten and become fibrous, preventing your child from extending his limb. Joint contractures typically occur in the knee and elbow because these joints are most likely to bleed. With a contracture, your child won't be able to stretch his arm out straight, straighten his leg, or squat down. He'll have a hard time walking. Contractures also cause him to put more stress on other joints as he overcompensates for the affected joint.

> *We've tried scheduled activities for our son, but that hasn't worked out, as he missed a lot. Because of joint damage and lost ROM in his left knee, it's harder to do activities that require bending his knee past 80 or 90 degrees.*
> *—Shari Luckey, Michigan*

When PT begins, the physical therapist will measure your child's joint ROM to determine the severity of the contracture. This allows the therapist to track and measure progress over time. Eventually, if PT is implemented early and no bone problems are contributing to the contracture, your child's joint will regain ROM and he'll be able to bend and straighten it. Your child can use a variety of devices—elastic bands, small weights, rubber balls—to work the stiffened limbs back to functioning.[4] His therapist may also use heat, ultrasound, or diathermy to help stretch the joint.[5] *Note: Never use heat on a joint or muscle with an acute bleed*, or if you even suspect a bleed. Always use ice!

Hydrotherapy can be both a relief and an effective way to rebuild muscle tone and flexibility. That's why swimming is rated the number one sport for children with hemophilia. Water provides natural resistance while supporting your child through buoyancy. He can also achieve resistance—so important for muscle strength—through weight lifting. Even if your child has no joint contractures, he should regularly stretch and lift small weights to keep his joints and muscles toned and functioning well. This helps prevent muscle tears and builds up the area around the joint to protect it from bleeding. Your HTC can give you simple exercises to do at home to keep joints supple.

Supportive Devices

During an acute bleed, your child needs to rest. Because it's hard to make young children rest a joint, your physical therapist may recommend a splint—a device like a cast, usually removable. Splints immobilize the bleeding area so the body can heal. Splints can be made by the HTC physical therapist or nurse, or in your hospital's emergency department. Splints can also be quite hi-tech and expensive, and may be covered by insurance.

Even when the bleeding joint is immobilized and your child has received factor, a bleed can take a long time to resolve. Until the joint has healed or regained ROM, your child might need extra support from a wheelchair, splint, or crutch to allow the joint to rest and heal, and to prevent further damage.

> *I've used crutches since age three. I use them when I have a bleed, and lately only when a knee bleed is bad enough that my knee is bent. —Nathan Fatula, Pennsylvania*

> *Splinting, icing, and immobilization are required to stop any bleed. It usually takes at least a week of rest, treatment, and splinting until a bleed is under control. We splint twenty-four hours a day. —Debbie Porter, California*

Be sure to get instructions from your HTC when using any supportive device. Though they're a source of valuable support, crutches that are too tall or too short can make a bleed worse or cause bleeds in the arms or shoulders.

■ ■ ■

> *I was told I would never walk again due to severe damage to my left knee. I was told to just use a wheelchair. There was nothing to live for. I went to a church service, and the priest, a recognized faith healer, laid his hand on me and I started to walk again. This is documented in the hospital records. I had been getting PT and electrotherapy. I left on Friday and returned Tuesday, and the PT staff almost fell off their chairs! My body started getting stronger, I returned to college, started dating, and got married. My life became so different! —R. H., Connecticut*

Inhibitors can cause many setbacks, sometimes thwarting all your efforts and progress. But stay hopeful: most children with inhibitors *can* do some activities. Your child won't have a perfect quality of life, but thanks to advanced treatments, experts in the field, positive motivation, and even personal faith, he'll have a shot at a good one. ■

■ NOTES

1. Recent reports in inhibitor literature discuss using bypassing agents during prophylaxis, similar to prophylactic treatment in non-inhibitor patients using factor VIII or IX. These studies are emerging, and at the time of this writing, a clear recommendation cannot be made.
2. See *Playing It Safe: Bleeding Disorders, Sports and Exercise* from the National Hemophilia Society, available at www.hemophilia.org.
3. The Universal Data Collection (UDC) is a surveillance project of the CDC that monitors the safety of the blood supply and the occurrence of joint complications. BMI is a measure of obesity determined by using weight and height to calculate a number called the "body mass index." An adult who has a BMI between 25 and 29.9 is considered overweight. An adult who has a BMI of 30 or higher is considered obese. Source: www.CDC.gov.

    U.S. Department of Health and Human Services, Public Health Service. Report on the Universal Data Collection System (UDC) [Internet]. Atlanta: Centers for Disease Control and Prevention, National Center for Infectious Diseases; 1999 Mar;1(1):16 [cited 2010 Feb 16]. Available from: http://www.cdc.gov/ncbddd/hbd/documents/UDCReport3-99.pdf
4. These techniques would be useful in preventing or treating the first stages of contracture, but they would not be useful for moderate to severe contracture. Moderate contracture requires serial casting (when a cast is applied and removed weekly, with each cast gradually increasing the range of motion), dynamic splints, or joint-active splints (which are spring loaded), or wedging. Severe contracture can be resolved only by surgery.
5. Diathermy is the application of local heat to body tissues using electromagnetic radiation at high frequency, electric currents, or ultrasonic waves.

SUMMARY 12
Keeping Joints Healthy

- Joint health is key to overall good health and improved quality of life.
- To minimize or delay joint destruction, infuse early and aggressively.
- Symptoms of an early joint bleed include limping, tingling, or warmth in the joint.
- Left untreated, symptoms of a joint bleed include pain in the joint, stiffness, heat, swelling, and limited range of motion.
- Engage your child in some kind of regular physical activity: strong, flexible muscles help stabilize joints and decrease joint and muscle bleeds.
- Warming up and stretching properly will help prevent muscle bleeds, and are just as important as exercise.
- Try to find other ways for your child to participate in sports when he can't participate physically.
- Promote healthy weight with a healthful diet.
- Physical therapy can help keep muscles strong to protect joints, and can ease stiff joints into flexible joints after a bleed.
- Support devices like a wheelchair, splint, or crutch can help rest a joint to prevent further damage, giving the joint time to heal.

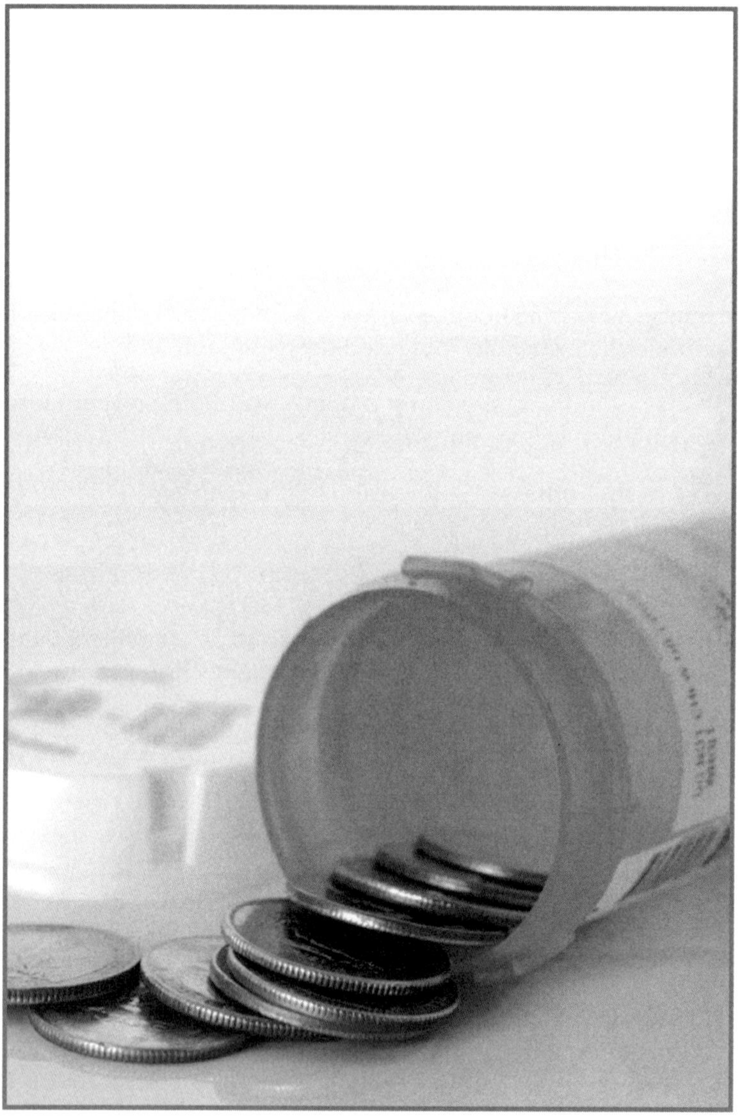

13 Insurance and Inhibitors

Hemophilia is expensive to treat, but hemophilia with an inhibitor is extraordinarily expensive. Why? Higher doses of standard factor VIII or IX; more costly bypassing agents; more frequent and longer dosing; more hospital visits; ITI; and prophylaxis with bypassing agents for some patients—these all add to the cost of treating hemophilia with inhibitors. It's essential to have some form of insurance to help pay for your factor concentrate and healthcare services. Indeed, new healthcare reform will make it mandatory to have insurance in the coming years. Make sure your coverage includes inhibitor treatment, and monitor your coverage for changes that threaten to limit hemophilia and inhibitor care. You'll need to know these essentials:

- Who pays for your hemophilia care?
- How might ongoing insurance reforms affect your policy?
- Which kind of plan do you have?
- What does your plan cover and not cover?
- How can you manage costs?
- How much are your co-pays?
- Are there restrictions on where you can get treatment, lab studies, or products?

Above all, families with inhibitors have three main concerns: (1) understanding limits (caps), (2) managing out-of-pocket expenses, and (3) keeping insurance.

> *The insurance challenge we face is that we will cap out sooner than we would have if our son hadn't developed an inhibitor, because he went through ITI. His current medical expenditures total $535,000 and he's only three!* —Sasha Cheatham, Oklahoma

Who Pays for Insurance?

In a nutshell, here's how the hemophilia business works: factor concentrates are made at a pharmaceutical manufacturing facility, sold to a distributor (home care company, specialty pharmacy, or HTC), and then delivered to you. The distributor invoices the total cost of the factor to your payer—the private insurance company or state or federal program that pays for factor and hemophilia healthcare. The distributor is eventually reimbursed by your payer for each shipment or "sale."

Private insurance companies include Blue Cross Blue Shield, Cigna, and Aetna. These companies sell policies to employers, who then cover their employees' medical expenses. Policies are also sold to individuals.

Public programs include Medicaid, which insures low-income people, and Medicare, which covers people aged sixty-five and older, and those with certain chronic conditions. Of Americans with hemophilia, approximately 65% use private insurance (group and individual policies), 25% use Medicaid, and 7% use Medicare.[1]

> We have only used Medicaid. Kyler is close to having used $1 million of insurance. Thankfully, Medicaid pays for everything! —Anonymous

Hemophilia High on Insurance Radar

Right now, healthcare insurance is undergoing massive change in America. On March 22, 2010, President Obama signed into law H.R. 3590, the Patient Protection and Affordable Care Act. Some believe that this legislation represents the biggest change in the U.S. healthcare system since Medicaid was introduced in 1965. And it will radically change insurance for people with chronic disorders.

Even with new laws in place, payers may try to cut their escalating costs by looking for new ways to limit your healthcare options, including limiting choice of factor product, factor provider, or treatment regimen. Why? Hemophilia is one of the most expensive of all chronic disorders. Factor concentrate is a specialty pharmaceutical—an injectible, biological product. It's fragile and must be carefully manufactured, transported, stored, and distributed.

And factor is only one biological product. There are hundreds, all with big price tags. Total costs for all biological products have risen at a shocking rate, and state and private insurer budgets haven't kept up with rising costs. Law requires state budgets to be balanced, and on average today, Medicaid alone consumes 20% of all state budgets. As more advanced factor products entered the market and more patients started prophylaxis, hemophilia costs began to crush state Medicaid budgets. Private employers begged insurance companies to negotiate with manufacturers for lower prices. And payers have responded by employing various methods to cut costs, including these attempts:

- Lowering reimbursement price per unit of factor
- Limiting choice of factor provider, such as home delivery service
- Requiring prior authorization of factor shipments
- Increasing co-payments for medicine
- Limiting choice of factor product brand through formularies or preferred drug lists (PDL)[2]

Healthcare costs must be reduced even further in the future, but cost cutting could harm your child's treatment. Why? Unfortunately, payers may not know enough about hemophilia or inhibitors when they make budget-cutting decisions. So it may be up to you to educate them. You can best educate them when you know their language and understand your policy, so you can challenge payer policy changes that might affect you.

> Most of the insurance reps you contact regarding claims have no idea what you're talking about. When one called and wanted my son's infusion logs, she couldn't believe any kid costs this much. She didn't know what hemophilia was, and I told her she needed to get educated. —Anonymous

Which Kind of Plan Do You Have?

If you have private insurance, you need to know the kind of plan you use: traditional *indemnity* plan or nontraditional *managed care* plan. Your human resource department at work or your HTC social worker can help you determine this. Here, we provide a quick review.

Approximately 10% of hemophilia patients with private insurance use traditional indemnity plans, also called *fee-for-service* (FFS). Compared to other types of plans, these plans generally allow more freedom of choice of doctors. Most American employees use some kind of nontraditional managed care plan. There's a good chance that if you have private insurance, your child with hemophilia will be insured through a *managed care organization* (MCO). MCOs usually allow less freedom of choice of doctors than FFS plans allow. If you have a managed care plan, you'll have one of three basic types:

- Health Maintenance Organization (HMO)
- Preferred Provider Organization (PPO) or Exclusive Provider Organization (EPO)
- Point of Service (POS)

The differences among these plans? Coverage and cost. Your best bet is to first identify the kind of plan you have, and then ask specific questions about coverage and how much treatments will cost. Then you can estimate your annual costs, prepare your budget, and find ways to help cover costs.

> We have a private plan, Blue Cross Blue Shield. I'd say we have spent so far about $40 million on our son's care. Mostly on factor, but we have had two wheelchairs, physical therapy, many hospitalizations, orthopedics, specialists, and prescription drugs. —Joyce Hewitt, Michigan

Which Services Does Your Plan Cover?

Whether you have a traditional or nontraditional plan, you need to know exactly which services and products are covered under your policy. The insurance company should explain your coverage in writing, in either a summary of benefits document or a letter. *Never assume that coverage exists for any aspect of hemophilia.*

> Read your insurance policy carefully. Simply reading the summary of benefits is not enough. I once had to direct the customer service rep to a certain page, paragraph and sentence in our policy in order to get a $250-per-month prescription covered. Know your exact policy: one person's United Insurance plan can be vastly different from the next person's United plan. —Sonji Wilkes, Colorado

Any health insurance plan has two parts, representing two different budgets:

1. ***Medical benefit (major medical):*** covers all clinical services including doctor visits, diagnostic tests, and surgery

2. ***Pharmacy benefit:*** covers outpatient drugs

> Beau started ITI when he turned age twenty-two months. We worried about insurance, but factor costs were applied to the pharmacy benefit, not to major medical. Under pharmacy, we had only a $40 co-pay for one month's supply, and no lifetime cap. We felt very fortunate! —Kari Atkinson, Iowa

So in addition to knowing what's covered, be sure you know what's covered under each budget—medical and pharmacy. Ask these questions to find out what your plan covers:

- ***Is factor covered?*** If factor isn't considered a drug, it may be covered under the medical benefit. Does your major medical have a lifetime cap? What is the limit? For most people with hemophilia, factor is covered under the medical benefit.

Our expenses have been about $2.4 million this year. —Derek Nelson, Utah

- *Is there a co-payment?* A co-pay is a flat dollar amount you'll need to pay for a medical service, such as a $10 co-pay for an office visit.

- *Is there a co-payment for prescriptions?* When factor is covered under the pharmacy benefit, you may need to pay a percentage of the drug cost, such as 25%, out-of-pocket each time you get the drug. This adds up; and when you reach the policy's maximum, typically $3,000 to $5,000, prescription drugs are then covered at 100%.

- *What is the coinsurance?* This is the amount of money (or a percentage of costs) that you must pay out-of-pocket before the insurance plan will cover all costs at 100% in a given year.

- *What is the deductible?* An amount of money that the insured patient must pay before the insurance provider's coverage begins.

- *Are there brand restrictions?* A *formulary* or *preferred drug list* (PDL) is a list of prescription drugs that are approved and covered by an insurance plan for its members. Before you enroll in a new plan, find out if the plan uses a formulary, and if your factor brand is on it.

- *How is factor delivered?* Is it delivered by hospital outpatient pharmacy, 340B program (HTCs that sell factor), specialty pharmacy, home care company, or mail-order company? Do you have choice? Does your payer try to influence you to use its preferred provider?

- *Is there a pre-existing condition clause?* This allows insurance companies to restrict or deny coverage if you have an illness or chronic disorder before you sign up. Fortunately, the federal Health Insurance Portability and Accountability Act (HIPAA) of 1996 began protecting patients with pre-existing medical conditions from being denied insurance when switching to a new group policy. H.R. 3590, the Patient Protection and Affordable Care Act, eliminates pre-existing condition exclusions for children and for all new plans, effective six months after enactment, and for all Americans beginning in 2014.

- *Is there a limit (cap)?* This is the maximum amount of money a payer will allow for healthcare services during a certain time period, if you use the same plan. Once you reach this cap, you are no longer covered. The Patient Protection and Affordable Care Act prohibits insurers from imposing lifetime limits on benefits. But you may still have an annual cap.

Always be aware of the cap and try to save in every way possible to keep costs down in order to keep from capping out. —Sasha Cheatham, Oklahoma

- *Is prophylactic treatment covered?* Prophylaxis may be required if your child successfully completes ITI, and it can dramatically increase the cost of hemophilia treatment.

- *Is home treatment covered?* Treating your child at home can significantly reduce medical costs. Will your plan allow you to infuse at home? Store factor concentrate at home? Use a home care company to deliver factor? Hire a home infusion nurse?

- *Does the policy have riders?* Riders are legal documents that modify or amend coverage under an insurance policy. Sometimes riders are used to exclude pre-existing conditions. How will riders affect your standard benefit package?

- *Does the policy include catastrophic illness coverage?* This is coverage for a major healthcare expense, such as an organ transplant, or for an expensive disease or disorder, such as hemophilia.

- *At what age will your child no longer be covered under your policy?* Federal law now allows dependent children up to age twenty-six to be covered by a parent's insurance, even if the child is no longer living with a parent, or is no longer a student, and regardless of the child's marital status.

Mind-boggling, isn't it? The American insurance system is complicated, and it's essential that you learn about it to protect your child's healthcare. The new Patient Protection and Affordable Care Act has changed many of the rules. This legislation attempts to make healthcare affordable for all, especially people with chronic disorders—like your child. At the very least, remember this: never accept a medical insurance policy without first knowing the answers to the questions above—in writing.

HIPAA: Protecting Against Pre-Existing Clauses

Most parents worry about their insurance payer's reaction when they add a newly diagnosed baby to their existing health insurance plan, or decide to change plans. Ironically, insurance companies don't always want to insure those who need it most. A pre-existing medical condition like hemophilia used to disqualify applicants. But there is good news now.

HIPAA was created to protect you against pre-existing condition clauses when you want to change jobs or insurance plans.

HIPAA regulations mean that individuals who are eligible for group health plans can't be denied coverage or have their coverage cancelled if they have pre-existing medical conditions, as long as they meet two criteria:

1. They have had at least twelve months of continuous coverage.
2. They have had no lapse in coverage for sixty-three days.

HIPAA also makes it easier for you to switch plans. It provides continued coverage through a group or individual private plan, Medicare, Medicaid, SCHIP,[3] Tricare (military), and any state or local public health plan. And it's especially easy to switch plans during your payer's open enrollment period. Many insurance plans offer open enrollment periods, usually once a year, when anyone can join regardless of pre-existing conditions.

And as we've just discussed, the Patient Protection and Affordable Care Act eliminates pre-existing condition exclusions for all children and for all new plans, effective six months after its enactment, and for all Americans beginning in 2014.

If your insurance company has a pre-existing condition clause that requires a waiting period, you will be eligible for insurance after that time is up. In the meantime, you are financially responsible for the monthly premiums and all medical bills. The waiting period could be three months to one year, so be prepared with a supply of factor or alternate forms of coverage.[4]

Managing Costs

Even when you have a great insurance policy, understand your coverage, and have answers in writing, you'll still need to contain costs, especially if you have to pay some expenses yourself. The greatest cost in hemophilia treatment, even without an inhibitor, is factor. You must know the price per unit of factor. If you don't know, *call your factor provider and insurance provider today*.

To learn how to estimate out-of-pocket costs in advance, be sure you know the following:

- annual policy premium
- annual limit (cap)
- percentage of co-payment
- annual deductible per person

- annual out-of-pocket maximum
- annual prescription costs

We maxed out a $2 million cap in nine months. And we still got a bill for $400,000 for medicine shipped to us after we maxed out. I called the specialty pharmacy and told them nobody could pay this. They wouldn't let me use the home care company I wanted, and they charged me for saline, heparin, everything! I was furious. They wouldn't tell me what they charged for factor. —Debbie Branch, Kansas

Some costs, such as emergency surgery or hospitalization, are unpredictable. Other costs, such as clinic visits, prophylaxis, and even specific bleeding patterns, are predictable. Try to calculate predictable costs:

average number of infusions per month	X	average IU of factor required per bleed	X	cost per unit of factor	=	total factor costs per month

Even our homecare company went into a tizzy when we calculated costs: $1.15 per IU x 1,300 IU three days a week = $4,485 a week! —Carri Nease, Maryland

I don't know for sure our child's lifetime expenses, but in the last three years alone it has been several million. He's been having a joint bleed for so long I believe last month alone was probably $800,000 with hospital visits, factor, medical supplies, casts, and a brace. —Cicely Evans, Massachusetts

Here are strategies to help you manage costs:

- ***Question healthcare providers.*** Make sure that all services are medically necessary. Ask in advance why a procedure is being ordered and how much it will cost.
- ***Know your cost per unit or microgram.***
- ***Investigate reimbursement programs.*** Many home care and pharmaceutical companies offer help if you can prove financial hardship. They may waive fees or portions of the bill, or even provide free product.
- ***Explore home (or self-) infusion.*** Home infusion saves money. Avoid the ER whenever possible.

- *Get an MSA (pretax medical savings account).* Estimate costs, and put money toward the MSA, which also covers new eyeglasses, ancillaries, and OTC medications.
- *Consider secondary insurance.* Obtain a policy through your employer or on your own.
- *Coordinate benefits.* Do this through your spouse's insurance plan when possible.
- *Eliminate unnecessary items or services.* Fancy packaging or home nursing services, for example, can add extra cost.
- *Compare the prescribed dose with the dose delivered.* "Dose creep" happens when your factor provider delivers more IU per vial than you need, costing you extra money unnecessarily.
- *Examine your Explanation of Benefits (EOB) carefully.* Request itemized hospital bills to be sure you're charged only for what you used or ordered.

> We are getting financial assistance from hemophilia foundations to help us make our $2,000 deductible. My husband has neurofibrosis, and he's the main moneymaker. It's been a stressful time. I've been working three jobs. We called Patient Services, Inc. [see appendix A] and they helped. Don't ever be afraid to ask for help, especially financial assistance. —Ashley Druckenmiller, Iowa

Record, Document, File

Each visit to the doctor or hospital, each lab test, each service, and each factor order generates medical expenses and medical bills. Eventually, the medical service provider or factor provider will invoice your payer. Your payer will reimburse your provider. Your payer may send you an EOB showing how much was paid and whether you owe a co-payment. The medical provider will bill you if you owe a co-pay, or bill you for any product or service not covered by your insurance policy.

> Insurance companies have no knowledge about hemophilia and inhibitors, and you have to fight for your son's medication. I've had bill collectors calling because insurance companies would not pay on time for Austin's medical needs. I've had to fight many times to get our physician covered under our plan. I've had to fight for our rights at hospitals, and for the home care company we wanted. —Julie Baker, Nevada

> I've developed a relationship with our case manager. We tell him about changes in therapy, why we make changes, why he will see product usage go up, why there will be no factor VIII claims for a few months; we pass along clinical information so he knows there is a clinical basis for what we do. I want my insurance company to be part of my care team. —Derek Nelson, Utah

From day one, you must keep comprehensive, accurate records of all your EOBs, your insurance policy, and any other relevant information. To track your expenses and services, *now* is the time to set up a filing system, perhaps in a portable file case or on your computer. You never know when you'll need your records as evidence of coverage and payment, to discuss with your payer, or even to present in court.

> We've been aggressive with our insurance company. We monitor everything; we have SevenSECURE[®5] to monitor our caps. We track our son's EOBs and started a spreadsheet to list reimbursements. It paid off! I had to fight the payer when it didn't cover his brain surgery because we used a non-PPO provider. It took eighteen months to get our money back. Track your bills, and don't automatically think the bill sent to you is right. Question everything. —Corby Lust, Arizona

Always keep accurate records of these essentials:

- all medical procedures
- any phone calls with your payer
- all correspondence with your payer

Keep records of everything to help you . . .

- determine whether your deductible has been met,
- know your portion of costs,
- record any billing errors, and
- track how close you are your annual limit.

Records are essential when your child has many bleeds or is covered by two insurance policies. You also rack up extraordinary charges when your child is on ITI, and you may be asked to defend these charges.

> Insurance companies will wait as long as possible to pay claims. My son recently started using tons of factor for a bleed, so I took pictures in case they gave us a hard time about payment! —Julie Baker, Nevada

Insurance and Inhibitors

> **Keeping Good Insurance Records**
>
> - Read and file the EOBs generated when your payer covers the medical bill for any treatment.
>
> - Photocopy all your claim forms and any correspondence with the hospital or insurance company.
>
> - Take notes on phone conversations with your hospital or insurance company. Document full names, titles, time and date of call, subject, and conclusion. Get direct phone numbers, not just extensions. Ask for and record the case number for each call.
>
> - If you call to ask about alternate insurance policies, you don't have to identify yourself. Don't reveal information that may disqualify you or lead to discrimination.
>
> - Once you've received satisfactory answers from the insurance company, follow up: get all those answers in writing.

To the Max

Regardless of the evolution of American healthcare, we should never forget that for many years, inhibitor families struggled with the challenge of capping out.

> *In seven weeks, I've ordered $300,000 of NovoSeven just for ankle bleeds.*
> —Anonymous

> *Leland underwent the Malmö protocol for ITI, for eighteen months. Eventually we had to accept that we wouldn't beat the inhibitor. We had a $2 million cap when we started; we went through $1.5 million just doing ITI, and then my husband's insurance changed—and thankfully, we had no cap.*
> —Jane, Massachusetts

But even with the end of lifetime limits, you'll still face annual limits—the dollar amount of healthcare products and services you can use in one year. You'll need to learn about your policy's annual limits, and carefully monitor your expenses.

When You Have No Insurance

If you have no insurance, your family may be eligible for Medicaid, the state assistance program, which covers all expenses for hemophilia and inhibitor treatment and has no limit. But to be on Medicaid, the family income may need to be very low. This is actually a sacrifice for some families, who normally would be able to earn good wages but would easily hit their insurance caps and run out of insurance. Check your state requirement, as each state differs. Currently in Pennsylvania, for example, all children with hemophilia are eligible for Medicaid until age eighteen without regard to family income.

> This is not a cheap disorder. We are charged about $2,000 a dose for factor, incurred $72,000 for one hospitalization, and need medical equipment and home care. —Jessica Herren, Pennsylvania

> We've had several caps. The first was $1 million, which Matthew exceeded when he was eighteen months old. My husband's employer paid $13 million out-of-pocket for his care, gave us an additional $2 million, and then said we had exceeded all they could offer. Since then Matt has been on public assistance through California's Genetically Handicapped Persons Program. —Debbie Porter, California

The good news is that under the Patient Protection and Affordable Care Act, uninsured American adults and legal immigrants with pre-existing conditions will be able to obtain health coverage through a new program that establishes a temporary national high-risk pool. So if you have lost your insurance for six months, and have hemophilia and inhibitors, you will be eligible to enroll in the high-risk pool and receive subsidized premiums for insurance. This means that under the 2010 healthcare reform bill, you should never be without health insurance.

Trying to Keep Insurance

When asked about her insurance challenges related to the inhibitor treatment, one mother voiced her main worry: "Keeping it." Even if you have great insurance, insurance plans and policies change every year. What's working one year may not be available the next, even from the same employer.

> My husband worked for a large, multinational company. We always believed that working for a large company would protect our coverage. We found out that was wrong. —Debbie Porter, California

Warning: Your employer might change plans without your consent. This means you'll need to again ask the questions listed earlier in this chapter about coverage and cost.

> I was working for Kmart, where we used Humana insurance for seven years—they were wonderful. When it came time to renew, Humana wasn't offered; Kmart chose someone else. So we selected Coventry. We had a grace period to line everything up so Coventry would cover everything. There were phone calls and getting through to right person, and they didn't understand hemophilia, but we finally got a case manager who was like a guardian angel. Lee was the only hemophilia patient on the plan. —Eleth Ridenhour, Kansas

Some families even must switch employers to maintain coverage. This is always challenging, but it's easier if you live in an urban area and have a reliable work record, solid experience, or a good education. Many families live in rural areas or don't have extensive education, and their insurance options may be limited.

> Over the years, I changed jobs when we found that our son was capping out his policy. We've had at least nine different policies over the past fourteen years. I estimate Austin's medical bills at around $9 million. After we capped out my policy, his father's insurance had to back us up. We currently have $7 million left on this cap. It's enough to get Austin through high school and his first two years of college, unless his factor costs increase. —Julie Baker, Nevada

Ironically, and perhaps hardest to comprehend, our insurance system makes it easier for people with chronic conditions to stay on welfare than to have paying jobs. The burden on families—to handle inhibitors, treat their child, worry about costs, and plan for the future—becomes a nightmare.

> When I wasn't working, there was no problem. I was on Medicaid and didn't have a co-pay. All of our hemophilia expenses were covered. Once I went back to work, my insurance became an issue. I work part time, so I am limited—we can make only $2,100 a month. When I do get a full-time job, insurance may become our nightmare. —Anonymous

Simply understanding your basic health insurance policy is daunting. You need help navigating this maze, and help is available from many sources (see appendix A). You'll never have to go it alone. But do your part: know your insurance coverage, keep accurate records, update your child's personal medical information annually, and question everything. Health insurance is a necessity for people with hemophilia and inhibitors. Never be complacent or assume that someone else will take care of it. Each family with inhibitors is different, and only you can know your plan and your needs. Only you can monitor changes and prepare for the future of healthcare. ■

Managing Your Child's Inhibitor

■NOTES

1. Many other state insurance programs are not covered here.
2. Formularies and PDLs define which prescription drugs are covered and reimbursed. Formularies are used by insurance companies and can include both generic and brand-name drugs. PDLs are used by state Medicaid offices and limit approval of brand-name drugs, usually within a therapeutic class. For example, a plan may have a PDL that lists and approves for reimbursement only one brand of recombinant factor VIII. A PDL differs slightly from a formulary. For example, the formulary might allow any recombinant factor brand, but the PDL restricts your choice to one or two brand names of recombinant product.
3. State Children's Health Insurance Program (SCHIP) provides health insurance coverage to uninsured children under age nineteen in families that meet certain financial guidelines: incomes too high to qualify for Medicaid but too low to afford private family coverage.
4. See appendix A for manufacturer information about compassionate care programs.
5. SevenSECURE is a program of Novo Nordisk that assists patients with inhibitors. It helps with health insurance and coverage, offers educational grants and scholarships, and provides reimbursement assistance with medical and dental expenses.

SUMMARY 13
Insurance and Inhibitors

- It's essential to have some form of insurance to pay for factor concentrate and healthcare services.

- Families with inhibitors have three main concerns: (1) understanding limits (caps), (2) managing out-of-pocket expenses, and (3) keeping insurance.

- Private insurance companies sell policies to employers, who then cover their employees' medical expenses. Policies are also sold to individuals.

- Public programs include Medicaid, which insures low-income people, and Medicare, which covers people aged sixty-five and older and those with certain chronic conditions. Public programs also include state high-risk pools.

- Know exactly which services and products are covered under your policy. *Never assume that coverage exists for any aspect of hemophilia.*

- A health insurance plan has two parts, representing two different budgets: (1) the medical benefit covers all clinical services including doctor visits, diagnostic tests, and surgery; (2) the pharmacy benefit covers outpatient drugs.

- The 2010 Patient Protection and Affordable Care Act eliminates lifetime limits and pre-existing condition exclusions. Speak with your insurer or social worker about the details of this new law.

- Know the answers to these questions: Is factor is covered? Is there a co-payment? Coinsurance? Deductible? Catastrophic illness coverage? Annual limit? Coverage for prophylaxis? Home treatment? Are there riders? Brand restrictions?

- Your dependent child with hemophilia can be covered by your insurance up to age twenty-six even if he is no longer living with you, or is no longer a student, and regardless of his marital status.

- Manage costs by knowing the cost for factor and estimating out-of-pocket costs.

- Keep comprehensive, accurate records of all your EOBs, your insurance policy, and any other relevant information.

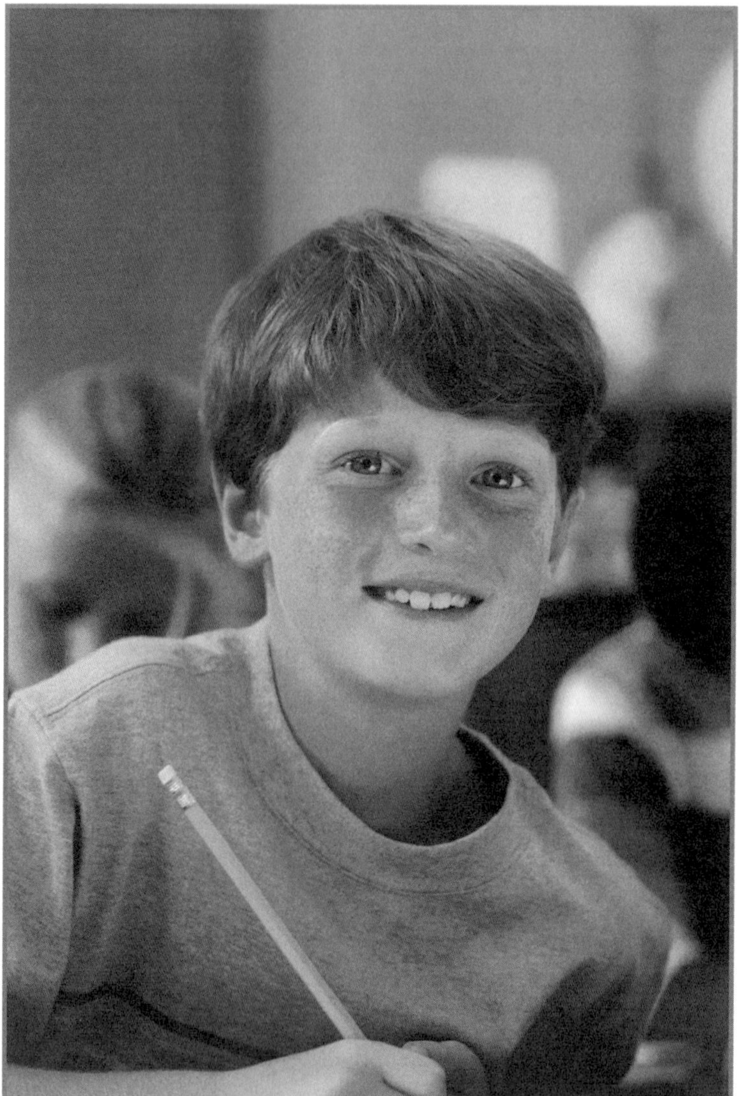

14 Attending School When You Have Inhibitors

Attending school is at once a triumph and a challenge for families with inhibitors. But it's vitally important that your child attend school through twelfth grade, and preferably on to college, because one day he'll need a job that provides good heath insurance. A solid education will open more doors for him; offer more selection in jobs and locations; give him confidence and purpose; and allow him to be independent. At the same time, school is one of the greatest developmental hurdles for parents and children. Trying to maintain attendance and good grades while battling inhibitors, and sometimes chronic pain, is difficult and draining. Many children with inhibitors attend school regularly with little interruption, while others may miss a significant number of school days. Planning ahead and working closely with the school and your HTC are the keys to success.

You may have mixed feelings as your child enters school for the first time and must be away from your protective care, mingling with other children and teachers who know little about his condition. Like all children starting school, your child may be anxious about this venture into independence. Your attitude is the best predictor of how he will handle the transition. If you show confidence and excitement about his new adventure, then he will too. Many families with inhibitors have overcome school challenges and succeeded, and so can you.

> *Everything depends on how the parent handles the introduction of a bleeding disorder. At the beginning of the school year, I always meet with school staff to refresh their memory about bleeding disorders. I stress that I prefer they call me to check out an incident rather than ignore something or worry about bothering me. This makes them feel at ease and gives them a huge sense of security.* —Cazandra Campos-MacDonald, New Mexico

> *Colton loves high school. Teachers have always been receptive to my speaking with them, letting them know what's going on.* —Debbie Branch, Kansas

Some school issues that many families with inhibitors encounter:

Working with school staff: how to educate them about inhibitors; how to coordinate communication

Dosing: how to reduce disruption in the daily school routine

Missed school: how to get lessons and homework done during hospitalizations bleeds, and recovery

Special education considerations: how to determine if a 504 plan, an IEP, or an IHP is right for your child (see "Accommodation Plans" section)

Alternative schooling: does your child need a tutor or access to "distance learning" via the Internet?

Being different: how to help your child fit in with peers

Working with School Staff

Making sure your child is happy, confident, and healthy at school is a team effort now. It involves you, your child, your HTC, and school staff. What, how, and when should you tell staff about his hemophilia and inhibitors? How will his disorder be explained to classmates? What special needs must be addressed?

School staff must handle a dual diagnosis: hemophilia and inhibitors. Both are rare, so don't be surprised if staff members know little, if anything, about hemophilia. They may imagine profuse bleeding and emergencies. They may worry about liability. They may wonder . . . *Can he use scissors? Can he play at recess? What happens when he gets hurt? Will he bleed excessively? Will I be blamed?*

> Reece is three, and he recently started preschool. I think the director and teachers were apprehensive at first, but my husband and I met with them, explained some misconceptions, and gave them the facts of Reece's condition. By the end of the meeting, they felt comfortable about handling the issues.
> —Sasha Cheatham, Oklahoma

When you first learned the diagnosis, remember how much better you felt when you armed yourself with knowledge? Your child's teachers will, too. But how should you educate them?

- Invite your HTC nurse or social worker to give a talk at school.
- Bring resources about school and hemophilia.[1]
- Provide a cell phone number for emergencies or questions.
- Stress normalcy, whenever possible.
- Arrange a meeting with school staff *before* school starts.
- Meet with school staff again in four months to review.

The initial meeting should include your child's head teacher, assistant teacher, teacher's aides, principal, administrative assistant, physical education (PE) teacher, playground aides, and school nurse. Ask your HTC nurse coordinator to attend. He or she may also want to meet with school staff in private to answer any questions they are reluctant to ask in front of you. Your child doesn't need to be present at either meeting, although he should be told about it. Ask your child if he'd like to attend.

> We gave the school written information, and our outreach worker visited them to talk about hemophilia. We try to build a good relationship with teachers and office staff so they feel comfortable approaching us, asking questions, and calling. We gave them many contact numbers including the hospital, HTC, and extended family and friends. —Richard and Lynley Scott, New Zealand

Keep your messages simple. Staff must believe your child when he says he needs to call home or needs treatment. They should never single him out, announce that he has hemophilia without your permission or his, or make an issue of his medical identification bracelet, CVAD, wheelchair, or bruises. They should take normal precautions and observe normal safety practices. Remind them to follow standard first-aid procedures, if needed, while they are trying to notify you.[2]

> We stressed that if there is any concern, it's important to call us so we—not they—can do the decision-making. At first we had lots of phone calls, mostly out of fear. But now that staff are more knowledgeable, they call us less often. During Andrew's second year of school, he had lots of nose bleeds. Initially we were called the minute one started, and we would tell them to sit him quietly for five minutes and call us back. Each time they became more confident, until gradually they could handle basic nose bleeds without calling us. —Richard and Lynley Scott, New Zealand

> Thomas attended preschool two days a week. We went to a staff meeting the week before school started and did an hour-long PowerPoint presentation on hemophilia and inhibitors. Our main concern: the playground—it scared me. Our main point: call us! And they never have, because he's done well there. —Sonji Wilkes, Colorado

Later in the school year, you can meet again. School staff will have more questions and may be more comfortable and eager to learn, as you once were.

The Teacher-Parent-Child Partnership

Many teachers have students with special needs; they may be completely comfortable with your child. Still, chances are your child is the first with hemophilia that his teacher has met. A teacher may develop concerns when left alone with your child for the day. Afraid of injury, fearing the sight of blood, and anxious about being held responsible, a worried teacher might intentionally or unintentionally be overprotective, single out your child, deny a bleed, or overreact.

To avoid overprotection based on the fear of a bleed, ask the teacher to be proactive and watch for symptoms of a bleed. Provide a list of all school activities that are allowed for your child, and a list of activities that are off limits. Ask staff to find creative ways to include your child in an activity, despite a bleed that sidelines him.

To avoid singling out your child, the teacher can arrange a face-saving way to exclude him if he must avoid a particular activity, such as PE. This should be something that doesn't shame him or draw attention to his disorder.

> For school trips, we assess the risks. Sometimes one of us needs to go as a parent helper. If the risk isn't so great, we don't go. If Andrew has a bleed or is recovering from one, we might have him sit out from an activity such as PE. But we try to encourage him and the teachers to participate as fully as possible.
> —Richard and Lynley Scott, New Zealand

On some days, your child can participate in school and show no outward signs of bleeding, particularly if he is recovering from a bleed. His teacher may not recognize the need for rest. Be sure to inform your child's teacher of what's happening at home, and in general, that he or she will not be expected to diagnose your child. The teacher can trust your child's assessment of a bleed or his recovery, with or without notes from home.

> We had arrangements with PE: Jake will tell you when something is wrong, and believe him! He never fakes. If he says he can't do something, then believe him. But try to find ways to allow him to participate. —Molly A. Eppenbach, Nebraska

Your child's teacher may overreact to bleeds and injuries, or even long absences. But teachers need to model emotional maturity for all. Injuries, bleeds, and absences should be handled calmly and competently, with concern but with minimal fuss.

Teachers give us information about how our children are adjusting to school. They can alert us to signs of depression, such as withdrawal or slipping grades. Communication, trust, and respect between parent and teacher are key building blocks of a positive student-teacher relationship. Keep communication channels open by scheduling periodic meetings to answer staff questions. Keep his teacher up-to-date with events at home, such as a traumatic bleed while on vacation, the birth of a sibling—anything that might cause stress and lead to a bleed, or might be reflected in school participation and attitude. Many teachers have voicemail or email, and you can use either as a way to stay in touch.

> *Email is an easy way to send the teacher a note about what's happening: "Thomas said his foot hurt when he went to bed last night. He appears fine this morning, but I just wanted to give you a heads-up in case anything arises at school today." —Sonji Wilkes, Colorado*

> *It's important to get to know the teachers and office staff well. They see your child the most and will address any issues if your child becomes unwell or has a bleed. —Richard and Lynley Scott, New Zealand*

Your most important team member may be the school nurse. Find out what the nurse knows about hemophilia, and then supply any missing information. Is the nurse willing to be involved with hemophilia and assume some responsibility for your child? Can you infuse in the nurse's office, involve the nurse in the infusion, or store factor in the nursing office?

> *Logan missed the first seven weeks of preschool due to an ankle bleed. He attended the rest of last year, did well, and loved it. He had no bleeding issues. The staff was not apprehensive. The school nurse told me she had seven other kids in district with hemophilia, and she knew quite a bit. I was leery at first. I waited hours for the phone to ring, but it rang only twice, and they were minor things. —Anonymous*

Check with your school nurse about state regulations that might prohibit infusions at school, and find out if the nurse is allowed and licensed to infuse your child.

Accommodation Plans

Chronic disorders place an extra burden on families who are trying to comply with school logistics, policies, and classroom assignments. Sometimes the disorder demands so much attention that schools must make special accommodations for the child to maintain his student status. Accommodations are a must for a child with hemophilia and an inhibitor.

All public schools in the United States are required by federal law to provide services for children with special needs. The eligibility criteria and implementation of services vary by state and school district. Your state's special education department should have a website and information about its accommodation plans and state laws. You can also call your local school district and speak to the special education department.

A school district may be required to provide one or more of these accommodations:

- home schooling and tutoring
- specialized instruction
- modifications to the curriculum
- accommodations in nonacademic and extracurricular activities
- adaptive equipment or assistive technology devices
- an aide
- assistance with health-related needs
- school transportation

And the district may provide other related services and accommodations. Your child might need special environmental changes, such as a wheelchair ramp, extra time to get to class after the bell, or help boarding the school bus. Schools are usually anxious to work with you to meet your child's educational needs, and agreements about special accommodations are often reached without rancor. But sometimes the child's problems are particularly severe, or the school may not be flexible enough. Fortunately, the law protects your child's needs in these cases.

Accommodation plans include an IHP (Individual Health Plan), an IEP (Individualized Education Plan), and a 504 plan.[3]

IHP

This plan ensures access to education for students with special healthcare needs, regardless of whether the student is classified as eligible for special education. It's a formal written agreement involving the school administration and licensed registered school nurse, the student's family, the student, and the student's healthcare providers. The plan's goal is to coordinate health and nursing services at school, to and from school, and at home. The IHP describes the student's health needs and specifies how the school will meet these needs during the school day, on field trips, during special events, and in sports. The plan also details procedures for health emergencies. For example, your child's IHP might allow for infusions to be done on school property, or for your child to keep his cell phone on at all times.

IEP

An IEP is designed to meet a child's unique academic and functional needs, offering a program that is fundamentally different from the way other students are learning. The federal government reimburses the school for providing services under an IEP. This plan is a legally binding document created by teachers, parents, school administrators, related services personnel, and students (when age appropriate). An IEP outlines the child's present levels of academic and functional achievement, and provides a statement of measurable yearly goals, listing any special and appropriate accommodations. An IEP requires progress reports. For example, an IEP might provide a home tutor for a child who misses school regularly, or may allow for extended absences because of medical treatment.[4]

> When Matthew was little, he had a full-time aide during the school day. By fifth grade we felt he no longer needed the aide, but he has certain teachers looking out for him. Currently he receives extra time between classes and can eat lunch in the classroom when needed. —Debbie Porter, California

> Eshton is sometimes given extensions based on the assignment. He has a small refrigerator reserved specifically for his ice packs, supplies, and factor. —Joyce Hewitt, Michigan

504 plan

This accommodation plan prohibits discrimination based on disability. It requires schools to ensure that students with disabilities have full opportunities to participate in all aspects of regular school on an equal basis with students without disabilities. This means that if your child needs access to the regular curriculum, his school must make sure he has access. No evaluations or progress reports are required. A 504 is offered to students who don't qualify for special education services, but who have needs that require some accommodation to allow access to regular educational services. Such plans are not federally funded and come directly out of the school's budget. A 504 plan might mean that your child receives extended time on tests or assignments, or peer assistance with note-taking.

■ ■ ■

How do these plans compare? An IEP offers more rights and protections than does a 504 plan. Any child covered under an IEP is automatically covered under Section 504 laws, but the opposite is not true.

IEPs are rarely needed for children with hemophilia, even with inhibitors, but 504 plans may be helpful, especially if the child is absent often or has trouble navigating in school. All plans must be reassessed annually. If your school system is facing budget cuts, your child's plan might be denied. You can always appeal any decision by the school system to try to reinstate your child's plan.

Jake has an IEP in place, and they know his condition, but he still needs to do the appeal each quarter for the whole high school. The burden is on us. We work full time, and we can't do these things after hours. We have to complete paperwork and make an appeal during work time, and we already have burdens. —Molly A. Eppenbach, Nebraska

Dosing

An inhibitor often requires a demanding dosing schedule when you're treating a bleed or undertaking ITI. If you use FEIBA to treat a bleed, you'll be treating approximately every twelve hours, so the doses can be scheduled to be given at home before and after school. If you use NovoSeven, you could be dosing every two hours. You may need to visit the school, take your child out of class to the nurse's office, and infuse him. You'll need to coordinate logistics with the school: Can you store factor at school? Can you infuse on school property? Can your child infuse himself at school? Some families do megadose infusions to increase the interval between infusions (see chapter 3).

We treat every six hours if it's a bad bleed. We used to infuse every two to three hours with small doses (90 mcg/kg) but that was difficult when our son started school. When he had a bleed, we had to go to school every two hours to infuse, so he missed a ton of elementary school. To stretch the treatments out, we went to higher doses. On school days, we infuse before he leaves and right when he gets home. —Shari Luckey, Michigan

Missed School

One of the main challenges in schooling a child with inhibitors is the amount of school missed. Almost every family experiences this to some extent. Unresolved bleeds, hospitalizations, and frequent infusions can interrupt the school day. Most children with inhibitors will miss so much school that it affects their education.

Excessive absences are an ongoing problem. From second through fourth grade, Matthew attended less than half the school year. He usually misses at least one week a month. It's very difficult to keep up on his schoolwork. Now that he's in middle school, it's even more challenging. —Debbie Porter, California

> On average, Ethan misses ten to fifteen school days every year. But he's on the honor roll, and he hates missing school. —Kim Stubbs, Mississippi

Children sometimes miss school not because of an active bleed, but because of constant pain or surgeries.

> Leland was in pain every day, all day, for eighteen months from sixth to seventh grade, with lots of bleeds and a major surgery. The inhibitor took over our lives. He missed an incredible amount of school. He only misses school now due to pain. He misses on average forty to fifty days a year. A tutor comes to our house. —Jane, Massachusetts

Inhibitors can be all-consuming. You may begin thinking of school as a luxury, or as less important than the day-to-day struggle of treatments, hospitals, and appointments. But remember, it's always better for your child to be in school whenever possible, for his education, his socialization, and his self-esteem.

> If you are on ITI, you get so focused on the medical side of things; you don't even try to normalize his day-to-day life. If he misses fifteen school days, you think, oh well! He can't sit through it in pain. —Kerry Fatula, Pennsylvania

There are ways to keep your child up-to-date with school. Work with the school to create a plan to help him stay on track with his peers and complete the required work. If your child must miss school, alert the classroom teacher. You may want to put this information in writing, and estimate the amount of time: one day, one week, two weeks? Alert your child's other teachers or aides: special education teacher, art instructor, PE teacher.

Ask your child's classmates to bring his work home. Many schools are online, and homework can be emailed. Give the teacher weekly updates while your child is absent, and ask for weekly updates on the returned work. Ask for classroom news about special events, field trips, or new students so your child doesn't feel left out.

> I get the assignments from Matthew's teachers and work with him to complete them. Some teachers have voluntarily come to our home to tutor him. Sometimes he stays after school to catch up on missed work. —Debbie Porter, California

Alternative Schooling

Despite your best attempts to keep your child in school, sometimes it's impossible. Frequent bleeds mean frequent infusions and bed rest. He may spend days in constant pain. ITI might mean frequent hospital trips. You may need to consider home tutoring as an option, especially as your child gets older and homework becomes more complex.

> Tyler is in second grade in a wonderful school. He started bleeding a lot this year. Previously, if he missed a week, he could do the work and catch up. Now he's getting more serious schoolwork, so he gets tutored once a week. —Anonymous

Some parents consider home schooling. This can be a great option when parents are properly trained, have the right resources and support, and have a stable home environment.

> As the mother of a child with an inhibitor, my role became nurse, physical therapist, counselor, teacher, coach . . . Too many roles! Stephen missed so much school in fifth grade that I tried to tutor him myself, but it was too much. Finally I had a conference with the school counselor, who said I should just be Mom. —Janet Brewer, Massachusetts

Since 1998, another option has opened: distance learning, or cyber school. Students attend school online, from the comfort of home or a hospital bed. As of this writing, about forty states offer some kind of cyber schooling. In this type of education program, students must log on for a certain number of hours per week and have their attendance checked daily by "mentors." Students can take classes in real time, and many cyber schools give the student a laptop, microphone, and electronic writing pad. Cyber schools offer flexible schedules—perfect for families whose lives are often interrupted by inhibitor treatments. Quizzes and tests are scheduled to keep students at a specific learning pace, so they don't get too far ahead or behind the class.

> I've missed a lot of school due to bleeds—more than half of seventh grade. Now I attend cyber school. Public school wasn't helpful. I don't miss it. And we can still socialize because there are chances to get together with others in our area for field trips. —Nathan Fatula, Pennsylvania

I'm Different

We've discussed several ways to accommodate your child's educational needs, but accommodations do signal how different he is when compared to his peers. The influence of peers is very strong during the school years. Although your child always may have known that he's different, when he's with his peers, it really hits home. This realization may affect his mood, self-image, and progress in school.

Most children want to fit in and be liked. Your child's steady friends probably grew up with him—and his hemophilia and inhibitor—but new friends may bombard him with questions: Why didn't you come to school for three days? Are you sick? How did you get that bruise? Why are you in a wheelchair? The spotlight is on him, sometimes in an uncomfortable way.

> In second grade, I fell on wet floors at school and was hospitalized for two months with a bad knee bleed. The school decided I shouldn't come back; they were afraid my parents would sue. Tutors came to my house. My mother said, "My boy needs to go to school." So I returned, but I wasn't allowed to go to PE. I couldn't use scissors. The other kids avoided me. We lived in a small town, so I was the big target. New kids learned quickly: "Don't go near him." Rarely was I invited to birthday parties. —R. H., Connecticut

The realization that he's different can be positive or negative. One child may feel proud to be different; another may feel proud that he's not squeamish about needles, or he's tough about handling pain. But some children may not be comforted or strengthened by this kind of pride. Particularly if a child isn't well prepared for other people's reactions, has a poor self-image, or was taught to hide his hemophilia, he may be uncomfortable with his differences. And he may start ignoring his bleeds to prove that he's not different (see chapter 15 for more on denying bleeds).

> Friends have been a long, hard-fought battle. Our son is much more comfortable around adults. But as his peers mature and stop being so physical with each other, his ability to have friends is growing by leaps and bounds. —Joyce Hewitt, Michigan

> Kindergarten was the first time Thomas really began to notice he was different. He started "hating hemophilia." I first tried to put a positive spin on it: "But think about all the cool things about hemophilia: camp, trips to fun meetings, new friends." That approach didn't work. Then I started saying, "Everybody has something. Some kids wear glasses. Some wear hearing aids. Some have peanut allergies." That hit home, especially when he realized his best buddy had a peanut allergy. —Sonji Wilkes, Colorado

Be sure that your child doesn't use bleeds as a way to hide from his peers. Stress personal responsibility. He can be infused, and still make up a math test later that day or week. He can still attend PE even if he's sidelined. He can complete classwork that his friends bring home.

> *In school, I became manager of the basketball team. Having friends who played basketball, I had to choose a lower road. I tried to stay involved as much as possible.* —R. H., Connecticut

What should you tell your child's peers about hemophilia? And who should tell them—you or your child? Try letting your child make that decision. Remind him that there's no need to make announcements, but probably no need to hide hemophilia either. Generally, children are compassionate toward classmates when the situation is explained in terms they can understand.

> *Matthew has always been like a little adult because of everything he's been through. He gets along well with the teachers, but he doesn't interact much with other kids. He has one or two friends. He does not discuss his hemophilia at school.* —Debbie Porter, California

If you prepare him well, you can leave it up to your child to tell his friends. Here's how you can help him:

- List only a few key points that he should tell his classmates.
- Avoid crisis mode. Don't focus on worst-case scenarios.
- Emphasize what he *can* do. Minimize differences.
- Be relaxed and casual. Your attitude is contagious!

Having a close circle of friends is a great way for your child to gain stability when hemophilia and inhibitors get rocky. True friends accept him unconditionally. And your child will meet kids with other disabilities or disorders; kids from single-parent and two-parent homes; and kids from different ethnic, racial, and religious backgrounds. Hemophilia with inhibitors can be a great opportunity to learn tolerance, acceptance, compassion, and community spirit! ■

Attending School When You Have Inhibitors

■ NOTES

1. See appendix A.
2. Visit the American Red Cross at www.redcross.org and search for B.A.T. (Basic First Aid).
3. Section 504 of the Rehabilitation Act of 1973 (PL 93-112) is a civil rights law prohibiting discrimination against people with disabilities in any program or activity receiving or benefiting from federal financial assistance. An IEP falls under IDEA (Individuals with Disabilities Education Act) and is an educational law. Visit http//idea.ed.gov for more information.
4. For more information, visit www.ed.gov/parents/needs/speced/iepguide/index.html.

SUMMARY 14
Attending School When You Have Inhibitors

- Meet with school staff before school starts. Ask your HTC nurse coordinator to attend.

- Give staff some simple hemophilia books as an introduction. Select three main points to discuss.

- Tell staff how to reach you at all times: phone, pager, cell phone.

- Discuss with teachers the importance of avoiding overprotecting, singling out your child, denying hemophilia or bleeds, and overreacting.

- Turn to the school nurse as your first line of defense when seeking medical assistance at school for your child.

- Review and apply for accommodation plans like IHP, IEP, and 504.

- When your child misses school, have homework emailed or brought home.

- If absences are excessive, consider a full-time tutor, home schooling, or cyber school.

- Your child will realize that he's different from his peers. Beware of your child ignoring bleeds to fit in.

15 Adolescence and Beyond

You've had success nurturing your child, learning to infuse, and mastering the details of his care. You've successfully navigated some rocky roads, including the hemophilia diagnosis and inhibitor diagnosis; attitudes of family and friends; perhaps port surgery and prophylaxis; and of course, insurance problems. Now your child has hit the teen years, the gateway to adulthood and independence. In this stage, you'll find some of the same struggles—physical therapy for joints, clinic visits, school attendance. But new concerns appear as your child prepares for life on his own.

> *He's getting more freedom. He's driving, away more often, off to college soon. My goal is to prepare him to take care himself: he must do well in school to do well in college to get insurance.* —Shari Luckey, Michigan

One major concern now is how to foster emotional and physical independence when your child may be so dependent. All his life you've been trying to prepare him, but his inhibitor has made this hard, at times even impossible.

> *How do you become independent when you have to depend on someone?* —Joyce Hewitt, Michigan

The good news is that you have encouraged him to learn about hemophilia and his inhibitor, recognize symptoms of a bleed, and know how to infuse. Perhaps you've also prepared him by helping him learn his strengths and limitations, by including him in treatment decisions, and by letting him explore activities. After all this preparation, plus his medical challenges, your teenager is probably more mature than most, and he takes hemophilia and inhibitors seriously.

> *I think I'm a little more mature than a lot of my peers, because I've been through a lot. I hardly complain about my chores: inhibitors have definitely shaped me. I am 100% happy with who I am.* —Nathan Fatula, Pennsylvania

But don't be too surprised when your child acts like a normal teen. All teenagers, including those with hemophilia, share common traits that stem from a dramatic change in physiology, a broadening social base, and a relentless desire to be independent. And if his inhibitor prevents him from doing all he wants to do, he'll probably be frustrated, angry, withdrawn, or rebellious. Being sensitive to your teen's changing needs can help you survive these years, and can help him mature. Your goal: encourage your teen to be independent and responsible, and to avoid taking needless personal risks.

Biological Changes

The distinct biological, chemical, and physical differences between males and females are vividly obvious in adolescence. Biological changes can be quick and dramatic, as your child seems to transform before your eyes. In adolescence, a boy's testosterone levels may jump tremendously. Testosterone is the hormone that changes boys into young men. It stimulates facial hair growth and boosts muscle mass. It fuels aggression, energy, and sexual desire. The intense hormonal changes that develop a child's body into a man's body can also cause lots of stress and upheaval in his brain and nervous system. No wonder teens can be moody, defensive, withdrawn, and argumentative! Add hospital visits, infusions, restricted activities, pain—and your teen could be pretty prickly to live with.

When you observe emotional or behavioral changes in your teen, keep in mind what's happening in his bloodstream. Along with infusions of factor, he is receiving continual "infusions" of testosterone—affecting his behavior and emotions. Your job is to help him understand and manage these physiological changes.

Don't forget that by the time your child is a teenager, you might be undergoing your own biological changes. Are you approaching forty? Fifty? Your hormones, metabolism, and appearance are all changing. Your metabolism slows down just as your teen's is revving up. You seek peace and quiet, but your testosterone-charged teen is looking for some action. You want to continue traditional family activities or vacations, but your teen wants freedom, even though he loves his family. Physiological and psychological changes can derail communication and interrupt family dynamics, impacting hemophilia management and your child's health. Let's examine how adolescence affects your teen with hemophilia.

Independence, Privacy, and Secrecy

A teenager longs for independence: a goal he's been striving toward since he learned to stand. He may want to try to "separate" from his family. To separate emotionally, he may need to separate physically. He may withdraw, talk less, and stay in his bedroom more. He may prefer to hang out with friends, not family. Door closed, computer password protected, warning sign posted. Why? He's creating a buffer, a neutral zone where he can relax, experiment, and protect his developing personality without challenge or criticism. It may be hard for you to respect his privacy when you believe he's not yet mature enough to make good medical decisions about his hemophilia and inhibitor.

But you may have to learn to let go a bit, and give him some space. It helps to voice your expectations while acknowledging his needs: "We know you want the car to join your friends at the beach, but only if you bring your factor with you."

> *The most important lesson I learned as a teen: take your factor as soon as you have a bleed. Parents, don't hold your child back, but insist that they must do factor right away.* —Nathan Fatula, Pennsylvania

> *One thing I have learned is that regardless of whether you have an inhibitor, you need to take extra factor with you if you are going on a distant trip. You never know when an accident may occur.* —Colton Branch, Kansas

There are limits to the kind of behavior you will accept from your teen, but where can you be flexible? How can you compromise? Perhaps he no longer needs to tell you every time he has a bleed or infuses, but he must keep a log of his infusions for hospital and insurance records. He has permission to drive the car or go to the concert if he has his medical identification bracelet or wallet card. Encourage your teen's input and responsibility. Make each decision less a personal conflict—you versus him—and more a choice.

> *Our son has to learn his own limitations. He is very determined and stubborn! We supported him, and let him play flag football as a high school junior. But he kept jamming his fingers. He was frustrated. This year he wanted to try out for basketball but got a bad elbow bleed. He was devastated, but he understood. Every day after school now, he lifts weights. If you saw him out playing, you'd never know he has hemophilia or an inhibitor.* —Molly A. Eppenbach, Nebraska

Although you need to grant him privacy, privacy can be dangerous when it becomes secrecy—especially if he spends excessive time with peers or on the Internet, at the expense of real-life interactions. A teen who spends long periods withdrawn from his family may learn about relationships, privacy, and communication in inappropriate ways. Be sure to monitor your teen's time, and look over his shoulder occasionally. He needs to develop healthy relationships with others *in person*.

Self-Image and Denial

Concern about self-image peaks during adolescence, a time of intense self-scrutiny, self-criticism, and experimentation with looks. Even teens with no medical problems, who fit accepted physical norms, can be hypercritical of their bodies and abilities. Because he has hemophilia and an inhibitor, your teen may suddenly find many things to dislike about himself. Hemophilia is an "imperfection" that makes him different, and many teens don't easily tolerate differences. Some teenagers hide hemophilia from their peers, especially when dating.

> We worry that he will develop his self-esteem based on society's opinions of what it means to be a man. And that no one will want to commit to a relationship that will be difficult, and he'll end up alone. —Joyce Hewitt, Michigan

> My girlfriend doesn't care that I have hemophilia, though her mom did call my doctor! —Lee Ridenhour, Kansas

Your teen may be crushed when it truly hits him that hemophilia is forever, or that ITI hasn't worked to eradicate his inhibitor. He may imagine scenarios where hemophilia interferes with his life: dating, high school sports, getting a job, health insurance, marriage.

> Sometimes I still deny that I have a bleed. Sometimes I think I don't need factor. But I know I can't go without it completely. Don't be in denial about factor. But don't let hemophilia take over your life. —John Salierno, New Jersey

If a teen denies his differences and tries to be just like his peers, he may deny his bleeds. Some teens hide hemophilia successfully and manage to discreetly infuse when needed, so no one ever knows. But denial can lead to neglect: ignoring bleeds, not infusing to stop a bleed, or refusing to wear safety equipment to prevent bleeds.

> In middle school, when we talked about genetic diseases, I never told anyone. In high school, my coaches knew, and they told the other kids. Hemophilia doesn't bother me now. Inhibitors made me grow up faster; I had to be more responsible. If kids ask me if I have something wrong, I say yeah, but I usually don't volunteer it. No one understands hemophilia—they think we will bleed to death. —Lee Ridenhour, Kansas

Start early to help your child accept and tolerate his hemophilia and inhibitor. Don't hide it, but don't make it the defining point of his life. Let him decide when and who to tell. To keep his disorder in perspective, offer positive but realistic messages:

- What's important is not what happens in our lives, but what we *do* about what happens.

- Hemophilia isn't the reason that good or bad things happen, and it's never a reason to limit our enjoyment of life.

- Our differences are what make us unique.

My high school coach told us that Coach John Wooden once said, "Do not let what you cannot do interfere with what you can do." I always remember that. So many things are possible. Just because something is in your way, it may create an opportunity for something else. When I was hurt and home, I learned to play the piano. —John Salierno, New Jersey

Risk-Taking Behavior

His testosterone pumping, and with a natural sense of invulnerability, a teen with hemophilia may want to push his limits, despite an inhibitor.

We constantly worry about our children. When Austin was several months old, I asked an adult with hemophilia for advice. He told me to let my son set his own limits as he gets older. —Julie Baker, Nevada

When I was young, my parents told me that I couldn't play touch football with friends or head-butt the ball in soccer, but I did it anyway. I wanted to know what my limits were and how far I could take them. Sometimes I got bleeds, and other times I didn't, but just the freedom to let me know for myself was the main goal. —Colton Branch, Kansas

Some risk-taking is healthy. Moving to a new city, making new friends, starting a business, breaking with tradition—these risks involve some anxiety or fear but can bring immense rewards. Challenging the body and mind stimulates growth. When challenged, a teen can discover his strengths and limitations and learn to be responsible for his actions.

How can you encourage *safe* risk-taking? Recommend activities in a healthy, structured environment, preferably with an adult mentor. Certain sports provide plenty of risk under safe conditions with experienced adults. Enroll your teen in driver's education classes. Help him choose activities that come with the warning, "That's safe, but only when . . ." instead of, "No, that's not safe—you'll get hurt." Translate the second warning into teen-speak, and he hears, "I don't trust you to be competent and to learn." When he has positive outlets for adventure and risk, your teen will build skills, self-control, and confidence.

If your teen is not prepared or guided, he may find danger, particularly if he doesn't accept his hemophilia. He may rebel against parental restrictions. He may seek his peers' approval of risky behavior. He may try to seize control of a life too rigidly structured by adults. If this happens, the same activities that could challenge him, test his endurance, and build maturity may cause injury or permanent damage.

Of course, some rebellious or experimental activities should never be attempted by anyone, regardless of hemophilia. High-speed driving, drinking and driving, and drugs are real dangers to our youths.

Why do teens take dangerous risks? Sometimes it's curiosity, sometimes peer pressure. It could also be a reaction to overprotective parents. After thirteen years of parental limitations, constant monitoring, and living with an inhibitor, he's frustrated. He wants to make up for lost time. Our challenge is to recognize our children's needs but set clear limits and consequences.[1]

> We knew that as a teenager, Scott might make some poor decisions. Alcohol and drugs were concerns because they could impair his decision-making and memory. During his senior year of high school he had a bad experience with excess alcohol consumption: he learned what it can do physically and mentally. —Laura Shumway, Virginia

On the other hand, a high degree of parental control may have the opposite effect. Teens may give up trying to take control of their activities, lives, and decisions. So allow your teen some freedom and responsibility, including the freedom to choose activities. This may mean pushing the envelope and taking risks. Prepare him by reviewing safety rules. You'll encourage the confidence and self-esteem he needs to take greater control of his life as he matures.

> Scott had a rough last half of senior year: he had several panic attacks and was really unsettled, but he wanted to go to college far from home. Home was safe, things were predictable, and dealing with hemophilia was commonplace; he had help. At college, he'd be on his own. He needed to find a way to feel safe at school. We sent him packages and called often until he said, "Enough, already." That's when we knew he had things under control. —Laura Shumway, Virginia

How to Encourage Responsibility and Independence

Children with hemophilia depend on their parents for a time, like all children. Your goal is to gradually decrease your teen's dependency, increase his feeling of competence, and enhance his sense of responsibility. You can do this in many ways:

Let him make some decisions. Begin after age three or four, when he can better understand consequences. Teach him how to detect bleeds. Explain the consequences of untreated bleeds. Tell him which activities will benefit his body and which will hurt. Show faith in his judgment. Instead of, "It looks to me like you're having a bleed. Let's get some factor," try saying, "Do you think you're having a bleed? Will you tell me when you need factor?" Offer him choices: Treatment in the kitchen or dining room? What color bandage?

Introduce him to other teens and adults with hemophilia and inhibitors. Your teen may be less likely to hide hemophilia when he knows he belongs to a community that supports him. He'll meet others with hemophilia and inhibitors who are successful, involved, and responsible. But don't promote a peer group solely of boys with hemophilia. Your teen will become a part of the community in your neighborhood, school, or religious institution, which is healthier for him in the long run.

Educate him about risk-taking behavior. Drinking causes loss of inhibition, which may lead to more risk-taking behavior, such as speeding. Examine with your son your state government's website listing laws and consequences of drinking, driving, and underage sex.

Involve him in making rules. What time does he suggest for curfew? Negotiate. Show that you respect his opinion—even if you choose not to follow it.

Expect him to learn about hemophilia and inhibitors. He should know how to prevent bleeds, detect bleeds early, comply with HTC treatment guidelines, take safety precautions, and keep good records.

Expect him to self-infuse. Help him understand that self-treatment means more than sticking himself. It means taking responsibility. He needs to know when and how to treat, how to calculate appropriate doses, and when and who to call for help. He needs to be informed about his treatment product, and to be responsible for regular evaluations at the HTC. He's also capable of ordering his own factor. Give him phone numbers and product information, and walk him through his first order. Don't wait until he's about to go off to college to teach him everything. Along with the myriad adjustments of a college freshman, he may not be able to handle the additional stress of learning to infuse.

Managing Your Child's Inhibitor

Expect rebellion. View some rebellion as a developmental milestone, a necessary rite of passage. His rebellion is more about him than about you. Don't take it too personally, but don't let it go too far. Set and post clear family rules about consequences for disrespect and disobedience—and be sure to enforce them.

Encourage a sense of ownership of his body. His body belongs to him, and his actions directly affect his health. When he was a child, you checked for bleeds, administered factor, called doctors, made appointments, ordered supplies, talked to HTC staff, logged infusions, and selected his factor brand. Which of these tasks can he do now?

Checklist: Topics to Discuss with Your Teen

- ☐ Internet usage: how often, how much, sharing private information online
- ☐ Driving: permit, driver's education, license, rules of the road, seatbelts
- ☐ Sex: education, ethics, birth control, legal consent, responsibility
- ☐ Drugs: types, peer pressure, legal consequences, health consequences
- ☐ School: grades, college preparation, extracurricular activities
- ☐ Peers: choice of friends, social activities, dating
- ☐ Spirituality: teen's beliefs, family's beliefs, tolerance
- ☐ Hemophilia: review facts, diagnosis, level, inhibitor titer, appropriate product and dosage, log books, self-infusion
- ☐ Factor supplies: ordering, storage, travel pack, logging infusions
- ☐ Work: finding first job, work ethics, insurance
- ☐ Health: eating well, sleep habits, physical exercise, insurance
- ☐ Risk-taking: appropriate activities, dangerous choices, reasons why

When you teach your child to be independent, you're teaching him how to manage his life, and you're also saying, "I respect your intelligence and abilities. You know best when you are having a bleed. You are able to care for yourself. You are competent."

We are teaching our thirteen-year-old to be more independent about his care. We work on having him log his infusions, mix his factor, and be responsible for ordering his supplies—with our supervision. —Shari Luckey, Michigan

Transition: Adolescence to Adulthood

Adolescence flies by as your child grows more independent and busy. You'll help him reach goals like practicing for his driver's license test and applying for jobs. Here's a checklist of milestones, with approximate ages.

Checklist: Teen Milestones

☐	Driver's permit	16+
☐	Driver's license	16–17
☐	SAT or ACT (college entrance exams)	16–17
☐	Prom	16–18
☐	College applications	17–18
☐	High school graduation	17–18
☐	Select Service System registration (even a teen with hemophilia must enroll)	18
☐	Health insurance changes	18+

I was scheduled to take the practice SATs as a sophomore, and I couldn't. Sitting was too painful. I missed a month of school. —John Salierno, New Jersey

Achieving these milestones may be complicated by the inhibitor. Treatments, hospital stays, ITI, protracted bleeds, and recovery periods can all delay transitions. And your teen may fall behind his peers because he is so dependent on his parents.

You can help him through tough times by discussing these milestones and explaining that it's normal to delay some transitions. Help him find ways to make up for lost time. Show you appreciate his perseverance by celebrating when he finally achieves a milestone—plan a "License Luau" or "SAT-urday Night at the Movies."

Health Insurance Changes

Parents of children with hemophilia and inhibitors excel in the area of insurance. Now is the time to start teaching your teen what you know. Someday he'll need to monitor his own insurance and fight his own insurance battles. Understanding insurance is essential for families with inhibitors: insurance concerns will surely affect your teen's choice of a career. Teens may dream of being rock stars or fighter pilots, but you must be realistic. Explain the value of having a job with insurance.

> I think about insurance. Since I turned sixteen, I've known I will go on disability when I hit eighteen. I know I can't make more than $900 a month. I want to major in music at college, and eventually teach. —Nathan Fatula, Pennsylvania

After high school, the 2010 Patient Protection and Affordable Care Act allows him to stay on your private group and non-group plan (in place prior to March 23, 2010) until age twenty-six even if he is no longer living with you, is no longer a student, and regardless of his marital status. But he can't have a job that offers insurance, and he must be claimed as a dependent on your tax returns.

Help him think through what to do after high school. Will he remain a student by attending college, or will he land a job with good health benefits?

> Insurance is an ongoing, wake-you-up-in-the-middle-of-the-night worry. We've told the boys, since they were old enough to understand, that they will have a minimum of seventeen years of school. Without career options, they're destined for heartache, resentment, and hopelessness. —Joyce Hewitt, Michigan

Transitioning to Adult HTCs

By age eighteen, a hemophilia patient is normally self-infusing, working or attending college, and ready to accept personal responsibility for his care, including ordering factor

When he turns eighteen, if your HTC allows it, your teen can keep the hematologist and comprehensive HTC team he had as a pediatric patient. But in some cases, he will be transitioned to the adult hematology department. Your HTC team will work with you for several years before the actual transfer, to help you and your teen successfully transition to adult care. Your teen's social worker can help with this transition.

One major change is that your teen is now seen alone at the HTC. Patient confidentiality is paramount now that he is considered an adult. Your teen will be expected to give his own medical history and speak directly to his hematologist, nurse, physical therapist, and social worker. He'll need to share information about his sex life to prevent disease and unwanted pregnancy. And he'll be asked about drug and alcohol use, nutrition, career planning, and insurance.

It's hard for some parents to accept their child's independence. At the HTC, you are no longer privileged to know all about his private life.[2] Take courage from the fact that the professional, experienced HTC team will advise and monitor him well. You may be consulted as needed; but if all goes well, you'll have only a small role in his ongoing healthcare. He may be happy to know that he can always come to you for advice and guidance.

Career Choices

If you want your teen to grow into a truly independent adult, you both need to think seriously and early about his career. More than anything else, he'll need a good job that provides good medical insurance. The best way to accomplish this, though not the only way, is to get a higher education.

> My son knows he must go to college. Manual labor is not an option. He knows he'll need a job that provides insurance. He's seen what we've gone through with insurance. He's considering teaching, nursing, or working in a home care company to help people with hemophilia. —Debbie Branch, Kansas

You and your teen should consider career inclination, job satisfaction, and general happiness. What are his interests and skills? Job satisfaction is based on enjoyment, challenge, competence and contribution, not just security or financial reward. Introduce your teen to a variety of activities to uncover his skills and passions: chemistry, music, art, medicine, writing, engineering, travel, acting—the list is endless! Ask if your HTC team can refer him to a vocational or educational counselor.

> Picking a major was a big deal because I was thinking about jobs: I want to be covered. I want to go to law school. I also know state employees get insurance. —John Salierno, New Jersey

> *The inhibitor caused me to change schools—my first college was too rural— and career paths—I abandoned meteorology. You can't let inhibitors control your life, but it must affect your life. At twenty-two, transferring to another school, I felt like a freshman again. Having an inhibitor helped me grow up faster than my peers, and understand how to keep fighting and not give up.*
> *—Richard Pezzillo, Rhode Island*

> *Deciding on a major was always a challenge because of different things I wanted to do. I had to decide on a major with a high employment rate and good healthcare benefits. Living with inhibitors had very little effect on what I decided to do. I've lived with it my whole life and it hasn't slowed me down yet, and it's still not going to today! —Colton Branch, Kansas*

Career choice directly affects medical insurance coverage. Working for the government provides excellent coverage. Large companies, banks, and hospitals normally offer a wide range of coverage. Private companies, self-employment, and small firms may provide less coverage. When possible, your son should get a copy of a prospective employer's insurance policy before accepting a job, and should have it examined by a social worker who is familiar with insurance as it applies to hemophilia.

> *I wonder how my son's hemophilia and inhibitor will affect him in the workforce. Will it keep him from getting a job? He wants to go to college and study business. —Kim Stubbs, Mississippi*

The decision to attend or skip college has a major impact on insurance coverage. If your teen isn't going to college, he'll need to identify a source for his insurance coverage. If he does attend college or university, he must maintain full-time status or he will likely be dropped from your employer's plan! A solid education is the foundation of many opportunities in life, including job satisfaction, job choices, and excellent health insurance. Encourage your child to stay in school and consider college.

Alternatives to College

Not all young adults want to attend college or can afford it. There are many alternatives: family businesses, clerical positions, trade schools. Scholarship programs exist just for students with hemophilia attending college or trade school.[3] Consult your child's high school to find volunteer or summer jobs that offer career experience: working in an office or store, coaching sports, being a camp counselor, and applying for professional internships can all open doors to a bright future.

We worry that our son doesn't realize the impact of his actions on his future. He's not doing well in school. We tell him that employers may look at grades. We'd like him to go to college. He loves art, and is talented. —Molly A. Eppenbach, Nebraska

When your son finds an appropriate job with good medical coverage, he'll need to decide what to tell his employer. If hemophilia affects his job performance, through absences or inability to do heavy labor, he should consider informing his employer about hemophilia. If his job is flexible, he might be able to make up hours outside his regular shift. It's a difficult decision. He may risk discrimination if he reveals his hemophilia too early. He may face resentment if he reveals it too late, after many job absences.

Prophylaxis has a tremendously positive influence on securing and keeping jobs. If your teen must stop prophylaxis because of inadequate or limited insurance coverage, he may still be in excellent condition for work because his joints will be preserved. If he can continue prophylaxis, then his range of job opportunities widens because his bleeds are prevented.

Loving Enough to Let Go

When raising our children, we often forget this fundamental fact: it's our children's goal in life to become independent of us.

It's easy to forget about looming independence when you're engrossed in the busy life of a family with inhibitors. But one day, you'll gasp to see your young adult standing before you!

Independence. It's the path your child started down when he first learned to walk. It's the pride that surges when he gets an award for achievement at school. It's the glow he feels when he does his first infusion. Independence is his horizon as he sets off for college or his first job. And you can help him.

Start when he's young. Help him make good decisions by setting him up for success, with choices that encourage positive outcomes. Success builds on success. And with each success, your child's self-esteem grows. Inspire him: give him books about people who have triumphed over physical disabilities—like Franklin D. Roosevelt or Helen Keller.

> Some of the world's greatest men and women have been saddled with disabilities and adversities but have managed to overcome them. Cripple him, and you have a Sir Walter Scott. Lock him in a prison cell, and you have a John Bunyan. Bury him in the snows of Valley Forge, and you have a George Washington. Raise him in abject poverty and you have an Abraham Lincoln . . . Strike him down with infantile paralysis, and he becomes a Franklin Roosevelt. Burn him so severely . . . that the doctors say he will never walk again, and you have a Glenn Cunningham, who set the world's record in 1934 for running a mile in 4 minutes and 6.7 seconds. Deafen a genius composer and you have a Ludwig van Beethoven.
>
> —Ted Engstrom, *The Essential Ted Engstrom*
>
> ■■■

Having inhibitors is tough. It can be a trial. But so many people emerge from their trials stronger, with greater perspective and wisdom. As your child grows, show him positive ways to handle problems, maintain grace through hard times, advocate for his own healthcare, and care for himself. When he's ready to leave home as a young adult, he'll be confident, healthy, and educated about hemophilia and inhibitors. He'll feel mature and positive, and one day—if not now—he'll appreciate all your efforts, sacrifice, and love through the years. ■

> *To parents: absolutely don't hold your child back. If it's bad enough that they sometimes can't play sports, or do things that other kids can do, don't hold them back. Encourage them. Support them. My parents did a good job raising me. I'm happy with who I am. —Nathan Fatula, Pennsylvania*

Adolescence and Beyond

■ NOTES

1. One mother wisely notes, "Risk-taking can also be the result of depression or bipolar disorder. Remember that even people with hemophilia have other stuff going on, and that manic behaviors like risk-taking might need evaluation."
2. Your child can authorize you to have access to medical files or specific information by signing a Statement of Authorized Representative and Release of Medical Information. The age at which a child can make his or her own medical decisions is called the *age of majority*; this may be as young as twelve for results of AIDS tests and some other procedures.
3. Visit LA Kelley Communications, Inc., online for a list of scholarships for students with bleeding disorders.

SUMMARY 15
Adolescence and Beyond

- Teenagers undergo dramatic changes in physiology and emotions.

- A teen strongly desires independence. He may try to "separate" from his family emotionally and physically.

- Inhibitors may delay or interfere with a teen's driving need to be independent, causing frustration, anger, or rebellion.

- Concern about self-image peaks during adolescence. Hemophilia and inhibitors may give your teen things to dislike about himself.

- If a teen denies his differences and tries to be just like his peers, he may deny his bleeds.

- A teen with hemophilia may want to push his limits and take risks, despite an inhibitor.

- Encourage healthy risk-taking through activities in a structured environment, with an adult mentor.

- High-speed driving, drinking and driving, and drugs are real dangers to our youths.

- Encourage independence by letting your teen make some of his own decisions, and by educating him about risk-taking behavior.

- Expect your teen to self-infuse.

- Achieving ordinary milestones, like getting a driver's license, may be complicated by the inhibitor.

- Your teen can now stay on your insurance policy, even if he is no longer living with you, is no longer a student, and regardless of his marital status.

- Career choice may directly affect medical insurance coverage. Working for the government or a large company with a group policy can provide excellent coverage.

APPENDIX A
RESOURCES

Publications

Books

The Great Inhibinator (2006)
I Am Nate! (2007)
Quest for Infusion: Nate Goes to Camp (2008)
>Chris Perretti Barnes
>Stories about a boy named Nate who has inhibitors. For children ages 4–7.

>Available through BioRX: www.biorx.net
>Sponsored by Bayer HealthCare: www.kogenatefs.com

All About Inhibitors
>62-page booklet with Q&A about inhibitors.

>Canadian Hemophilia Society: www.hemophilia.ca

Magazines

HEMAware
National Hemophilia Foundation
www.hemaware.org

Parent Empowerment Newsletter (PEN)
LA Kelley Communications, Inc.
www.kelleycom.com

PEN's Insurance Pulse
LA Kelley Communications, Inc.
www.kelleycom.com

Bloodstone Magazine
Hemophilia Health Services
www.hemophiliahealth.com

Dateline Federation
Hemophilia Federation of America
www.hemophiliafed.org

COTT Washington Update
Committee of Ten Thousand
www.cott1.org

Equipment and Supplies

Cryo/Cuff
Nylon wraps with an attached cold water cooler system designed to apply cold, safe compression to minimize hemarthrosis, help control joint and muscle swelling, and reduce pain.
www.cryocuff.com

MedicAlert Foundation
Necklaces, bracelets, and ID tags for people with chronic illnesses. Yearly membership can be purchased that includes 24-hour call-in services for doctors and ER staff to receive diagnosis and treatment information about the patient.
www.medicalert.com

Compassionate Care Programs

CARE Program (Baxter)
www.thereforyou.com

SevenASSIST℠ (Novo Nordisk)
www.novosevenrt.com

Recommended Websites

- **National Hemophilia Foundation (NHF)** www.hemophilia.org
- **Hemophilia Federation of America (HFA)** www.hemophiliafed.org
- **LA Kelley Communications, Inc.** www.kelleycom.com
- **Patient Notification System (PNS)** www.patientnotificationsystem.org
- **Patient Services, Inc. (PSI)** www.UneedPSI.org
- **World Federation of Hemophilia (WFH)** www.wfh.org
- **Canadian Hemophilia Society** www.hemophilia.ca
- **Baxter BioScience** www.thereforyou.com
- **Novo Nordisk Inc.** www.novosevenrt.com

APPENDIX B
HOW THE BETHESDA INHIBITOR ASSAY WORKS

The Bethesda Inhibitor Assay is performed by mixing a hemophilia patient's plasma (which has little or no factor VIII or IX) with normal pooled plasma, which contains a normal level of factor activity. If there is no inhibitor present, then a 50:50 mixture of hemophilic and normal plasma should result in approximately 50% of normal factor levels. That's because the hemophilic plasma has diluted the normal plasma by half. If an inhibitor is present, it will reduce the level below 50%, because the inhibitor has inactivated some of the factor in the normal plasma.

The Bethesda Unit (BU) number indicates how many times you can dilute the patient's plasma and still see a reduction in the clotting efficiency of the normal plasma to about half of what you'd expect. For example, a BU level of 4 means that if the patient's plasma is diluted four times when mixed with normal plasma (1 part patient plasma, 3 parts normal plasma), the clotting level will drop to about 50% of what you would expect without inhibitors. A level of 500 BU means that even if you dilute the hemophilia patient's plasma 500 times (1 part patient plasma, 499 parts normal plasma), you'll still have enough antibodies in that very small sample to inactivate half of the factor in the normal plasma. ∎

APPENDIX C
MATHEMATICAL AND MEDICAL SYMBOLS AND ABBREVIATIONS

In medicine, we must often quantify an amount—we must make *measurements*. The type of measurement we make is a *quantity*. To measure a quantity, we must compare it to a known amount called a *unit*. For example, length is a quantity, and inches are units.

For convenience, the names of units are often abbreviated using letters or symbols. In medicine, poor penmanship when writing abbreviations can result in medical errors that could be life-threatening. This is especially true in the United States, where we straddle two measurement systems. Almost all other countries use only the metric system for measurements: it's easy, and it produces fewer errors. In the United States, science and medicine use the metric system. But our official, everyday measurement system is the U.S. Customary System, also called the English system or standard system. Because we use both the Customary System and the metric system, this increases the chance of medical errors from misreading units. The chart on the next page lists the units used in this book.

Appendix C

Symbol/ Abbreviation	Unit Name	Quantity	Equivalent Measure	Notes
BU	Bethesda Unit	measurement of the ability of an inhibitor to inactivate factor		Inhibitor plasma that contains 1 BU antibodies per mL will neutralize 50% of factor VIII or factor IX activity in an equal volume of pooled normal plasma
C	Celsius	temperature		Human body temperature is 37 degrees C
cm³ or cc	cubic centimeter	metric unit of volume	one-thousandth of a liter; 1 mL	Although cc is a common abbreviation for cubic centimeter, it is not an official metric abbreviation; medical professionals use the equivalent measure, mL
g	gram	basic metric unit of mass		
IU or U	International Unit	measurement of the amount of a substance, based on its measured biological activity or effect		IU is not a fixed amount but varies with the substance being measured; FEIBA is measured in U
kg	kilogram	metric unit of mass	1,000 grams; 1 kg is approx. 2.25 lb	
L or l	liter	basic metric unit of volume	1 liter is approx. 1 quart	In English-speaking countries and especially in medicine, the uppercase L is preferred to avoid confusion with the number 1
lb	pound	English unit of weight	1 lb = 16 oz	
mg	milligram	metric unit of mass	one-thousandth of a gram	NovoSeven is sold in vials by mg
mL or ml	milliliter	metric unit of volume	one-thousandth of a liter or 1 cm³	
ng	nanogram	metric unit of mass	one-billionth of a gram	
oz	ounce	English unit of weight	16 oz = 1 lb	
µg or mcg	microgram	metric unit of mass	one-millionth of a gram	The Greek letter µ is the internationally recognized metric symbol for the prefix micro, but the unofficial abbreviation mcg is preferred in medicine to avoid misreading the symbol; NovoSeven is dosed in mcg

APPENDIX D
ANATOMY OF A JOINT

It's helpful to know the basic anatomy of a joint and what happens to it after repeated joint bleeds. A joint is a place where two bones meet. All bones connect to other bones through joints. Joints allow the skeleton to move.

Joints are classified by the amount of movement they allow:

Immovable (fixed or fibrous) joints join bones that are normally independent (separated) in babies and that fuse together to form a solid structure by adulthood. Example: skull.

Slightly movable (cartilaginous) joints connect bones to each other by pads of cartilage and connective tissue, and can move only a small amount. Examples: ribs and spine.

Freely movable (synovial) joints allow a lot of movement. Most joints of the skeleton are synovial joints. Examples: knee, ankle, and elbow.

Not surprisingly, the freely movable synovial joints are also where most of the bleeding occurs. These joints share four main features:

Joint capsule: sheet of fibrous connective tissue that encases the joint.

Synovial membrane (synovium): innermost lining of the joint; secretes a lubricant called synovial fluid. With the help of immune cells called *phagocytes*, the synovium helps remove unwanted substances from the joint cavity. The synovium also contains many small blood vessels that supply nutrients not only for the synovium, but also for the cartilage covering the ends of the bones, which has no blood vessels of its own. The synovium surface may be flat or covered with tiny finger-like projections called *villi*.

Synovial fluid: slimy, viscous lubricant secreted by the synovial membrane; fills the joint or articular cavity (the space in the joint between the bone ends). Serves as a lubricant to prevent friction between bones. Normally, there is little synovial fluid in a joint, with the cartilage on the ends of the bones covered by only a thin layer of synovial fluid. Synovial fluid is held in the joint by the synovial membrane.

Hyaline (articular) cartilage: layer of smooth, rubbery cartilage covering the ends of the bones. Along with synovial fluid, the smooth cartilage allows frictionless movement of bones.

Synovial joints may also be classified by their structure and by the types of movement they allow. Three joint types are especially important to people with hemophilia because of their tendency to bleed:

Hinge joints allow movement of about 180 degrees in only one direction, like a door hinge. Examples: knee and elbow.

Ball-and-socket joints allow circular movement and provide the greatest range of motion. Examples: hip and shoulder.

Gliding joints are mostly flat surfaces that slide past each other and are held in position by ligaments. Although they allow movement in multiple directions, gliding joints have a relatively limited range of motion. Examples: ankle (foot) and wrist. ■

Glossary

Most terms in this glossary are defined as they relate to hemophilia and inhibitors. Some glossary terms do not appear in the text, but we have included them here because they are terms familiar to parents and medical professionals who work with hemophilia and inhibitors.

A

Acquired hemophilia: rare autoimmune disorder resulting in a noninherited form of hemophilia. Usually triggered by an illness that causes the body to mistakenly attack factor VIII.

Activated: chemical reaction that makes a clotting factor ready to participate in the clotting process. Clotting factors, produced mainly by the liver, circulate in the blood in an inactivated form, until an injury to a blood vessel occurs. *See* clotting cascade.

Activated prothrombin complex concentrate (aPCC): special factor concentrate used to stop bleeding in patients with inhibitors. Type of bypassing agent. Also called anti-inhibitor coagulant complex (AICC).

Adhesion: scar tissue that joins two body parts where there should be no bond. Common complication after some kinds of surgery, such as a synovectomy.

Adjuvant analgesic: loose term for many medications, including some antidepressants and anticonvulsants, that have little or no analgesic action when used alone, but can enhance painkilling effects when administered together.

Albumin: most abundant protein found in blood. Purified and virally inactivated albumin is added to plasma-derived and first-generation recombinant factor concentrates to make the factor more stable and add bulk.

Allergic reaction: response by the immune system to environmental contaminants such as pollen, animal dander, or food. Symptoms may include sneezing, itching, hives.

Analgesic: any drug used to reduce pain without causing loss of consciousness.

Anamnestic response: the immune system's memory of foreign substances (*see* antigen) it has previously encountered, triggering the formation of antibodies to the antigens. In high-responding inhibitor patients, anamnestic reaction is the rise in inhibitor titer (*see* Bethesda Unit) that accompanies an infusion of a factor product.

Anaphylaxis: severe allergic reaction to a foreign substance. A small percentage of hemophilia patients, mainly those with factor IX inhibitors, may experience anaphylaxis after infusion with factor concentrate.

Ancillaries: medical supplies used during an infusion, including syringes, needles, medical tape, adhesives, alcohol swabs, gauze.

Ankle fusion (arthrodesis): surgery in which cartilage is removed from the ends of some of the ankle bones, and the bones are joined together with screws, allowing the bones to fuse, or join together.

Antibody: blood protein produced by the immune system in response to bacteria, viruses, and foreign substances in the blood. Created for specific invaders, antibodies attack a certain virus or protein, and no other. *See* antigen.

Antifibrinolytic: medicine that slows the breakdown of blood clots; used mainly for mucous membrane bleeding, such as bleeding from the mouth, nose, uterus.

Antigen: bacteria, virus, foreign protein, or foreign substance in the body that causes the immune system to produce specific antibodies.

Antihistamine: OTC medicine that counteracts mild to moderate allergic reactions. Benadryl is a well-known brand.

Arterio-venous fistula (AVF): surgical procedure in which an artery in the lower part of the arm is connected to a vein, causing enlargement of the vein. Allows easy venous access by a regular needlestick, without using a tourniquet.

Arthrodesis: *see* ankle fusion.

Arthropathy: chronic arthritis in a person with hemophilia; caused by repeated bleeding into a joint.

Arthroplasty: joint replacement surgery.

Arthroscopic synovectomy: surgical removal of the synovium with pencil-sized tools inserted into the joint through small incisions. Also called a closed synovectomy.

Aseptic: technique to reduce the risk of bacterial infection; includes washing hands, using sterile gloves, cleaning the infusion site with topical antiseptics, and using only sterile equipment.

Assay: laboratory test to measure the quantity and/or quality of a substance. A clotting factor assay measures a specific clotting factor in blood.

Autoimmune disorder: condition in which the immune system mistakenly attacks the body itself. Examples: lupus; acquired hemophilia.

Auto-injectors: syringes for intramuscular injections (typically of epinephrine) that automatically inject when triggered by pressure, avoiding the need for the patient to push a plunger. Can be jabbed through clothing for immediate effect.

B

Ball-and-socket joint: allows circular movement and provides the greatest range of motion. Examples: hip; shoulder.

Ball-valve clot: complication of catheters in which a blood clot acts like a one-way valve, plugging the entrance to a catheter when someone is checking for a blood return.

Bethesda Inhibitor Assay: measures an inhibitor's ability to inactivate factor. The strength or concentration of the inhibitor is the inhibitor level, which is reported as a titer and expressed in Bethesda Units (BU).

Bethesda Unit (BU): the measure of an inhibitor level. Reflects the ability of the inhibitor to neutralize factor: the higher the BU, the more powerful the inhibitor, and the less effective will be a factor infusion. *See* titer.

Biofilm: thin colony of bacteria, often resistant to antibiotics. Typically colonizes foreign material in the body, such as catheters, port reservoirs, and artificial joints.

Bolus: administration of an intravenous drug in a single dose, as opposed to continuous infusion.

Bonn protocol: immune tolerance induction regimen requiring 200 IU/kg factor VIII every day. Highest dosage of ITI protocols.

Breakthrough bleed: bleeding that happens when a person with hemophilia is on prophylaxis.

BU: *see* Bethesda Unit.

Bypassing agent: blood-clotting product that skips the steps in the clotting process where factor VIII or IX is needed. Useful for inhibitor patients, who often cannot use regular factor.

C

Carrier: person who has a gene for a certain trait, but usually, one who does not exhibit that trait.

Cartilage: flexible connective tissue that provides structure and support for other tissues, without being as hard or brittle as bone.

Catheter: tubing that is inserted and positioned within a vein. *See* port.

Ceiling dose: maximum safe or effective dose of a drug. All NSAIDs have a ceiling dose.

Central line: *see* central venous access device.

Central venous access device (CVAD): catheter that avoids the need for peripheral infusions and makes infusions easier. It has a large target for the needle on one end, connected to tubing that is placed inside a big, central vein.

Chemical synovectomy: injection of a caustic chemical into the joint to destroy overgrown synovium, with the goal of decreasing frequency of bleeds in the joint. *See* synovium.

Chemotherapy drug: cancer therapy drug, such as rituximab, that may be used during ITI to suppress the immune system and reduce inhibitor titer.

Christmas disease: hemophilia B or factor IX deficiency.

Classic hemophilia: *see* factor VIII deficiency.

Closed synovectomy: *see* arthroscopic synovectomy.

Clot (blood clot): combination of platelets and fibrin fibers that seals off a leak in a blood vessel. *See* fibrin.

Clotting cascade: the sequential cellular and chemical reactions among the thirteen blood-clotting factors in response to a blood vessel injury. Results in the formation of fibrin fibers within the platelet plug, creating a fibrin clot to repair the vessel.

Clotting factor (coagulation factor): any of thirteen proteins, found in the plasma portion of blood, that help form blood clots.

Coagulation: formation of a blood clot. Also called hemostasis. *See* clotting cascade.

Compartment syndrome (acute): compression of blood vessels and nerves, caused by pressure from a bleed within an enclosed space, resulting in reduced blood flow to an extremity.

Complementary and alternative medicine (CAM): any adjunct therapy, like massage, used along with conventional medicine to help reduce pain and speed healing.

Comprehensive care: healthcare that covers all aspects (mental, emotional, physical) of a patient's health. The model used at HTCs usually includes members from hematology, psychology, social services, dentistry, orthopedics, physical therapy.

Comprehensive visit: appointment to see the hematologist and complete HTC team to examine physical, social, and overall health.

Computed tomography (CT scan): medical test that uses hundreds of cross-sectional X-ray images of the body to detect abnormalities and bleeds. Often used in hemophilia to detect intracranial bleeds. Also called computerized axial tomography (CAT scan). *See* intracranial hemorrhage.

Consolidated Omnibus Budget Reconciliation Act of 1985 (COBRA): legislation passed by Congress requiring insurance companies to allow an individual to pay for continuing insurance coverage temporarily, at the group rate received through the employer.

Continuous infusion: method of receiving factor replacement therapy continually through a pump, which can we worn on the patient's body.

COX-2 inhibitor: NSAID specifically developed to target only COX-2 (an enzyme responsible for inflammation and pain), reducing the risk of gastrointestinal bleeding and ulcers for people taking the drug for an extended time. *See* NSAID.

Crush injury: the squeezing and damaging of a body part under force or pressure, usually under a heavy object, against an object, or between two heavy objects.

CT scan: *see* computed tomography.

CVAD: *see* central venous access device.

D

Deep vein thrombosis (DVT): potentially dangerous condition in which clotting occurs in one or more of the major veins of the body.

DIC: *see* disseminated intravascular coagulation.

Disseminated intravascular coagulation (DIC): rare but dangerous complication of treatment with bypassing agents in which small, unwanted blood clots form throughout the body. The increased clotting may deplete clotting factors and platelets, leading to excessive, uncontrollable bleeding.

DNA (deoxyribonucleic acid): chemical name for the genetic instructions found in the nucleus of most cells, which control the development and function of all living organisms and some viruses.

Dutch protocol: immune tolerance induction regimen that calls for 25 IU/kg factor VIII every other day. Lowest dosage of ITI protocols.

DVT: *see* deep vein thrombosis.

E

Edema: observable swelling caused by fluid retention in body tissues, especially the feet and ankles; may involve any body part or the entire body.

Efficacy: effectiveness, or the capacity for a beneficial effect. Example: how well factor concentrate controls a bleed.

Epinephrine: same as the hormone adrenaline. Used to treat anaphylactic shock to help keep the airway open and increase blood pressure until patient can get to a medical facility.

Exposure day: a day on which a patient receives factor.

Extravasation: leakage of drugs or fluids from the reservoir of a port into surrounding tissues.

F

Factor VII deficiency: blood-clotting disorder caused by a lack of functional factor VII in the bloodstream.

Factor VIII: one of the clotting factors found in blood. Important in forming the fibrin clot. Deficiency of factor VIII causes hemophilia A.

Factor VIII deficiency: *see* hemophilia A.

Factor IX: one of the clotting factors found in blood. Important in forming the fibrin clot. Deficiency of factor IX causes hemophilia B.

Factor IX deficiency (Christmas disease): *see* hemophilia B.

Factor concentrate: commercially prepared biological drug to treat bleeding that results from a factor deficiency. Either produced from human plasma (*see* plasma-derived factor) or genetically engineered (*see* recombinant factor).

Fibrin: final protein produced by the clotting cascade. Needed to form a fibrin clot, or blood clot. *See* fibrin clot.

Fibrin clot (blood clot): intertwining network of fibers and platelets forming a blood clot that stays in place until the blood vessel wall heals.

Fibrin glue: medicine applied directly to a bleeding area to help form a clot. Made from human plasma that has been screened and treated to protect against viruses.

Fibrin sheath: fibrin coating along a CVAD catheter, sometimes causing obstruction of the catheter.

Fibrosis: formation of excessive collagen after damage to a tissue or organ.

G

Gene: sequence of DNA composing the basic unit of heredity. Located in chromosomes, in the nucleus of each cell. Genes contain the "blueprint," or chemical instructions that direct cell functions throughout life. *See* DNA.

Genetic mutation: change in a gene that scrambles or deletes the genetic instructions for cell functions. Hemophilia is a genetic mutation that scrambles the instructions for producing a clotting factor.

H

Half-life: average time required for the body to consume half the amount of a drug. Many factor VIII products have a half-life of about twelve hours: only half the factor is available twelve hours after being infused.

HCV: *see* hepatitis C.

Hemarthrosis: bleed into a joint.

Hematoma: tissue bleed; bruise.

Hematuria: presence of blood in the urine.

Hemophilia A: blood-clotting disorder caused by a lack of functional factor VIII in the blood. Also called factor VIII deficiency or classical hemophilia.

Hemophilia B: blood-clotting disorder caused by a lack of functional factor IX in the blood. Also called factor IX deficiency or Christmas disease.

Hemophilia treatment center (HTC): a medical facility staffed with a team of specialists who provide diagnosis, treatment, support, and information to people with bleeding disorders and their families.

Heparin: blood-thinning medication often used to flush catheters after an infusion.

Hepatitis: viral disease that causes inflammation and potential deterioration of the liver. Common types include hepatitis A, B, C.

Hepatitis A (HAV): viral liver disease usually transmitted by drinking water, eating food, or touching a surface contaminated with infected fecal matter, or by contaminated blood products. HAV is preventable by vaccination.

Hepatitis B (HBV): viral liver disease usually transmitted through contact with infected blood or saliva, sexual contact with an infected person, or IV drug use with contaminated needles. HBV is preventable by vaccination.

Hepatitis C (HCV): viral liver disease usually transmitted by direct contact with blood or contaminated blood products. Causes chronic liver infection and, after many years, cirrhosis of the liver. There is no vaccine for hepatitis C.

High responding: inhibitor titer that rises above 5 BU several days after a patient is exposed to factor.

High-titer inhibitor: inhibitor level greater than 5 BU.

HIV: *see* human immunodeficiency virus.

HTC: *see* hemophilia treatment center.

Huber needle: special non-coring needle used to infuse through a port to avoid damaging the port septum.

Human immunodeficiency virus (HIV): the virus that causes AIDS. HIV weakens the immune system, leaving the patient susceptible to infections. HIV is transmitted through unprotected sexual contact, intravenous needle sharing, breast feeding, prenatally through the placenta, and through shared blood and blood products.

I

Ibuprofen (Motrin): common OTC NSAID for treating pain and inflammation. Like all NSAIDs, ibuprofen has a ceiling dose (*see* ceiling dose).

Iliopsoas (psoas): large group of muscles in the hip area that help flex the thigh. Bleeding into these muscles is serious because of the large volume of blood that can be lost and the potential for nerve or muscle damage. *See* compartment syndrome.

Immune system: the body's system of biological processes and reactions that protect against disease by identifying and killing or inactivating pathogens. *See* antibody.

Immune tolerance induction (ITI): one of several therapies for inhibitor patients. Involves administering high, frequent doses of factor in an attempt to desensitize the immune system to factor VIII or factor IX infusions with the goal that the body will "learn" to recognize factor over time and stop producing inhibitors.

Immune tolerance therapy (ITT): *see* immune tolerance induction.

Immunoadsorption: the removal of substances such as proteins (factor VIII) or antibodies (inhibitors) from blood plasma.

Immunoglobulin (IVIG): mixture of antibodies isolated from blood plasma. Intravenous administration of immunoglobulins temporarily reduces an inhibitor.

Immunosuppressive drugs: medicines that depress the immune system. In patients with inhibitors, these drugs decrease inhibitor titer, in preparation for ITI or during ITI.

Incidence: frequency with which a disease or disorder appears in a certain population.

Inhibitor: antibody to factor VIII or factor IX that inhibits or neutralizes their function.

Inhibitor assay: laboratory test that determines the presence and activity of an inhibitor. *See* Bethesda Inhibitor Assay.

Inhibitor level: *see* Bethesda Unit.

Inhibitor titer: *see* Bethesda Unit.

International Unit (IU): standardized measure of the activity (functional amount) of a substance. One IU of human factor VIII or IX is approximately equal to the amount of factor VIII or IX in 1.0 mL of pooled human plasma.

Intracranial hemorrhage (ICH): a bleed inside the skull, usually caused by a head injury. Treated as a medical emergency.

ITI: *see* immune tolerance induction.

ITT: *see* immune tolerance therapy.

IVIG: *see* immunoglobulin.

J

Jugular veins: four large veins in the neck that drain blood from the head.

Joint: place where two bones meet that allows the bones to move.

Joint capsule: sheet of fibrous connective tissue that encases the joint.

Joint fusion: *see* ankle fusion; arthrodesis.

L

Ligaments: bands of connective tissue that hold bones together.

Line occlusion (obstruction): blockage that results when something disrupts the flow of factor into or out of a catheter.

Low responding: inhibitor titer less than or equal to 5 BU, and remaining at or close to that level after a patient is exposed to factor.

Low-titer inhibitor: inhibitor level less than or equal to 5 BU.

M

Magnetic resonance imaging (MRI): test that visualizes the internal structure and function of the body. Provides greater contrast than computed tomography between different soft tissues of the body, and with no X-ray exposure.

Malmö protocol: intensive two- to four-week inpatient ITI regimen. Uses high doses of factor VIII in conjunction with immunosuppressive drugs in an attempt to shorten ITI treatment time and achieve immune tolerance in about a month.

Medical benefit (major medical): portion of an insurance policy that covers all clinical services, including doctor visits, diagnostic tests, surgery.

Megadose: single, high dose of NovoSeven RT, greater than 200 mcg/kg, that allows for fewer follow-up doses.

Mild hemophilia: classification of hemophilia in which 5% to 50% of factor is active.

Mixing study: diagnostic test for inhibitors in which a hemophilia patient's blood plasma is mixed with normal plasma, and the clotting time is measured. A normal clotting time means the patient does not have an inhibitor.

Moderate hemophilia: classification of hemophilia in which 1% to 5% of factor is active.

Monoclonal antibodies: group of identical antibodies that bind to a specific antigen. Used in factor production to separate factor from plasma or, with recombinant products, from cell culture medium.

MRI: *see* magnetic resonance imaging.

Mutation: a change in one or more inherited characteristics, caused by a change in a gene or chromosome.

Myocardial infarction (MI): heart attack; blood vessels that supply blood to the heart are blocked.

N

Nephrotic syndrome: condition in which kidneys become plugged with microscopic solids (precipitates) that form when inhibitors combine with factor IX, causing fluid retention, high blood pressure, and possible kidney damage.

Neuropathic (neurogenic) pain: caused by damage to the nerves. Continues long after bleeds have resolved, and is hard to treat.

Nonsense mutation: one of the simplest kinds of genetic mutations, in which a single base of the DNA of a gene is changed. Results in an incomplete, nonfunctional protein, such as nonfunctional factor VIII or factor IX. Causes 10% to 30% of cases of severe hemophilia.

Non-steroidal anti-inflammatory drug (NSAID): pain reliever that also helps reduce swelling and inflammation. All NSAIDs have a ceiling dose. Can cause gastrointestinal bleeding, ulcers, and liver or kidney damage. *See* ceiling dose.

Nontunneled CVAD: short, large-bore catheter inserted through the skin into one of the deep veins of the body. Not used for long-term infusion therapy.

NSAID: *see* non-steroidal anti-inflammatory drug.

O

Off-label: therapeutic use of a drug that has not been approved by the U.S. FDA.

Open synovectomy: joint surgery to treat chronic synovitis; involves a large incision to remove the synovial membrane. Removes more synovium than does an arthroscopic synovectomy. Because of high cost and difficult rehabilitation, now rarely performed on patients with hemophilia.

Opioid (narcotic): type of prescription painkiller; safe and effective for treating moderate to severe chronic pain. Has no ceiling dose; does not cause kidney or liver damage, as NSAIDs can. Examples: morphine, codeine. *See* ceiling dose.

Over-the-counter (OTC): medications that are available without a prescription.

P

Partial thromboplastin time (PTT): laboratory test that determines how long it takes blood to clot. An abnormally long PTT indicates a bleeding disorder.

Peripherally inserted central catheter (PICC): device that allows the infusion of liquids into a vein. Inserted directly into a peripheral vein, and threaded through the length of the vein into a large vein near the heart. Usually temporary.

Pharmacy benefit: the portion of an insurance policy that covers outpatient drugs.

Physical dependence: adjustment of the body to a drug taken regularly. Withdrawal symptoms (sweating, rapid heart rate, nausea, diarrhea, anxiety) occur if the drug is suddenly stopped or the dose is lowered too quickly. Physical dependence is not addiction.

PICC: *see* peripherally inserted central catheter.

Plasma-derived factor: factor concentrate created from pooled human blood plasma.

Plasmapheresis: blood collection process in which whole blood is removed from a donor while red blood cells are separated from the plasma and then returned to the donor. Can be used to lower the inhibitor titer to prepare the patient for ITI.

Platelet count: test to determine the number of platelets in blood. A low platelet count may indicate a bleeding disorder.

Platelets (thrombocytes): irregularly shaped cell fragments manufactured in the bone marrow and essential to blood clotting. Platelets circulate in the bloodstream, and are needed to form a platelet plug at the site of injury to a blood vessel.

Point of Service (POS): insurance plan that offers options for more flexibility in choosing providers or specialists.

Porcine factor VIII: factor VIII concentrate derived from pig plasma. Once used to treat hemophilic patients with inhibitors to factor VIII, porcine factor was discontinued as treatment in 2004 because of the risk of viral contamination. A recombinant product is under development.

Port: CVAD surgically implanted under the skin in the chest wall and used for infusion. *See* central venous access device.

Prevalence: proportion of individuals in a population who have a disease or disorder at a specific point in time, like a snapshot.

Protein: class of compounds manufactured by cells. Proteins make up essential parts of organisms and are involved in every body process. Clotting factors are proteins.

Prothrombin complex concentrate (PCC): plasma-derived bypassing agent. *See* activated prothrombin complex concentrate.

Protocol: detailed formal plan of a clinical research trial, treatment, or procedure.

Pseudoaddiction: drug-seeking behaviors that occur when pain is undertreated, and that look like signs of addiction.

Psoas: *see* iliopsoas.

Pulmonary embolism (PE): blood clots in the arteries leading to the lungs. *See* thrombosis.

R

Radial head excision: surgery that removes the end of one of the bones in the forearm. Preferred surgery to treat hemophilic arthropathy of an elbow.

Radical synovectomy: *see* open synovectomy.

Radioactive synovectomy: surgery that injects radioactive material (isotope) into the joint, which slowly kills the cells of the synovium, causing it to dissolve. New, healthy synovium replaces the dying synovium. Also called radionuclide synovectomy or synoviorthesis.

Recombinant factor: factor concentrate produced by splicing the human factor gene into a nonhuman cell, which is then cloned and cultured in large vats. The inserted gene instructs the host cell to produce human factor. Recombinant factor is not derived from human blood sources.

Recombinant factor VIIa: activated recombinant factor VII; type of bypassing agent used to control bleeding in people with inhibitors.

Recovery: the concentration of functional factor in the plasma after administering a dose of factor. Recovery is used to help determine how much factor needs to be infused prophylactically, following a bleed, or to prepare for surgery.

Red blood cells: disk-shaped blood cells that carry oxygen to tissues in the body.

RICE (Rest, Ice, Compression, Elevation): adjunct treatment that helps reduce pain from bleeds and speed healing.

Rituximab: a monoclonal antibody used to treat some cancers and autoimmune diseases. Its use for inhibitors is off-label, but it may help to treat factor VIII inhibitors, though its effect is not permanent. *See* monoclonal antibodies.

S

Sepsis: severe blood infection. Symptoms include high fever, chills, lethargy, confusion, delirium, shaking, rapid breathing, elevated white blood cell count, and sometimes redness around port or catheter site. Considered a life-threatening emergency.

Septum: part of a port made of self-sealing silicone through which the needle is inserted.

Severe hemophilia: classification of hemophilia in which less than 1% of factor is active.

Severity level: amount of functional clotting factor active or present in the bloodstream. *See* mild hemophilia; moderate hemophilia; severe hemophilia.

Specialty pharmacy: licensed distributor of biologic products.

Spontaneous bleed: bleeding that occurs with no apparent injury, usually in people with severe hemophilia.

Steroid: immunosuppressive drug used to treat hemophilia inhibitors. Helps to reduce inflammation and suppress the immune system.

Subcutaneous: under the top layer of the skin. In children with hemophilia, inoculations should be given subcutaneously to reduce the risk of bleeding.

Surgical synovectomy: *see* open synovectomy; radical synovectomy; closed synovectomy; arthroscopic synovectomy.

Survival: blood test to monitor the half-life of infused factor.

Synovectomy: surgical removal of overgrown synovium to decrease the number of bleeds in a joint. Reduces frequency of bleeds, but may not stop progression of joint disease.

Synovial fluid: slimy, viscous lubricant secreted by the synovium. Lubricates the joint to prevent friction between the bones.

Synovitis: inflammation of the synovium that causes swelling of the joint.

Synovium: inner layer of the joint capsule. Composed of a thin layer of connective tissue that may be flat or may contain villi, and which surrounds and lubricates the joint cavity. Contains small blood vessels, and supplies nutrients to the cartilage covering the ends of the bones. *See* synovial fluid.

Systemic infection: infection that spreads to and affects multiple parts of the body and can cause organ failure and death.

T

Target joint: joint that suffers repeated bleeding. Over time, target joints usually develop arthritis.

Thrombosis: formation of a blood clot in a blood vessel, causing loss of circulation to the body part served by the blood vessel. Thrombosis increases the risk of heart attack and stroke.

Tissue factor: factor III; a protein involved in blood clotting. Tissue factor is exposed by injury to a blood vessel wall.

Tissue plasminogen activator (tPA): special clot-busting medicines administered through a central line.

Titer: laboratory measurement of the amount of a substance in solution. In hemophilia, usually refers to inhibitor antibody level. *See* Bethesda Unit.

Tolerance (drug): when the body adapts to the continual presence of a drug. Results in decreased sensitivity to a particular effect of the drug, so increasingly larger doses are needed to achieve the same effect.

Tolerized: when a patient's inhibitor is eradicated through ITI. *See* immune tolerance induction.

Tract infection: painful condition caused by a bacterial infection along the outside of a catheter.

Transient inhibitor: low-titer inhibitor that goes away on its own.

Trough level: lowest level of factor in a patient's blood between infusions.

V

Venous access device (VAD): infusion device used to protect veins, prevent scarring and scar tissue buildup, and make it easier to find a vein. *See* CVAD.

Villi: tiny finger-like projections. Inflammation of the synovium after a bleed increases blood flow to the synovium, engorging the villi and making the joint more likely to rebleed.

von Willebrand factor (VWF): blood protein that (1) helps platelets stick to each other and to the blood vessel wall at the site of injury and (2) stabilizes factor VIII and transports it through the bloodstream. Patients with VWD either do not have enough VWF or the VWF they produce does not function properly.

Acknowledgments

It has been an incredible privilege to write this book. First and foremost, I thank the forty families with inhibitors whose insights are included in this book. They allowed me to witness their struggles and pain, and to represent them in these pages. I spent hours interviewing them, learning about their lives, and trying to understand what they endure. Many of them also spent hours writing answers to a questionnaire about their experiences, easing my job as author. Before this book was published, I don't think many of us in the bleeding disorder community understood the challenges faced by these inhibitor families, or appreciated how well the families hid them. During several interviews, parents broke down and cried, just remembering some tough days. One young man wept when recalling the pain he had experienced ten months before. If I have done my job well, then many families around the world will empathize and learn from these shared stories.

Writing this book allowed me to work closely with some people I highly respect. Paul Clement not only provided the meticulous research that went into the first half of the book, but he also drafted and wrote those chapters. Paul's writing skills and breadth of knowledge are remarkable, and he is gifted in making complex, medical text simpler for all of us to understand.

I am also privileged to work with an exceptional production team. Sara Prisland Evangelos, editor with JAS Group Editorial and Writing Services, has worked with me for more than a dozen years. Sara takes the huge amount of text we give her and makes much better sense of it by ensuring that it flows coherently, is consistent and organized, and has correct grammar. She constantly challenged us on every bit of the text, to find any weak spots or lack of logic. Long ago I decided I could not write a book ever without her skilled guidance. She is more than an editor; she is an integral part of the entire writing, strategic thinking, and production process.

Tracy Brody, our designer, has also worked with me for years. Tracy takes the finished text and makes it look beautiful in her appropriate, attractive designs. She's the most cheerful person to work with, despite our many drafts and changes. And special thanks to Zoraida Rosado, Manager of Production and Projects, my long-time assistant who keeps everything running smoothly in the office, even in the midst of chaos. Zoraida helped pull together the necessary paperwork, calls, and trips to make the book complete. Thanks to Paul, Sara, Tracy, and Zoraida for being such a great team.

Acknowledgments

Many thanks also go to our two physician medical reviewers: Prasad Mathews, MD, Medical Director, University of New Mexico, Department of Pediatrics, Albuquerque, New Mexico; and Leonard Valentino, MD, Director, Pediatric Hematology/Oncology, Rush University Medical Center, Chicago, Illinois. I've known and worked with Dr. Mathews and Dr. Valentino for years, and I hold them in the highest regard. Beloved by their patients, they are also counted among the top hematologists in our country for hemophilia.

I'd also like to thank one of my favorite hemophilia nurses, Regina Butler, Clinical Manager, Division of Hematology, Children's Hospital of Philadelphia. Regina is an incredible professional—always ready to help, always knowledgeable, easy to work with, and always on time! Like Dr. Mathews and Dr. Valentino, Regina is treasured by her patients.

I'm especially grateful to my peer reviewers, Kerry Fatula and Sonji Wilkes, both mothers of sons with hemophilia. They each read the manuscript twice, and offered excellent insights that only parents living with inhibitors can impart. Kerry has four children—three with inhibitors—and a full-time job. How she found time to squeeze me in for a weekend visit to Pittsburgh to see life with inhibitors at her home—ground zero—I'll never know. Sonji's son has many complications, and is often in and out of hospitals, yet Sonji made the time to review the manuscript and offer her own story. Thanks to both these wonderful ladies, and to their families.

Many thanks go to Colton Branch, a young man with an inhibitor, who reviewed my teen chapter to offer his insights. Also thanks to Jeff Kallberg, who has hemophilia and is a physical therapist, for his excellent comments and suggestions for the chapter on joints.

My deepest gratitude to Novo Nordisk, worldwide supplier of NovoSeven RT, a bypassing agent used to treat acute bleeding in inhibitor patients. Novo Nordisk provided the funding for this book, the first ever on inhibitors. But beyond their generous funding, I am grateful to Novo Nordisk for opening my eyes to the plight of families with inhibitors. I was blind to their struggles until I was asked to help create the Novo Nordisk Consumer Council in 2005. The council was a gathering of inhibitor families that offered feedback and suggestions to the marketing team at Novo Nordisk. The idea for this book was born at this first meeting. Thank you, George McAvoy and Ian Tu, members of the marketing team, who initiated the idea for the council, and who invited me to participate and facilitate. This brilliant idea has sent positive ripples throughout the years. Thanks also to Gar Park and Tanya Hill, who kept the council going after George and Ian moved on to different positions in the company.

And finally, special thanks again to George McAvoy. In addition to the Novo Nordisk Consumer Council, George also envisioned the Novo Nordisk Inhibitor Education Summits, which I think became the most significant events in the hemophilia community in a decade. For the first time ever, inhibitor families had an event dedicated to them, an opportunity to meet, share, cry, connect, vent, and learn without worrying about how the non-inhibitor community would react. The importance of these summits can't be understated. They changed the lives of scores of families who had been isolated, hurt, and misunderstood. The summits revealed the power of community, the need for connection, and the success of one visionary idea from a very thoughtful and compassionate person. ∎

Index

Entries referring to figures are followed by *f* (for example, 115f).

Entries referring to end-of-chapter notes are indicated by *n* (for example, 67n3).

A

accommodation plans, 213–15, 222
acetylsalicylic acid (ASA), 88, 89, 100n6, 101n8,102
acquired hemophilia, 28, 38n1
activated prothrombin complex concentrate (aPCC), 43, 53n2
addiction, 91–93, 102
adhesion, 88, 89, 96, 100n6, 124, 134n8
adjuvant analgesic, 87, 90, 102
adrenaline (epinephrine), 73, 98
aerobic exercise, 183–84
albumin, 51, 77
allergic reaction
    factor VII and, 80*f*
    hemophilia B inhibitors and, 19, 30, 72–74, 80, 80*f*, 82
    ITI and, 77, 80
    nephrotic syndrome and, 78
    plasma and, 51
    product choice and, 44, 45, 50, 52*f*, 54, 75, 76
    severity of, 75
    symptoms of, 72–73
Amicar, 49, 50, 143, 150
analgesic, 87, 89, 102
anamnestic response, 32–33, 42, 44, 52*f*, 56*f*, 59, 132, 136
anaphylaxis, 19, 73, 77
ancillaries, 201
ankle fusion (arthrodesis), 130–31, 136
antifibrinolytic, 49–50, 54
antihistamine, 73, 82
aPCC: *see* activated prothrombin complex concentrate
arterio-venous fistula (AVF), 113–15, 115*f*
arthritis, 83, 85, 86, 102, 120, 123, 126*f*, 181
arthrodesis: *see* ankle fusion
arthropathy, 52, 120, 123, 125–26*f*, 130, 131, 136, 187

arthroplasty, 128
aseptic technique, 95, 108–9, 114, 115, 115*f*, 118, 129
aspirin: *see* acetylsalicylic acid
assay, 31, 37, 46, 53n8, 144. *See also* Bethesda Inhibitor Assay
autoimmune disorder, 29, 38n1
auto-injector, 74

B

B-cells, 80
bacteria, 29, 106, 107, 108, 109, 113, 116n6, 129, 150
ball-valve clot, 110
Bethesda Inhibitor Assay (or Bethesda assay), 31, 37, 38n2–4, 40, 74, 241
Bethesda Unit (BU), 31, 40, 41, 60*f*, 241, 243*f*
biofilm, 107, 113, 129
bleeds
    ankle, 79, 84, 123, 143, 186, 203, 213
    breakthrough, 17, 48, 50, 182
    buttocks, 142
    developmental milestones and, 120, 142–44
    head, 19, 72, 146, 147
    gastrointestinal (GI), 88, 89, 90, 143
    gum, 19, 143, 149, 150, 151, 152
    joint: exercise and, 94, 183–85; explained, 122, 123, 136, 244, 125–26*f*; pain and, 83, 85, 86, 90, 102, 155, 181, 183; prevention of, 181–82, 191; prophylaxis and, 52, 134n6, 182; mentioned, 120, 143, 187, 188, 200. *See also* joint
    kidney, 49
    mouth, 49, 50, 54, 143, 150
    muscle, 16, 53n9, 142, 143, 187, 188, 191
    nose, 49, 54, 143, 150, 152, 211
    patterns of, 142, 200
    spontaneous, 17, 19, 72, 89, 122
    tissue, 17, 142, 150
    tongue, 142, 150
    urinary tract (UT), 143
blood cell
    red, 122, 134n3
    white, 80

blood clot
  adjunct therapy and, 49
  Amicar and, 150
  antifibrinolytic and, 49
  non-opioids and, 89
  unwanted (thrombosis), 44, 52*f*, 76, 93, 110, 111, 115, 115*f*, 118, 129, 131, 135n16, 182
blood vessel, 58, 121, 122, 127, 136, 244
bolus, 19, 36
Bonn protocol, 56, 67n3, 67n5, 69
brand restrictions, 197, 207
Broviac, 104, 105, 106, 107, 111, 112
BU: *see* Bethesda Unit
bypassing agent
  overdosing and, 182
  in factor IX, 75–76, 77, 82
  use in surgery, 42
  use in treatment, 33, 41, 42–43, 52, 52*f*, 54, 86, 100n1, 190n1
  mentioned, 103, 119, 177, 193

C

career choice, and insurance coverage, 233–34, 238
ceiling dose, 88, 90, 91
central line, 93, 103–4, 108, 111, 115
central venous access device (CVAD)
  advantages and disadvantages of, 105–6, 115*f*, 116n7, 118
  complications of, 107–13, 118
  compared to AVF, 108, 115*f*
  hygiene with, 145, 150, 152
  in school, 211
  internal, 103–4, 106, 118
  external, 103–4, 105–6, 108
  reservoir, 104, 105, 107, 109, 111–12, 118
  septum, 105, 109, 110, 112
Christmas disease, 71. *See* hemophilia: hemophilia B
circumcision, 18–18, 27n5, 119
classic hemophilia, 71. *See* hemophilia: hemophilia A
clotting cascade, 42, 43, 44, 53n1, 90, 110, 113
clotting factor: *see* factor
coinsurance, 197, 207
compassionate care programs, 240
comprehensive care, 83
comprehensive visit, 16, 17, 37
complementary and alternative medicine (CAM), 94–96, 98, 99, 101n11, 102
contracture, 131, 187–88
co-payment, 195, 197, 199, 201
corporal punishment, 160

COX-2 inhibitor, 89
crush injury, 44, 76
Cryo/Cuff, 86, 240
CVAD: *see* central venous access device
cyber school, 218, 222

D

deductible, 197, 199, 201, 202, 207
deep vein thrombosis (DVT), 76, 111, 114, 116n10, 118, 129
dental work, 109, 116, 129
diagnostic test, 31, 196, 207
disseminated intravascular coagulation (DIC), 44, 76
distance learning, 218
DNA
  mutations and, 39n11, 81n4
Dutch protocol, 57, 69
DVT: *see* deep vein thrombosis

E

edema,72, 79
elective surgery, 33, 42, 50, 119
EMLA, 116n6
EOB: *see* Explanation of Benefits
epinephrine, 73, 74, 82
EpiPen, 74, 82
EPO: *see* Exclusive Provider Organization
Exclusive Provider Organization (EPO), 195
Explanation of Benefits (EOB), 201, 202, 203*f*, 207
exposure day, 16, 19, 28, 36
extravasation, 112

F

factor
  factor VIII deficiency and, 30, 43, 71
  factor IX deficiency and, 30, 71–82, 132, 136
  level, measurements of, 45, 60, 241
  protein in, 15, 30, 39n11, 40, 56, 58, 71, 110, 111
  plasma-derived, 19, 36, 43, 54, 58, 66*f*, 76
  recombinant: factor VIIa, 33, 43, 44, 53n6, 54, 78; factor VIII, 36, 50, 58, 66*f*, 111, 206n2; factor IX, 77–78
fee-for-service (FFS), 195
FEIBA VH
  factor IX and, 76
  prophylaxis and, 52
  dosing, 44, 46, 47*f*, 54, 144, 216
  off-label use, 48, 53n7
  side effects, 43, 44, 45, 50, 76

use: in treatment, 43–44, 58, 67n5, 76, 82, 100n1, 182, 243*f*; compared with NovoSeven, 45–46, 47*f*, 48–49, 50, 52, 52*f*, 54, 76
504 plan, 210, 214, 215, 221n3, 222
FFS: *see* fee-for-service
fibrin
    clot, 43, 44, 49, 110, 111
    glue, 151
    sheath, 110, 111
fibrosis, 123, 201
formulary, 197
frenulum, 150

G

genetic
    mutation, 35, 36, 39n11, 71
    counseling, 25

H

half-life, 45, 56*f*, 58, 59, 60, 65, 67n3, 75
Health Insurance Portability and Accountability Act (HIPAA), 197, 198–99
health maintenance organization (HMO), 195
helmet, 146–47, 152, 170, 181
hemarthrosis, 122, 136, 240
hemophilia A (classic)
    anamnesis and, 43, 45
    incidence and prevalence of, 18, 34–35, 35*f*, 39n10, 40, 71, 82
    ITI and, 55, 59, 60f, 81n14
    risk factors for, 35, 40, 71, 82
hemophilia B (Christmas disease)
    allergic reactions and, 18–19, 45, 72, 76, 77, 80, 82
    anamnesis and, 43, 76
    incidence and prevalence of, 18–19, 34, 35, 35*f*, 39n10, 71, 81n3, 82
    ITI and, 55, 67n4, 77, 80, 82
hemophilia, severity levels of
    mild, 19, 22, 30, 34, 35, 67n3
    moderate, 30, 34, 35
severe, 16, 19, 20, 30, 34, 35, 35f, 40, 67n3; development of inhibitors, 30; hemophilia B, 71, 72, 82; joint disease and, 120, 136
hemosiderin, 122
heparin, 109, 110, 129, 200
hepatitis
    hepatitis B virus (HBV), 64
    hepatitis C virus (HCV), 10, 62, 87
Hickman, 104, 112

HIPAA: *see* Health Insurance Portability and Accountability Act
HIV: *see* human immunodeficiency virus
hives, 19, 72, 73, 74
HMO: *see* health maintenance organization
home infusion (self-infusion), 198, 200, 230
home care company, 193, 197, 198, 200, 201, 233
Huber needle, 105, 109
human immunodeficiency virus (HIV), 10, 11, 62, 64
hydrotherapy, 94, 188
hypotension, 73

I

immune tolerance induction (ITI), 33, 55–69, 77–80
immune tolerance therapy (ITT): *see* immune tolerance induction
immunoadsorption, 51, 54, 77
immunogenic, 71
immunoglobulin (IVIG), 50, 62, 63, 67n6, 77
immunosuppressive drug, 50–51, 54, 56, 57, 62, 64, 69, 75, 77, 80, 82
incidence
    defined, 33–34, 38n6
    of inhibitors, 34, 35*f*, 40
Individual Health Plan (IHP), 214
Individualized Education Plan (IEP), 214
infection
    AVF and, 113, 115*f*
    blood, 44, 106, 108. See also sepsis
    CVAD (port) and, 61, 63, 106, 115, 115*f*. *See also* aseptic technique, sepsis, skin
    prosthesis and, 128–29, 135n14
    systemic, 63, 64, 128
    tract, 108
    viral, 44, 51
infusion
    needles: CVAD and, 103, 104, 105, 115*f*, 116n, 118; AVF and, 113; Huber, 105, 106, 109–10; sterile, 108
    supplies, 149, 200, 215, 230, 230*f*
inhibitor
    high-responding, 32, 33, 40, 42, 71, 75, 77, 82. *See also* Bethesda Unit
    low-responding, 33, 40, 41, 59, 75, 82. *See also* Bethesda Unit
    level, 31–33, 38n4, 41, 43, 59, 51, 66*f*, 67n3, 78, 132, 136
    titer: classification of, 31–33, 40; factor IX and, 74, 75, 77, 81n5, 81n6; immunosuppression and, 62, 63, 64, 69; surgery and, 128, 132; treatment of, 41–42, 46, 51, 55–

56, 56f, 65, 69
transient, 27n2, 33, 34, 35f, 40, 69, 71
Inhibitor Education Summit, 11, 27n8, 176–77, 264
insurance
    cap (annual), 10, 193, 197, 199
    catastrophic illness coverage, 198, 207
    coverage, 45, 48, 205, 206n3, 234, 235, 238
    maximum (lifetime cap), 132, 186, 196, 207
    reimbursement, 195, 200, 202, 206n2, 206n5
International ITI (I-ITI) study, 57, 67n3
intramuscular injection, 29, 74
ITI: *see* immune tolerance induction
ITT: *see* immune tolerance induction
IVIG: *see* immunoglobulin

J

joint
    ball-and-socket, 122, 123, 245
    capsule, 121, 122, 123, 127, 130, 136, 187, 244
    damage to, 83, 94, 99, 123, 127, 130, 181–88
    destruction, 52, 83, 99, 122–23, 125–26, 126f, 128, 186, 188
    disease, 55, 120, 136, 181
    exercise, 94, 184–85, 191
    pain, 83, 85–86, 88, 89, 90, 93, 99, 102, 132, 155
    replacement, 95, 119, 120, 128, 129, 132
    stiffness in, 94, 132, 183, 191
    target, 86, 122, 123, 131, 134n5
    types of, 121–22, 123, 130, 131, 240, 244–45.
    See also bleeds: joint

L

Leonard, 104
ligament, 122, 134n2, 185, 187, 245
line occlusion (obstruction), 109–10, 111, 118
Lysteda, 49, 143, 150

M

Malmö protocol, 57, 64, 66f, 67n6, 69, 203
managed care
    organization (MCO), 195
    plan, 195
MCO: *see* managed care, organization
medical benefit (major medical), 196, 207
Medicaid, 194, 199, 203–04, 205, 206n2-3, 207
MedicAlert, 149, 240
Medicare, 194, 199, 207
megadose, 47, 54, 216
mixing study, 31
monoclonal antibody, 51, 63, 77

morphine, 79, 86, 87, 90, 92, 102
muscle
    pain, 85, 86, 100, 102
    exercise, 94, 95, 96, 183, 184, 185, 187, 188, 191.
    See also bleed: muscle
myocardial infarction, 76

N

nephrotic syndrome, 78–80, 81n14, 82
neuropathic (neurogenic) pain, 97
nonsense mutation, 35, 39n11, 71, 81n4
non-opioid, 87–89, 102
non-steroidal anti-inflammatory drug (NSAID), 87–89, 90, 91, 100n4, 101n8,102
nontunneled CVAD, 104
NovoSeven
    compared to FEIBA, 45, 46, 47f, 48, 49, 50, 52, 52f, 54, 75–76, 82, 100n1
    disseminated intravascular coagulation and, 44, 45, 53n4
    dosing 46–47, 52, 53n5, 53n7, 53n12, 54, 145, 216
    half-life and, 45
    insurance and, 203
    megadosing with, 47, 48, 54
    product information, 8, 44
NSAID: *see* non-steroidal anti-inflammatory drug

O

obesity, 186–87, 190n3
off-label, 48, 53n4, 53n7, 63
open enrollment period, 199
opioid, 83, 87, 88, 89, 90–91, 92, 93, 101n9, 102

P

parvovirus, 50
PCC: *see* prothrombin complex concentrate
PDL: *see* preferred drug list
peripherally inserted central catheter (PICC), 104, 106, 107, 113, 118
physical dependence
    addiction and, 91, 92
    tapering and, 92
PICC: *see* peripherally inserted central catheter
plasmapheresis, 51, 54, 57, 61, 66f, 77, 81n11
platelet
    painkillers and, 88–89, 96, 100n6
    adhesion, 88, 89
    plug, 89
    count, and porcine factor, 50
Point of Service (POS), 195

Port-a-Cath, 105, 106
POS: *see* Point of Service
PPO: *see* Preferred Provider Organization
pre-existing condition, 197, 198, 199, 204, 207
preferred drug list, 195, 197
Preferred Provider Organization (PPO), 195
prevalence
    defined, 34
    of inhibitors, 34, 35*f*, 39n10, 71
protective gear, 142, 146, 147
prothrombin complex concentrate (PCC), 43, 53n2
pseudoaddiction, 92–93
pulmonary embolism, 76, 135n16

R

radial head excision, 129–30, 136
RICE, 86–87, 102, 183
recovery, and half-life, 56*f*, 58, 59, 67n3, 75
rituximab, 50, 62, 63–64, 77, 80

S

SCHIP: *see* State Children's Health Insurance Program
self-infusion (home infusion), 200, 230
sepsis, 107, 116n3
skin, breakdown of (erosion), 111–12
spanking, 159, 160, 161
specialty pharmacy, 193, 197, 200
State Children's Health Insurance Program (SCHIP), 199, 206n3
steroid
    anti-inflammatory, 52, 183
    immunosuppressive drug, and 50–51, 52, 59, 62, 63, 64, 183
    ITI and, 77–78, 80
    nephrotic syndrome and, 78, 79–80
synovectomy
    arthroscopic (closed), 124–27
    chemical, 123, 127
    radical (open), 124–28, 130
    radioactive, 123, 127, 134n10, 136
    surgical, 123, 124, 136, 183
synovitis, 123, 126f, 127, 131, 136, 183

T

teething, 150
thrombosis: *see* blood clot: unwanted. *See also* deep vein thrombosis
tissue plasminogen activator (tPA), 110

teeth
    care of, 109, 150
    loss of, 150, 152
tolerance, and addiction, 87
trough level, 17

V

venous access device (VAD): see central venous access device (CVAD)
villi, 121, 122, 344
von Willebrand
    disease (VWD), 10
    factor (VWF), 58, 66*f*
VWD: *see* von Willebrand, disease
VWF: *see* von Willebrand, factor